T0367148

PARKCHESTER

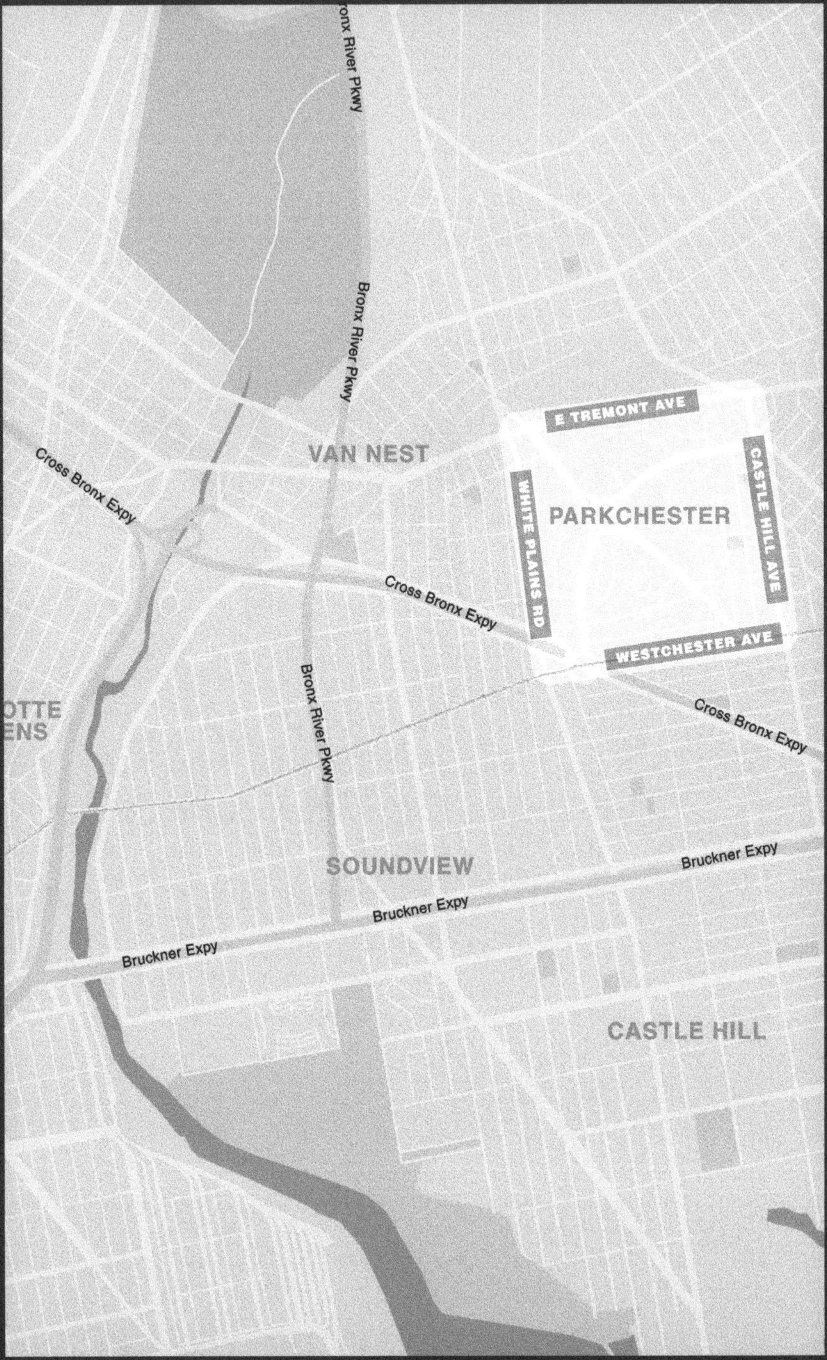
Bronx River Pkwy
Bronx River Pkwy
VAN NEST
Cross Bronx Expy
E TREMONT AVE
WHITE PLAINS RD
PARKCHESTER
CASTLE HILL AVE
Cross Bronx Expy
WESTCHESTER AVE
Cross Bronx Expy
Bronx River Pkwy
SOUNDVIEW
Bruckner Expy
Bruckner Expy
Bruckner Expy
CASTLE HILL

PARKC

A Bronx Tale of Race and Ethnicity

JEFFREY S. GUROCK

HESTER

WASHINGTON MEWS BOOKS
An Imprint of
NEW YORK UNIVERSITY PRESS *New York*

WASHINGTON MEWS BOOKS
An Imprint of
NEW YORK UNIVERSITY PRESS
New York
www.nyupress.org

References to Internet websites (URLs) were accurate at the time of writing. Neither the author nor New York University Press is responsible for URLs that may have expired or changed since the manuscript was prepared.

Library of Congress Cataloging-in-Publication Data
Names: Gurock, Jeffrey S., 1949–   author.
Title: Parkchester : a Bronx tale of race and ethnicity / Jeffrey S. Gurock.
Description: New York : New York University Press, [2019] |
Includes bibliographical references and index.
Identifiers: LCCN 2019001461 | ISBN 9781479896707 (cl : alk. paper)
Subjects: LCSH: Parkchester (New York, N.Y.)—Race relations—Case studies. |
Parkchester (New York, N.Y.)—History.
Classification: LCC F128.9.A1 G87 2019 | DDC 974.7/275—dc23
LC record available at https://lccn.loc.gov/2019001461

New York University Press books are printed on acid-free paper, and their binding materials are chosen for strength and durability. We strive to use environmentally responsible suppliers and materials to the greatest extent possible in publishing our books.

Manufactured in the United States of America

10 9 8 7 6 5 4 3 2 1

Also available as an ebook

Frontispiece: Maps of Parkchester. Courtesy of the Yeshiva University Office of Communications and Public Affairs.

For Adison Rae: it is her turn

Contents

Abbreviations

The following abbreviations are used in the text:

BHN	*Bronx Home News*
BN	*Bronx News*
BPR	*Bronx Press Review*
HO	*Home Office*
MLICA	Metropolitan Life Insurance Company Archive
NYAN	*New York Amsterdam News*
NYDN	*New York Daily News*
NYHT	*New York Herald Tribune*
NYT	*New York Times*
RFW	Robert F. Wagner Papers, Municipal Archives, New York City
YI	*Young Israelite*
YIP	Young Israel of Parkchester Papers, Yeshiva University Archives

INTRODUCTION

Parkchester and New York City's History

PARKCHESTER HAS BEEN HOME OVER THE PAST eight decades to tens of thousands of aspiring working- and lower-middle-class men and women. Amid an expanse of 129 acres of land situated in the East Bronx, its 12,271 apartments in 171 buildings, some rising as high as thirteen stories, are readily visible to motorists as their cars speed or crawl on the Cross Bronx Expressway eastbound toward the northernmost reaches of the borough or out to Queens or westbound toward New Jersey. No matter their direction, drivers are on the road to suburbia. This enclave has often been referred to as "a city within a city" by its founders, tenants, and the media since the day it opened with some fanfare in the early spring of 1940. Back then, its scale was compared to that of New Brunswick, New Jersey, or Bangor, Maine, except that Parkchester was even larger.[1]

Parkchester is a short subway ride from Manhattan—what its residents call the "city"—convenient for the army of civil servants, garment workers, salespeople, and small business owners who have daily marched together down Metropolitan Avenue, the area's main thoroughfare, to the 177th Street/Parkchester local and express stop at Hugh J. Grant Circle. Straphangers awaiting their trains at this elevated subway station have, for generations, looked down upon the bumper-to-bumper traffic, the onerous workday lot of suburban commuters.

In its early decades, this planned community—owned and operated by the Metropolitan Life Insurance Corporation (MLIC)—welcomed in, after a close investigation of applicants' behavioral and economic backgrounds, Irish Catholics (Parkchester's largest white ethnic group), many Italian Catholics, a minority of Protestants, and a substantial number of Jews. All felt fortunate to have secured a spot in the community. The management expected those "of any nationality and religion" whom they "carefully selected" would "fit into the Bronx as easily as Parkchester's street numbers." But during the new neighborhood's first thirty years, an egregious blot stained management's vetting process. Almost no blacks or Latinos were allowed to settle there.[2]

In keeping with the tenor of those times, in the 1940s and early 1950s the MLIC relied on the laws and the courts to maintain segregation. Subsequently, even when civil rights legislation was on the books, rental agents and the home office back in Manhattan used a variety of tactical subterfuges to forestall integration. While the chairman of the MLIC went on the record in 1943 to assert that "Negroes and whites don't mix," the company never admitted publicly that it, in fact, practiced institutionalized racism. Integration was not part of company chairman Frederick H. Ecker's "pet business and sociological dream." If anything, he and other officials frequently asserted that blacks were not among its more than forty thousand residents because they were not interested in living there. Those applicants who were turned away or steered away because of their race knew better. So did their advocates within and without the civil rights movement who struggled to break down the walls of racism in housing, often with no assistance from the municipal government.[3]

Starting late in the 1960s, the stain of segregation was finally removed from the neighborhood's buildings. Since the 1990s, community residents have been predominantly black or Latino, with a significant and growing population that hails from Asia, Africa, and South America. The whites who live in early-21st-century Parkchester are mostly elderly Christians; almost no Jews remain. One of Parkchester's former synagogues is now a mosque, one of the six Muslim places of worship that ring the community.

Over the decades, the neighborhood has been perceived as an idyllic setting. It is a place that folks of many backgrounds have wanted to be part of and it has been a source of frustration for those who were systematically excluded. Residents have largely been pleased to live in a bucolic environment within city limits replete with flowers, gardens, and well-kept playgrounds. The neighborhood's signature place is its magnificent Metropolitan Oval, situated in the very heart of the complex. This is the spot where, in summertime, people have sat out in the shade on park benches and admired the beautifully landscaped area while catching breezes from the sculpture fountain. During holiday seasons, passersby have admired both the Christmas stockings hung over a faux fireplace and the electric menorah on display, which also contributed to a sense that the residents lived in a peaceful preserve. Nonetheless, when tenants found themselves in disagreement with the management's policies, as tried and true New Yorkers, they made their complaints heard loud and clear. Indeed, the largest ball field was the site of many protest meetings. However, in the end, Parkchesterites have tacitly subscribed to a viewpoint that the MLIC articulated early in the development's existence. Unquestionably, from the 1940s through the 1960s, those who were admitted sincerely believed that they were better off than those who flocked to suburbia. Even beyond the daily commutation advantages of a subway whose fare until 1966 did not rise above twenty cents a ride, they liked the idea that they would not be obliged to rake leaves in the fall or shovel snow in the winter, not to mention arrive home late for dinner year-round after extricating themselves from traffic jams. During the MLIC's tenure, scores of skilled maintenance employees were on the premises to handle householders' chores. These crack workers were at the beck and call of residents, ready to fix electrical and plumbing problems or even to help hang photographs and mirrors.

Proud of where they resided and how they lived, Parkchesterites have long taken umbrage and responded with a "Bronx cheer" to any suggestion that their red-bricked, high-rise development was a "project." Such city-owned operations, built throughout New York around the same time as Parkchester and following years, often with the same color exteriors and similar asphalt playgrounds, would be tarred with the reputation of being poorly constructed, inadequately maintained, and eventually rife with criminality. Parkchester tenants knew of these residential areas. A few were located just a few subway stops southwest of their neighborhood, literally on the wrong side of the tracks. Until the 1970s, the uncharitable in Parkchester might also say that that was where the unwanted African Americans and Latinos lived. Subsequently, the fearful, drawn from among all racial groups, frequently expressed deep concern that troublemakers from the projects might prey on their community.[4]

In opting for apartment life in a neighborhood better than most in their borough and city, Parkchester's first settlers forewent the possibility of owning their own homes outside of the city, a touchstone of the American dream in the post–World War II era. Rather, many saw themselves as renters for life. In fact, in the early 1970s, when the Helmsley-Spear corporation, which in 1968 bought the development from the MLIC, initially tendered the option of tenants owning their apartments, most families did not buy in. Many, fearful that as renters they might be pressured or forced to leave, contested the new managers' condominium initiative. In all events, at least for the neighborhood's first generation, the intention was to stay put for the long haul within a generally salubrious setting in their home borough. In more recent times, there has been more movement in and out of the neighborhood. Still, notwithstanding critical issues that arose primarily with infrastructure as its buildings aged, problems that were laid at management's doorstep, Parkchester has retained its special character for generations. And, during the last two decades, residents have benefitted from a creature comfort that was not available to earlier tenants: their apartments are air-conditioned. When the neighborhood was built, the management did not address that structural imperfection. This crucial omission from the planned-community drawing boards was one of the reasons that the children of the first settlers looked elsewhere for housing once they reached their majority.

The story of choosing to live in Parkchester offers an alternative narrative to the oft-told tales of how long-time New Yorkers, almost all of whom were white, began exiting Gotham after 1945 for what was deemed a better life in suburbia, often also in segregated locales. This new East Bronx area—effectively for whites only—was a reasonable and affordable venue for those who were admitted. There they would raise their baby-boomer youngsters in what they deemed a special place in the city. During its first three decades, the community, with a robust spirit of neighborliness that prevailed among its young families, uncommon for an urban development of its dimensions, bore the nickname "Storkchester."

Parkchester likewise tenders an additional important dimension to the subsequent history of middle class migration of varying racial and ethnic groups within and out of New York City from the late 1970s through the 1990s. It has been widely noted that amid the maelstroms of financial crises, cutbacks in city services, deterioration if not destruction of old inner-city neighborhoods, and a concomitant spike in criminality, middle class whites fled Gotham en masse. In so doing, they took part in a second distinct era of movement toward suburbia. What took place in Parkchester complicates this narrative. This East Bronx enclave surely was not immune to the plights of the city; it too witnessed many older white residents and their children seek new homes out of town. But a now-integrated Parkchester simultaneously absorbed members of racial minority groups who fled into this relatively safe area without the violence and outcries that occurred in other parts of the city. The newcomers often came over from those "projects," extricating themselves from the city's more grievously afflicted areas. This aspect of the Parkchester story highlights the largely unrecognized phenomenon of African American and Latino flight *within* New York City to better areas of Gotham during this same troubled period.

In recent years, as the neighborhood increasingly has become home to a mélange of peoples from all over the globe, Parkchester's newest residents have deepened New York's cachet as an immigrant city, one of the proudest features of Gotham's long history. In opting for the now highly diverse East Bronx neighborhood, those from Asia, Africa, and South America have eschewed newcomers' generally presumed affinity for settling in substantially homogenous ethnic and national enclaves. Here and now, this community again limns the trail of groups moving within and without New York City.

Ultimately, however, Parkchester has been special not so much because people of varied and changing backgrounds, when they were permitted to reside there, chose to live in this neighborhood for similar reasons. Of far greater moment is that, for eighty years, those of diverse origins have generally lived together harmoniously. More often than not, Parkchester's many religious, ethnic, racial, and national groups have gotten along. This uncommon behavior demands the closest consideration. To begin with, early in its history, convivial life in the community constituted a turning point in interethnic relations in New York City, especially in the longtime contretemps between Irish Americans and Jews.

These groups' aggravated and sometimes violent history of conflict dates back to the close of the 19th century. As competing immigrants, they clashed over jobs, union memberships, housing, and frequently politics. One particular point of contention stemmed from the Irish perception, within downtown's congested and contested atmosphere, that they were losing control of the streets to Jews. One nasty way of getting even was to attack pushcart peddlers on East Broadway.

These tensions crescendoed exponentially in the decade or more of the Great Depression, during which Jews suffered economically but the Irish did even worse. In Gaelic neighborhoods, the word on the street, more than ever, was that the Jews were taking over civil service jobs, as police, firefighters, and teachers, that the Irish had maintained for generations.

Exacerbating matters, the rhetoric and organizations of Michigan-based radio preacher Father Charles Coughlin gave voice and action to local frustrations. His allegations about the supposed Jewish control of the American economy sat well with those who feared for their livelihoods. Members of Coughlin's Christian Front, and an even more violent group called the Christian Mobilizers, applied these teachings enthusiastically to the mean streets around them.

In the South Bronx, for example, young men from hard-hit Irish families attacked Jews and their businesses. Some Jewish tough guys defended their people. When one Irish American offender was arrested for his misdemeanors, he no doubt spoke for many others when he complained that the "Jews seem to be taking everything away. Most of the stores are owned by Jews. Practically everything is Jewish."[5]

Significantly, these angers and actions did not carry over to Parkchester, even though a sizeable number of original tenants actually hailed from the South Bronx. No Irish street gangs attacked against Jewish youngsters. Anti-Semitism was not preached from Christian pulpits. Yet in this generally tolerant neighborhood there still were discernible limits to interreligious conviviality. Jews and Christians rarely counted one another as their closest friends, even if synagogue leaders were concerned about the maintenance of Jewish identification in this new heterogeneous setting where there were no readily identifiable ethnic markers. In any event, the way these groups behaved toward one another with forbearance set their multiple-faith community apart from many other neighborhoods in the city.

Similarly, in the late 1960s and early 1970s, when Parkchester was finally integrated, the issue of race was roiling New York City and soiling the air all over its five boroughs. During this time of turmoil, there was in Parkchester some naysaying about integrated housing in line with the racist position that the MLIC had long maintained. This black mark on the community's history did not completely disappear. Indeed, incidents of nasty pushback from some white tenants about African Americans and Latinos residing in their buildings did occur. Still, while it is impossible to tease out what whites said privately to one another when previously excluded groups moved in, the change in the populace's coloration occurred without significant public discussion, rancor, or dispute. Nor was there an immediate mass flight of residents out of Parkchester. For the most part, the races lived among one another, in their initial encounters, without visible strife but also without much expression of the possible social and cultural bounties of integration. Even more notably, a few years later, when the neighborhood's own rapidly aging buildings began to break down and criminality seeped into the area, the onus of what was going wrong was not laid on the newest residents. In many other locales, acute urban problems led to social conflict and even violence. Here again, the Parkchester experience stood apart. Understanding why and how Parkchesterites have lived their lives as they have and what their encounters with each other and with the surrounding city have been is the key objective of this study.

This history of Parkchester identifies the factors that have made this Bronx neighborhood attractive to successive groups of residents as its mostly working-class families for the most part found ways to live harmoniously. It explores the dynamics of white, black, Latino, and new immigrant movement within and without the city and offers a nuanced examination of interethnic and interracial relations in Gotham over the past eighty years.

Our eight-decade-long story begins with a delineation of how Parkchester's founders successfully planned and created an imposing, affordable, and sustainable apartment neighborhood on virgin land in the East Bronx for white working- and middle-class families who, even before World War II, were contemplating suburban migration. There follows a discussion of the ethnic and religious range of the first residents who were fortunate enough to have passed the MLIC's vetting, as well as the efforts to establish religious institutions that would serve the neighborhood.

The lived lives of parents and their many children during its Storkchester era of the 1940s–1960s is the next consideration, as well as how Parkchester's people came together as neighbors, and often as friends, during World War II and in the first postwar decades. Here due attention is accorded to the behavior of some less-than-docile women tenants who organized those on their floors and in their buildings to protest so-called "voluntary" rent hikes. They also had their say about the controlling behavior of the MLIC through its unarmed but uniformed "Parkchester cops," who were hired to keep adults and children walking the straight and narrow on the development's streets. These officers were credited with helping to prevent the youth gangs that were so common elsewhere in the borough and city in the 1950s from either forming or invading their turf. But many parents were decidedly unhappy when their own children received summons for victimless bad behavior, such as picking flowers out of Metropolitan Oval's gardens, and when they were threatened with eviction because of their youngsters' minor malfeasances.

The issue of race in Parkchester takes center stage as the long road from segregation to integration is traversed. The coy statements and diversionary actions of MLIC's leaders designed to keep the neighborhood all white, within and then in violation of the law, are presented within the contexts of their times, as are the strategies that civil rights advocates used to open up this Bronx preserve. Collaterally, a sense is offered of how Parkchester's white Christians and Jews felt, though they did not say much publicly, about the status quo that the owners worked hard to maintain. Very late in the 1960s, the first non-whites entered Parkchester. Where they hailed from, why they chose Parkchester, and the mixed reception they received from established white residents is then explored.

The focus then turns back to tenant-owner relationships, with an examination of the disputatious episodes that took place during the three decades of the Helmsleys' control over the neighborhood. The combination of the Helmsleys' poor judgments, the problems of the city during their tenure that were beyond their control, and ultimately the corporation's neglect of Parkchester's infrastructure, which frequently brought the owners to grief with residents, are explained. Then follows an examination of how a new cohort of socially responsible urban redevelopers, beginning in the mid-1990s, took over the property from Helmsley-Spear and renewed the neighborhood.

Bringing the history of Parkchester up to the present day, the final chapters draw attention to the lived lives and efforts at integration of the neighborhood's contemporary racial, ethnic, and national residents, in all their diversity, while finishing the story of the aging of Parkchester's former majority: its elderly white Christians and Jews.

The book concludes with a discussion of and personal reflection on the theme that informs so much of this eighty-year neighborhood history: the special get-along spirit that has pervaded community life over generations and within an ever-changing array of group encounters.

FIGURE 1.1. Parkchester under construction, 1939. Courtesy of the Bronx Historical Society.

1

THE BUILDING OF PARKCHESTER

BY 1939, FREDERICK H. ECKER WAS ALREADY A LEGEND in the insurance industry. A veritable American "rags to riches" success story, in 1893, "as a boy barely out of grade school," he began his career as a clerk in the mailroom at the Metropolitan Life Insurance Corporation and rose to become president of "the largest financial institution in the world." Along the way, as he developed "a bent for the investment side of the business," he was controller, treasurer, and then director of a company that even during the era of the Great Depression could boast of having nearly fifty thousand employees and a "total business in force" consisting of more than forty-two million policies with a total worth close to $19 billion. One of his long-term business associates credited him with "safely . . . investing the funds entrusted . . . by its policyholders" to the company to ensure "a maximum yield." Indeed, over several decades, Ecker saw the New York housing market as a place where he could successfully grow the MLIC's profit base. In so doing, he became a respected and influential figure in the city's real estate hierarchy. It was said that "Mr. Ecker's career [was] monumentally proportioned as the fireplace of his handsome office in the company's famous building on Madison Square" in midtown Manhattan. As important as his business acumen, Ecker and his company were lionized as "a prime example of private enterprise productivity devoted to public service." The insurance giant's resources were frequently expended to allow "moderate income families [to] live in urban communities in a suburban atmosphere." Very late in his life, he would tell an interviewer that "social considerations" were a "prime motivating factor" in his housing initiatives. He saw himself as a city planner par excellence and was often honored for his contributions to Gotham's development and thoughtful expansion. From a corporate bottom-line perspective, it made great sense to do the utmost for industrious, law-abiding, working- and lower-middle-class New Yorkers to live in more salubrious settings. These environments would inevitably "reduce illness and mortality rates for policyholders and the general population." Those who applauded Ecker's efforts did not comment on how controlling his policies could be toward those whom he set out to assist in his housing initiatives. And only later on in his life were his attitudes regarding race closely scrutinized and roundly criticized.[1]

As early as the 1920s, Ecker was on the scene doing his part in overcoming the acute housing shortage that then troubled an overcrowded city. From 1915 to 1920, the population within the five boroughs rose by 600,000. Manhattan acquired a net growth of 146,000. Wartime industries had attracted hundreds of thousands of workers, many of them African American, from the South. Government restrictions during the European hostilities on the utilization of materiel had severely constricted new housing starts. Municipal authorities reported dolefully that "over twenty thousand of the worst dwellings in the city that were not in use in 1916" were back on the market because there were "practically no unoccupied apartments fit for human habitation." Fearful that with whites and blacks, old-time New Yorkers and immigrants alike, squeezed together in tight housing quarters, Gotham would suffer race riots like those in other American cities, the Empire State and the city passed legislation that encouraged new construction in underdeveloped parts of the city. Most critically, the new law decreed that such residential buildings be tax exempt for a decade. In time, the legislative go-ahead from Albany came to be known as the Metropolitan Bill.[2]

Capitalizing on this opportunity, the MLIC invested $7.5 million in building apartments in Queens, a borough with wide-open spaces. Occupants were afforded a sense of suburban living in the city as the buildings were situated "at the periphery of the blocks, interior spaces were developed as gardens and lawn use for use of the tenants." The commute to work in Manhattan was pitched as "fifteen to twenty minutes from Grand Central and the Times Square Theatre Districts, by two tunnels and the Queensboro Bridge, and for a five-cent fare." By 1925, their sponsored "five-story walk-ups," home to 2,125 apartments, were renting for "about $9 per room per month," complete with amenities like "steam heat and hot water . . . not ordinarily included" in such low-cost housing. Reportedly, "immediately after completion, the projects were 100 percent tenanted and for several years produced a net return of about 6 percent on the capital investment." Demand was so great that "at least 10,000 disappointed families could not be accommodated." In keeping with their social engineering agenda, the MLIC wanted not only to fill up their apartments, but also to have only what it deemed as the right kind of people in their domain. The company desired residents who were not too rich and not too poor and who possessed sterling reputations. A set of policy precedents would be codified that would inform the protocols of tenant selection in future, more expansive housing initiatives. The rental agent was told "no discrimination was to be made as to religion." However, left unwritten but clearly apparent was that the new development would be racially segregated. Men who had "worked on the buildings and had done their best were to have preference . . . persons with incomes above $4,000 were not to be considered," and special consideration was to be afforded to "families with children." Additionally, references of every prospective tenant "were to be investigated to insure the exclusion of persons found to be immoral or otherwise undesirable." Once approved, those granted apartments had to conform to "reasonable rules for the control of the property" and "undesirable offenders were subject to removal." In other words, the fortunate people who were granted apartments had to behave appropriately under the watchful eye of a vigilant landlord. The first families in the Long Island City area developments included "building trades" employees along with "stationery engineers, electricians, plasterers, plumbers, carpenters" and many "city workers," such as "sixty-one firemen and seventy-three policemen." The religious composition of those who lived in the new dwellings is not known. But it is certain that MLIC wanted the public to know that it "had solved all sorts of problems for its lucky tenants." A company-sponsored history boasted:

> A lithographer came with his family from four roach-infested rooms in Greenwich Village for which he had paid $55 a month; Metropolitan rented him a five-room apartment for $45 a month. An expressman had lived with his family in the same apartment in Harlem for fifteen years when rents began to soar and the district to change; Metropolitan rented him a four-room-and-dinette apartment at $42.75. A young student from Spain was low on funds; Metropolitan took care of him for $18 a month.

While the report did admit that these "homes for working people... had no elevators, no electric refrigerators and the rooms were small," still it asserted that "the millennium is not to be expected in New York." As it turned out, all would not be totally well during the very difficult 1930s. "Frequent vacancies, the expiration of the tax exemption and a modernization program" as the 1920s buildings surely needed repairs a decade later, "shaved the return considerably." However, toward the end of the 1930s, "the picture brightened . . . the projects were again producing a satisfactory net return."[3]

Convinced of "the wisdom of direct housing investment" in 1938, the MLIC turned to the state legislature for assistance once again to facilitate new construction. And this time, they had grander plans in mind. Now, they were out to build a "town" or a "city within a city" and to improve on the company's performance in the earlier Queens initiative. The target constituency, though, remained the same. Residents would be "big-town folk [who] have come to a small town." Children and grandchildren of immigrants, these "Native New Yorkers"—primarily of lower-middle-class station— were "the people who work in New York's offices, teach in New York's schools, serve in the New York Fire Department, coach New York's college basketball teams, work for New York's public utilities and run New York's small businesses." They would be selected with great care for their ability to live the type of life the company would demand.[4]

In a 1938 radio interview, Ecker was even more explicit in identifying his target resident population. He projected himself as an advocate for a class of people whom others in government and industry and city planners and developers had overlooked. "There are a tremendous number of people in New York and elsewhere in this country" he argued, "whose income are not so low that they cannot afford anything except the dingiest tenements, and not yet are a bit high enough to enable them to pay the relatively high rentals demanded for decent and comfortable apartments." These families, he had determined, "belong to the same economic class who do not have to go to the free clinic or charity hospitals . . . but find themselves pinched when they go to private hospitals. This enormous intermediate group has been neglected both by the government and housing projects and private builders. . . . Some of them will now be served by the apartment village." In the years to follow, the village idiom would serve Ecker and the MLIC well as they elaborated on and then publicized their endeavor[5]

Anxious to move ahead, the politically well-connected Ecker lobbied effectively for the passage of an amendment to the State Insurance Code that would allow companies like his to invest 10 percent of their "assets in low rent housing" over the succeeding five years. As the measure was under consideration, Ecker announced that his company was ready to invest "$100 million if and when permitted" and that it would commit itself to "housing for the lowest rental that would yield their desired six percent interest on investment." The MLIC's head did not have to push too hard in Albany as his objectives dovetailed with the legislators' dual desires to provide "decent, safe and sanitary dwelling accommodations for persons of low and moderate income" while combating massive Depression-era unemployment in the construction industry, which threatened social stability in the state. One month after the O'Brien-Piper Bill was passed, the MLIC announced that it "had already selected a site for a housing project to cost one-half of its 100 million promise and that the wheels of progress were already turning." In recognizing "astute Chairman Frederick Hudson Ecker" as its "Man of the Month" of May 1938, *Architectural Forum* noted how the honoree "sought and got the cooperation of numerous men high in the public, private and labor circles" in "pace set[ting] ... the development of social activities which befit large groups. Low rent housing [is] the greatest opportunity to further the well-being and health of the nation [as] it can combine social objectives with a secure reasonable return for its fifty million dollar investment."[6]

The site for what Ecker would proudly call his "special interest" was a 129-acre expanse in the Bronx, "an undeveloped estate of a Catholic orphanage for which [the MLIC] paid 71 cents per square foot." It was a bargain at the time as "apartment house land on small lots in the Bronx ran about $1 per square foot." And here there would be no need for slum clearance and the dispersal of an indigenous population, which had engendered controversy in other places. To achieve his objective, Ecker assembled a blue-ribbon team of experts with wide experience as both builders and real estate operators. The Board of Design included architect Richmond Shreve, whose company had designed the Empire State Building; Gilmore Clarke, a designer of both the 1939 New York World's Fair and the Westchester County Parkway; a landscape architect; and several real estate consultants, most notably Robert W. Dowling, president of the City Investment Company. Soon they would set out to construct the "largest housing project in the country." More important, the new residential space in the Bronx that would be named Parkchester was designed as nothing less than a suburb within city limits, boasting not only wide-open, tree-lined landscaped spaces maintained by teams of gardeners, but its own shopping center, banks, movie theaters, recreational directors, and even an unarmed police force.[7]

The construction concept of the New York urban planners of Parkchester was adapted from the architectural concepts credited to Auguste Perret and his renowned student Le Corbousier (Charles-Éduoard Jeanneret). These Parisian pioneers conceived of a new type of city with the usual grid "pattern of corridor streets and dense buildings" replaced by "tall widely-spaced towers" that would be able to provide both workers in offices and apartment dwellers a home with a maximum of "sun, space and green." What became known as the "tower in the park" concept envisioned large business skyscrapers situated at intervals from one another with park spaces in between. Similarly, housing developments could be of high stature, but it was essential to have greenery—parks and trees—all around the fortunate inhabitants. Parkchester would be "as close to the 'tower in the park' imagery as could be realized in New York City."[8]

Even as construction was not yet complete in May 1939, Ecker proudly showed at the New York World's Fair a scale model of Parkchester in his company's exhibit. The diorama displayed with "mathematical precision" not only "the general layout of the buildings, but also the parks, ball fields, stores, theatres, garages and central heating plant" that would transform the area bounded by East Tremont, Castle Hill, and McGraw Avenues and White Plains Road close to the 177th Street station of the Pelham Bay Line. Ecker declared in opening the exhibit that the name Parkchester had been chosen to suggest "open spaces" like those of suburban Westchester. (And he reminded his audience that, back in the 19th century, this portion of the Bronx had actually been part of the County of Westchester.) The name also evoked "Park Versailles" and "Westchester Heights," two existing neighborhoods that would border the new construction.

Visitors to the exhibit could see in miniature how "fifty-one groups of buildings averaging seven and eight stories in height" were divided among four quadrants, each with its own park and recreational facilities. With Unionport Road "cutting diagonally through the property," construction was under way "to accommodate more than 12,000 families or more than 40,000 persons" in 171 buildings. Another diagonal thoroughfare, Metropolitan Avenue, divided the community with a beautiful flower-laden and sculpture-bearing Metropolitan Oval as its centerpiece. Those who might have known of the MLIC's earlier endeavor in Queens would have noted right away that this new apartment village would afford youngsters plenty of both open and, as important, manageable space to run and play ball. Over in Long Island City, "children and gardens" had constituted "a difficult combination, and . . . iron fences were put up leaving the young ones only the streets in which to play." In Parkchester, while youngsters would be directed to recreate in assigned playgrounds, those who might venture into the streets would be protected from the dangers of large-scale traf-

FIGURE 1.2. Metropolitan Oval. Courtesy of the Bronx Historical Society.

fic because Unionport Road and Metropolitan Avenue were the only major thoroughfares in the development.[9]

In the months that followed, Ecker and his associates had to have been gratified when the *Architectural Forum* announced that Parkchester "is the scene of the world's most imposing residential building operation . . . the realization of one of Metropolitan Chairman Frederick H. Ecker's pet business and sociological dreams . . . an organized heap of 110,000,000 bricks, 120,000,000 pounds of structural steel, 15,000,000 sq. ft. of flooring . . . a big story for like its owner-company and the city of which it is part, Parkchester in significance as well as bulk is BIG [*sic*]."[10]

In a similar vein, the *New York Times* reported approvingly how "work [was] proceeding without serious interruption" on the $50 million endeavor ($750 million in present-day valuation) to construct a "veritable 'city within a city' which will eventually house more than 40,000 persons." As the development moved close to opening early in 1940, the *Times* described the venture as "overshadowing all else in significance in Bronx reality" and predicted that "if the project achieves the success as it now appears destined to attain, it may well be the forerunner of similar developments in the borough where vast areas of underdeveloped land and only partially improved low-cost land abound." Once Parkchester opened, the paper reported that "one of the largest jobs of landscaping in New York City [was] underway," yielding "3,700 trees, 35,000 hedge plants and shrubs and 300,000 ground-cover plants." A suburb was being created in the city even as this "town" was listed as "second only to Rockefeller Center as the most valuable property in New York City."[11]

By that time, this massive project was big news all over the United States. The MLIC collected and retained laudatory reports from more than one hundred newspapers from cities large and small. Typical of many, the *Kansas City Star* wrote about how "The Joneses Are About to Move into a $50,000,000 Home," while the Tacoma, Washington, *News-Times* spoke of Parkchester as a "New Saga of American Communities." Back home, in January 1941 the *New York Times* declared that this "City Within a City" is "to family life . . . what Radio City is to the business community. It is bound to be one of the show places of the city." In 1942, amid World War II, but looking ahead to the end of hostilities, a New York real estate broker told the *Times* that the Bronx "experiment" would "possibly set a pattern for post-war reconstruction." Around the time that the Bronx community commemorated its fifth anniversary, a letter writer to the *Hartford Times* called upon local insurance firms, located in the "Insurance Capital of America," to emulate the MLIC's lead with "a model suitably adapted" to the Connecticut city's needs. "A city within a city"—that expression was used very widely—was required "with its modern medium-rent apartment buildings and its own well-planned playgrounds, parking facilities and stores. They could employ the best architects and planners." Such a development, the writer argued, would "enhance the area and the adjoining region."[12]

Proud of what they were achieving, Parkchester's builders were happy to share their expertise with politicians, city planners, and students of urban development. Believing that "the planning and designing of Parkchester is an education within itself," the management fielded questions from a Chicago alderman who "was planning legislation to amend the Illinois insurance legislation . . . such as was done in New York," from graduate students searching for thesis materials, from social agencies who "desire statistics of all sorts," and from "nearly every housing authority in the United States." For those in the city who wished a comprehensive appreciation of the "problems of administration of large-scale housing projects," the development's resident manager proffered a graduate course at New York University. The course was "intended for those who wish to prepare themselves for large-scale housing projects." Covering all bases, guest speakers in the course included Parkchester's attorney, publicity director, operating supervisor, and recreational director.[13]

Several years later, with the Bronx community continuing to receive kudos and requests for advice from around the country, Parkchester inner-circle member Robert W. Dowling reflected on how crucial developments like Parkchester were for the future of the metropolis as immense suburbanization was becoming a fact of life in America. Dowling was much in favor of, and prepared to debate, the merits of the "vertical city" as distinguished from the "horizontal" community. In his view, "a way must be found to pro-

FIGURE 1.3. Aerial view of Parkchester, 1940. Courtesy of the Bronx Historical Society.

vide middle class housing if cities are to be restored as desirable and economically feasible places for middle-income families to live and to bring up children." Indeed, he critiqued "both the one-class middle-income suburbs and the city made up of the highest and lowest income groups" as "uneconomic, antisocial, un-American and undemocratic." Dowling was certain that "small ground coverage with high buildings has a tremendous advantage in densely-populated areas such as New York."[14]

Parkchester was not a perfect architectural construct, at least not in the opinions of design critics. Some architects and city planners argued, according to *Fortune Magazine*, that while the MLIC had "attempted to minimize the effects of density by building and confining buildings to 25% of the land" with the rest set aside for play areas, streets, and parkways, still "the buildings cast long shadows on one another's windows." Furthermore, "the sudden concentration of 35,000 residents on 129 acres of land . . . has disrupted subway service and necessitated building a new public school." Almost immediately after Parkchester opened, the Board of Transportation added twenty-six more rush-hour trains to the Pelham Bay subway line that serviced the new neighborhood. And in 1946, the station at 177th Street/Parkchester was favored with an additional track and was designated an express stop, helping speed commuters during rush hour into Manhattan. Nine local stations were passed in the South Bronx as the train made its way to 125th Street. The problem of school overcrowding would not be so quickly solved as Parkchester grew.[15] More sympathetic observers of the construction conceit recognized that to decrease "density per acre and the height of buildings" would have resulted in "the sacrifice of investment return" and "the upping [of] the rent scale."

No matter; Frederick Ecker and his associates had their "intended community." It was a place off of the city grid that would be later characterized as "an independent city, a new middle-class enclave well removed from the uncertainties of old inner city neighborhoods many of its residents left." Not said, but soon to be evident, was the truth that this special place within the metropolis would be the preserve of a select, white-only clientele who would be on the move into Parkchester in 1940.[16]

FIGURE 2.1. Irene and Julius Horowitz with their son Michael and nephew Mark Steiner, circa 1940. Courtesy of Rivka Horowitz.

2

FORTUNATE APARTMENT DWELLERS AND THE BEGINNINGS OF COMMUNITY LIFE

THE BACK AND FORTH BETWEEN ARCHITECTURAL design cognoscenti was of little moment to the thousands of families who flocked to see Parkchester under construction and to tender applications. In the fall and early winter of 1939–1940, even as much of the development was still being built, an estimated seventy-five thousand persons visited the renting offices. Coaches for transportation from midtown Manhattan to the Bronx were made available free of charge. A bus flyer also included driving directions for those who owned cars. Sometimes as many as four thousand people queued up on a Sunday to view "complete floor plans" and "model apartments decorated by leading department stores." Occasionally, the line extended well onto Westchester Avenue. The MLIC had thousands of names on file and many families waited months for an appointment. When their day to inspect the premises came, after strolling, wide-eyed, through "the curving, quiet, tree-lined drives" and looking at "artistically grouped buildings of different shades and no unsightly signs," anxious and excited prospective tenants were "greeted by an entrance hall large enough to be used as a dining space." They were shown "a clothes closet and . . . a living room 11 ½ by 17 ½ feet in size." The bedrooms were shown as "12 by 15 feet with a tiled bathroom." The kitchen that "adjoined the entrance hall" was described as "a cheerful and efficient workroom" with a combination "sink-laundry tub, metal cupboards, cabinets and broom closet." The refrigerator and range were of "popular make." Frigidaire was very pleased that "over 12,000" of its units were "chosen for the world's largest single apartment house development." The company boasted in a full page ad in the *New York Times* that it was proud to be associated with "the Town of Tomorrow."[1]

It was emphasized to those with "an eye out for . . . safety features . . . in these fire-proof buildings" that the elevators were "the last word in self-leveling, push button type." The stairwells had "abrasive treads" to prevent slipping and the front door of each apartment had "another kind of safety—burglary protection through the use of peep hole, chain and chime." Within the apartments, "flat-bottomed tubs were used to avoid slipping accidents, and there was even a built in compartment to store used razor blades. Men could shave without fear of cutting themselves, as bathroom lighting was designed so that shadows would not be cast under the chin." Perhaps most importantly for young families, the living quarters were child proofed. For example, the casement windows were designed to "have the effect of a high sill beyond the reach of a small child." It was said that nothing less could be expected from an insurance company.[2]

For in-home entertainment, "every building [was] equipped with a roof aerial and every apartment with a universal wall plug that gives power aerial and ground for radio sets." But, it was noted, "loud tuning at any time or receiving at all after eleven o'clock was frowned upon."[3]

Finally, visitors had to have been impressed when the agent rattled off how an army of workers would maintain the infrastructure of their "city within itself" with "equipment which includes

FIGURE 2.2. Frigidaire ad, *New York Times*, July 16, 1939.

snow-removal trucks, power lawn mowers, forty-six bicycles, a station wagon, a machine shop, an electrical shop for repairing motors and refrigerators and a carpentry shop."[4]

Among those most ready to sign a Parkchester lease were "couples and individuals who were starting out in housekeeping for the first time. Many . . . were newly-weds and some were married couples that had 'doubled up' by living with relatives." After an initial visit, some "young couples, newly-married, came back with 'in laws' whose appreciation was deemed advisable and desirable." Reportedly, one young man who filled out the application form wrote: "Please reserve one with a threshold, so that I can transport my spouse appropriately across." Fortunate new tenant, and new husband, David Hershkowitz did just that, early in April 1940, when after his honeymoon with Pearl, he carried her into their apartment on Unionport Road. For what it was worth, Ecker's design team was on the record as having "gone the last mile in the effort to simplify living and make matrimony painless."[5]

Maretta and Joe Krista surely felt appreciative of what the MLIC had produced. They would recall sixty-five years after they moved from the Melrose section of the Bronx into their apartment late in October 1940 that "through the eyes of newlyweds . . . Parkchester . . . was a veritable heaven. It was beautiful and there was a euphoria about the place. . . . Everything was so new and bright. There were shiny parquet floors, the smell of the new paint and new wood . . . the walls above the tiles in the lobbies were wall papered with high-quality, embossed paper that complemented the color of the tiles." For them, they were in "possession of our dream house."[6]

The Kristas and all of these first-comers also felt awfully fortunate to have secured a place, for it was very difficult for aspirants to get into Parkchester. Before the complex opened, some forty-eight thousand families applied to get into the highly desirable neighborhood, which could accommodate barely a quarter that number. The MLIC stated that it vetted on a "first come first serve" basis, though only "if the applicant's character and economic status are up to snuff." Such had been their policy back in the 1920s and 1930s in the Queens development. But now, Parkchester agents investigated applicants with even greater care and precision. All potential residents were fully vetted through a "six phase" process that began with the filing of an application and continued until those who were accepted deposited an extra month's rent as security.[7]

When Parkchester was under construction, Irene and Julius Horowitz lived at 1105 Manor Avenue, two subway stops away from the 177th Street station. After seeing a flyer about the development, they were captivated by the prospect of living in an apartment that would be available for $54 a month for two bedrooms, utilities included. Seemingly, they fit the type of family that the MLIC desired. Irene was in her twenties and Julius in his early thirties, and they had one child. Julius worked in the garment industry. Irene was a homemaker. Today, we might refer to her as a stay-at-home mom. Their family income was between $1,800 and $4,800 annually. The MLIC did not want residents who either earned more or less than this standard. Much as with their earlier Queens endeavor, pay stubs were important documents. But to gain a lease, the Horowitzes also had to be interviewed by a Parkchester "social worker" who ascertained their reputability through speaking to them and to their neighbors. The investigators were to determine through their "intimate and penetrating" questions, more than "any census enumerator has ever asked," whether the family was "neat and self-respecting or careless and uncouth. Decent and quiet folk, or likely to be loud and cantankerous neighbors."[8]

However, the MLIC was seemingly disturbed when their intrusive selection system became public knowledge. In August 1940, the MLIC strongly denied that "trained social workers" visited applicants' apartments. Rather, the company asserted quite vaguely "such investigation of applicants as is made is routine. It is performed by members of the management staff and merely follows the common practice in the renting of apartments." Still, four months later, in a matter-of fact, though complimentary, report on the development, a real estate journal identified a Parkchester Investigation Department that hired "an investigator that checks all references" and a tenant selection committee that "reviewed the data supplied [and] made the final determinations.[9]

The Horowitzes were both acceptable and felt fortunate at a time when "there were approximately four applicants for every apartment." It may also have crossed their minds that, as Jews, there were other places in the city where people of their faith were unwanted. What is certain is that "the management was particular in whom they chose to rent to and they could afford to be particular." Irene would recall some seventy years later that many young couples in their Manor Avenue building wanted to be in Parkchester. The Horowitz family was the only one selected. They moved in to a two-bedroom apartment on 2055 McGraw Avenue the day the development opened. The Horowitzes were among the several hundred families who entered Parkchester in late February–early March 1940.

When they looked around their floor and building, Julius and Irene found themselves among people whose lifestyles and concerns were remarkably similar to their own. Children were everywhere. Of the sixty-nine families who took up residence in the seven-story building, twenty were just like the Horowitzes, engaged in raising very young sons and daughters. Eight other families had preteens in tow. One family had three children. By the end of the 1940s, Julius and Irene would be blessed with an additional son and a daughter and then they too would have to deal with figuring out how to reside comfortably in a now crowded apartment. In time, many of the twenty-three husbands and wives of child-bearing age who, as of 1940, had yet to produce their own boys and girls would have youngsters who would add to the sounds that filled the building's halls.

To be sure, 2055 McGraw Avenue was also home to several older men and women, some singles, some couples with grown children who, in some cases, paid the rent. The MLIC preferred those in the Horowitzes' age group. But Ecker and his associates seemingly did not practice any sort of what we would call today institutionalized gender or age discrimination. Heads of households could be male or female, young or old, so long, of course, as they were white. We may surmise that some of the older folks may have doted on the little ones around them. Others may have complained to the management about noisy brats.

Occupationally, many of the families, no matter their age cohort, fit the pattern of workers, civil servants, and lower-middle-class clerks and salesmen that Parkchester was keen to welcome. As a sign of those times, none of the women raising children worked outside the home. Julius Horowitz passed away in 1972, but Irene was destined to live in her McGraw Avenue apartment until her passing at age one hundred.[10]

An Irish American family, the Grahams did not share the Horowitzes' nor the Kristas' good fortune. According to one son, John, his parents and three siblings were deemed socially suitable; there were no "monster children" in their Beach Avenue apartment situated only a few blocks from the new development. The problem was with his dad's occupation. He was a subway conductor and did not earn enough to qualify. Their rejection was seemingly arbitrary, as many transit authority employees did make the cut. Decades later, when Msgr. John Graham was called to the pulpit of St. Raymond's Church, situated on the outskirts of the neighborhood, he would frequently quip in introductory remarks to local groups that "I finally made it to Parkchester."[11]

When John Murray's more fortunate family moved into a building just a few steps away from the Horowitzes at 1959 McGraw Avenue during the community's first days, his family decorated the apartment without him. For more than two months, starting late in January, this teller for Con Edison had been stuck on jury duty, sequestered as he and his eleven compatriots considered the fate of the notorious Murder Inc. gangster Louis (Lepke) Buchalter.[12]

Similarly, "among the first to take up residence" was Albert L. Browne, a safety engineer who had been living in a "three-story brownstone house" in the Mott Haven section of the Bronx. Having kept tabs on Ecker's successful lobbying efforts in Albany, he wrote directly to the company indicating that he was "looking for an apartment for himself and his wife." He was called in for an interview, presumably passed the vetting tests, and signed Parkchester's first lease. The family moved into 1545 Unionport Road. Sadly, Browne died soon after settling in; his was arguably the first passing of a Parkchester tenant.[13]

On the other hand, good news abounded during Parkchester's inaugural days at 2001 McGraw Avenue when Sol and Sylvia Schwartz, who had lived formerly at 1691 Davidson Avenue, west of the Grand Concourse, brought home Carol, who was born on February 24 at Mount Eden Hospital. A local newspaper quickly awarded her the title of "Parkchester's first baby." Some six weeks later, the Wayukers, who lived in the same building, welcomed their own daughter. These two little girls would be the first of literally thousands of children in the years to come who would fill the community's buildings and play areas as Parkchester came to be known as "Storkchester."[14]

While as of July 1940, the majority of dwellers were "native New Yorkers and more than half of them from the Bronx itself," Parkchester also had become home to families from twenty-two states and several foreign countries. An employee of a large corporation who was in the process of being transferred from Boston "read an article about Parkchester, called management and soon took a train to sign a lease." It is not known whether an investigator traveled back with him to New England to check out his family and friends. Similarly, the precise selection process that brought a few couples from Iowa cannot be determined. However, upon settling in the East Coast neighborhood, these Iowans felt very much at ease when they found that neighbors from their hometown were, in fact, living in the same building.[15]

Meanwhile, very close to home, a Catholic chain migration from the South Bronx brought friends of long-standing to the new development. As designed, Parkchester did not provide room for houses of worship, or for that matter public or parochial schools. It has been argued, with much justification, that such facilities were excluded "in order to avoid a steady flow of 'unregulated' persons into the development on a daily basis." After all, these transient worshippers or students could never be vetted like residents. This design decision was another indication of social controls at work in the neighborhood. In the parlance of that 1940s era of racial segregation, "unregulated" may well have been a code word for keeping out persons of color.[16]

Francis Cardinal Spellman, archbishop of New York, did not question the MLIC's building policies even as he anticipated that "over 10,000 Catholics would live in the parish" within and beyond the strict boundaries of the new neighborhood. And he recognized that St. Raymond's Church, situated near the planned North Quadrant, was insufficient for the projected influx of worshippers, especially those who had just settled in the South Quadrant, the first part of Parkchester to be completed.

Initially, both Father Thaddeus W. Tierney of St. Raymond's and Father Edward A. Loehr of the Blessed Sacrament Parish in the nearby Soundview section of the Bronx were not thrilled with Cardinal Spellman's decision to create a new parish to be called St. Helena's. Tierney, apparently to protect his religious turf, recommended to the archbishop that the new church should be situated at the southwest corner of Parkchester "as far away as possible from his parish." He reasoned that his "plan would have given half of Parkchester's new Catholic residents to St. Raymond's." However, the priest deferred to Cardinal Spellman's judgment that St. Helena's would encompass the southeast corner of Parkchester. To bring peace and order to the neighborhood Catholic streets, Monsignor Arthur J. Scanlan of St. Helena's and Tierney signed a formal agreement in July 1940 setting forth "the dividing lines" between the two parishes "based on the walking distance between the two parishes to be determined by an engineer selected by the Archbishop." A subsequent document laid out by street and house number precisely which buildings in Parkchester would belong to each church. St. Helena's garnered the majority. In the end, St. Raymond's serviced the North Quadrant; St. Helena's worked with the other three segments.[17]

As it turned out, for at least a generation thereafter, a friendly rivalry grew between students and alumni allied with one or the other of Parkchester's two parishes. One partisan of St. Raymond's has contended that his parochial school was "one notch above St. Helena's" in the 1950s because the students at the other, overcrowded institution "went to school only half a day while we were there for a full day." For writer Peter Quinn, "we were academically superior while they were more athletic and tougher than us. We did not hangout with St. Helena's guys much." Or perhaps the differences among the pupils boiled down simply to their opinion that "my parish is better than your parish."[18]

Once the geographical question was officially decided, the archdiocese swiftly allocated $600,000 toward the purchase of a site at the corner of Westchester and Olmstead Avenues, running through to Benedict Avenue. A property that had housed a German beer garden became the home for St. Helena's Church and parochial school. The parish's first Mass took place on June 9, 1940, celebrated by Msgr. Scanlan. Those who attended the first series of services might have noticed that the beer garden's bar had been covered right before Mass began. Some 450 students were enrolled in the parish school when it opened the following September; classes were held in a slightly remodeled Loeffler's Tavern. St. Raymond's also did well in attracting the newcomers to the East Bronx community—in the 1940s, attendance at Sunday masses doubled and its parochial school enrollment increased from 867 students as of 1936 to 1,338 a decade later. In February 1951, the older parish opened a new, larger school building.

Peter and Anne Carolan and their young son, Peter Jr., were among a cohort of worshippers who like the Brownes, that first Parkchester applicant family, lived in the Mott Haven section of the Bronx. These Catholic families were members of the three churches in the area—St. Pius, St. Jerome, and St. Luke—situated within the same diocese. In the early 1940s, once St. Helena's was established, the Carolans moved on to the new neighborhood. Peter Sr., who was making a decent living as a plumber, and homemaker Anne saw it as a step up for them, especially as they perceived that their former neighborhood was "starting to change." Mott Haven had long been "a lower middle class market" with "many tenement and frame houses" and some "good apartment houses" occupied by "Russian Jews, Irish and Italians." But now, the Carolans and their friends had grown concerned about the movement of African Americans and other racial minorities into the district, even if blacks and Latinos were still less than 5 percent of the population. Like the Horowitz family, the Carolans were gratified that their application was accepted—they had close friends who were turned away and had to look to Fordham Road in the West Bronx for new housing. That latter unlucky couple would persistently seek out a spot in Parkchester for the next quarter century. Peter and Anne took an apartment at 1510 Archer Road in a community that, like the Mott Haven of the past, was composed of Irish, Italians, and Jews. Once young Peter was ready for school, St. Helena's was their unquestioned choice. He would be a student there from kindergarten in 1947 through high school.[19]

Sally and John McInerney, who moved to 1558 Unionport Road from the Highbridge area near Yankee Stadium in June 1940, immediately saw St. Helena's not only as a place to pray and to send their son to kindergarten but as a hub of their social life much like the church of their youth. Sally, a secretary at Columbia University, and John, a civil servant who worked "in the court system," viewed Parkchester as "a garden spot of the world" and were anxious to reconnect with friends from the old neighborhood who also had passed the vetting process. They were among the founding members of the Parkchester Christian Association, a social and recreational club that grew to between five and six hundred members. Not only did the association deepen St. Helena's hold on its parishioners, but on occasion the group's leaders met with Parkchester management to suggest improvements to the development's infrastructure.[20]

New Jewish religious institutions likewise were established right after the development opened. The founders of the Young Israel of Parkchester (YIP) on Virginia Avenue, just outside the West Quadrant, and Temple Emanuel of Parkchester, down the block from St. Helena's on Benedict Avenue in the South Quadrant, could tell their new Catholic neighbors similar stories about why they chose the area and what they hoped to do for their own young and old in the community. Similar to the Catholics, many of the Jews came to Parkchester from areas just a few subway stops away in the Bronx.

Much as St Raymond's had ministered to East Bronx Catholics until 1940, the Jewish Center of Unionport—also known as the "Ellis Avenue shul"—situated south of Parkchester in nearby Westchester Heights, and the Beth Jacob Congregation—the so-called "Leland Avenue shul"— located just a block west of the new development in Park Versailles, had served area Jews since the 1920s. Still, there was certainly space in these synagogues for newcomers. The Jewish Center, in particular, boasted 750 seats in its Orthodox sanctuary: 500 for men, 250 for women in the balcony. There also was a commodious hall in the basement for social events of all sorts. But the young couples who met in Kalman and Helen Winkler's apartment on McGraw Avenue in May 1940 for an organizational meeting wanted a congregation of their own. All of them had passed Parkchester's admission requirements and were precisely the type of lower-middle-class families the management wanted. Kalman Winkler was a pattern cutter in the garment industry. The hosts, much like Irene and Julius Horowitz, who were also at that initial gathering, had migrated several subway stops west over from the Soundview–Elder Avenue neighborhood. There they had been friends through association with the Young Israel of Bronx Gardens located on Ward Avenue, near

Westchester Avenue and 172nd Street. They wanted to bring the Young Israel style of worship and social conviviality to the new neighborhood even though the Winklers' brother-in-law, Rabbi Harry D. Silver, had just a year earlier been called to the Jewish Center's pulpit.[21]

Since its inception on the Lower East Side some thirty years earlier, this "young people's," modern Orthodox congregational movement had reached out to the American-born children of Jewish immigrants offering both the very observant and the less religiously committed, a panoply of educational, recreational, and, above all, social activities that complemented their decorous, participatory services. In fact, as true devotees of the Young Israel movement, Helen and Kalman and Irene and Julius had "double-dated," as it were, at Saturday night dances held in the storefront synagogue after the Sabbath ended. Helen's family belonged to the Bronx Gardens congregation; Kalman was her respectful suitor.[22]

Rabbi Silver, who ministered to an "older crowd" on Ellis Avenue, acceded to the YIP renting space in the Jewish Center's basement during the congregation's first eight years. Perhaps the Winklers and the Silvers, who were on very friendly terms, discussed these Jewish religious plans at their apartments at 1919 McGraw Avenue. What is known is that the generous Rabbi Silver served in the early years of the YIP as chairman of the education committee of the "competing" congregation situated downstairs. Back home, the two couples, their growing families, and the wives' parents, the Rosenblooms, all resided on the first floor of 1919 McGraw. In 1949, the YIP opened its permanent home on Virginia Avenue. By then, the congregation had grown from its original 24 members to 186. The synagogue was situated across the street from the Winklers, who had secured a larger apartment for their family of six.[23]

At the same time, even as the Horowitz family was instrumental in the growth of the YIP, they maintained an enduring
allegiance to their old synagogue on 172nd Street. For years after
they settled on McGraw Avenue, Julius and his two sons would
walk every week the mile and a half along Westchester Avenue to
the Bronx Gardens shul, passing at least three well-established
congregations and some storefront synagogues. As they walked
they may have mused that, in settling in Parkchester, they had
opted out of a neighborhood that possessed multiple Jewish institutions of long-standing to reside in a community where Jews
would be a minority religious group. Clearly there was work to
be done to create resolute Jewish life in this new heterogeneous
setting where there were no readily identifiable ethnic markers
beyond the synagogues situated outside of the complex. Still Julius retained a strong allegiance to his erstwhile synagogue and
its young rabbi. As president of the Young Israel of Bronx Gardens,
he had initially hired sixteen-year-old Solomon I. Berl as a youth
leader and Hebrew school teacher. Berl would assume the pulpit
in 1948 and would serve the Jews of the neighborhood until the
late 1960s.[24]

For Jews of more liberal religious persuasion, Temple Emanuel
of Parkchester opened its doors in 1942.[25] Initially, the Conservative
congregation occupied a corner storefront under the elevated subway tracks a few steps north of the 177th Street stop. Synagogue lore
has it that the congregation "scrimped and saved to build a stand
alone synagogue on Benedict Avenue." St Helena's tradition has it
that Temple Emanuel would not have become its friendly neighbor
without the intercession of Msgr. Scanlan. As the story goes, the
priest bought the property from an owner who would not sell to
Jews and then resold the large corner lot to Emanuel.[26]

Though the congregants were evidently pleased to have secured
a permanent home, its location, approximately one hundred feet

due north of the elevated subway tracks, proved a daunting challenge to its rabbis when they rose to preach. The rumbling of the subway cars, particularly the downtown trains that made the bigger racket, as they held forth from the rostrum was quite frustrating. The acoustic issue was particularly acute during the High Holiday season in pre-air-conditioning times when the windows and doors had to be wide open lest the large gathering of worshippers swelter. Even with a microphone, the rabbi strained to be heard above the din.[27]

In 1949, the Catholic church and the Conservative synagogue had a new neighbor, the Parkchester Baptist Church, also situated on Benedict Avenue. The members and clergy of this Protestant house of worship were very happy with its location. Its pastors could be heard without difficulty since apartment buildings across the street blocked subway screeching. St. Helena's, incidentally, got around the noise issue by always keeping the southern windows close to Westchester Avenue shut. It also benefitted from Msgr. Scalan's prescience in directing the installation of air-conditioning ducts as early as the 1940s. Sometime in the following decade, its now air-cooled environment became one of the community's most popular amenities. Outdoor ceremonies, though, still had to be timed to work around the subways passing through.

Far more important for the future of all the religious groups in Parkchester, the Building Committee of the Baptist church said "with a Jewish temple on the left and a Roman Catholic Church on the right, we felt there would be no harm in having a Baptist Church in the middle. We will work for peace and harmony with them all." Indeed, during a two-week period in September 1949, the YIP, Temple Emanuel, and Parkchester Baptist all celebrated groundbreaking events. A local newspaper appreciatively declared that "an interdependence of all of our people . . . contributes to a good, stable community."

Like its sister houses of worship, St. Paul's Lutheran Church started out modestly in 1946 when it relocated to the outskirts of Parkchester from Union Avenue and 156th Street in the South Bronx where it had been situated since 1898, beginning then as a German immigrant congregation. It rented space at the Circle Theatre close by the subway tracks and across Hugh J. Grant Circle from start-up Temple Emanuel and a Presbyterian church of long-standing located at the corner of Olmstead and Newbold Avenues. In 1954, church membership grew significantly when a Presbyterian church on Manhattan's Upper West Side merged with the Bronx institution and its pastor, Rev. Dr. Benjamin Farber, assumed the Olmstead post. Reportedly, many of his members joined him in the move away from West End Avenue because of "population change . . . a marked influx of Puerto Ricans in the area." In 1957, St. Paul's dedicated its own permanent house of worship on the corner of Virginia and McGraw Avenues, down the block from the Young Israel. Thus, by the mid-1950s, there were two "Interfaith Rows" right outside of Parkchester.[28]

Indeed, ecumenism was alive and well throughout the first decades of Parkchester's existence. Spiritual leaders of the Presbyterian church and the Conservative Jewish Temple Emanuel often exchanged pulpits on Thanksgiving and other holidays that the groups observed in common on a rotating basis. The local press praised this friendly practice. Some years later, Emanuel would conduct a Passover seder with St. Helena's. The YIP, in keeping with its Orthodox Jewish religious strictures, did not offer its rostrum to Christian groups, nor did its leaders speak in any churches. But the congregation was pleased that the MLIC saw fit to place an electric menorah in the middle of Metropolitan Oval, next to Christmas stockings hung over a faux fireplace. Although the Christmas decorations dwarfed the Hanukkah symbol, for those Jews who cared, it was a statement that their religious commemoration was recognized as part of the neighborhood's expression of holiday spirit.[29]

Meanwhile, living among these families who were carefully selected to reside in what a MLIC house organ called a "happy town and an asset to the city and the Metropolitan" were a group of special new neighbors who were not closely questioned. Even before Parkchester was completed, Ecker encouraged his own MLIC white-collar workers from the Manhattan home office to visit the new complex. And without pressuring his people to apply, he nonetheless asserted that "we have selected tenants chiefly on the basis of character and ability to pay rents, and if Metropolitan employees were interested, surely they could qualify in these respects." A year later, two months into Parkchester's existence, he reported to those whom he called his "veterans," those who had worked for the company for many years, that "250 Metropolitan employees were among the first 2,000 apartment dwellers in Parkchester." And he reiterated, "I can think of not one group of people who will meet these requirements better than the members of the Metropolitan family." In fact, there was one employee whom Ecker vetted or recommended himself: his chauffeur took an apartment on McGraw Avenue. This fine fellow was not only a source for inside information for the boss about what was going on in the neighborhood but also was known to drive children home when he was not on duty.[30]

Also contributing to the emergence of Parkchester as effectively a helpful company town was the legion of professional, maintenance, and service employees who personally resided in the development even as they kept the community running efficiently. In its first month, Meyer W. Greenwald, head of the legal department, moved in with his wife and three young children. He was assigned the complicated task of assisting tenants with their legal problems, like "when a family has a serious illness and can't pay the rent because of medical expenses," while protecting the financial interests of the management. In that latter role, it was warned, "let a tenant try to break his lease intentionally. Then he'll run up against a fiery Meyer ready to 'give him the works.'" The generally benevolent Greenwald also looked out for the concerns of the cohort of blue-collar workers who kept the neighborhood spick and span. For example, he relished going after "smooth talking salesmen" who tricked employees "into jams of one kind or another."[31]

In 1945, five years into Parkchester's history, the *Parkchester Press Review*, an organ that generally granted the insurance company favorable coverage, ran a series of profiles of the men and women who worked as service dispatchers, chief electrician, chief bookkeeper and assistant office manager, painting boss, and the like. The operating superintendent was referred to as the "Village Superintendent." The image of a suburban or even rural apartment village was again evoked. Readers were told that if they had a complaint in any of these areas, the problem solver was just a half mile away and at their beck and call. And when these well-rounded fellows were not on the job, one might be seen in the neighborhood with a fishing pole in his hands ready for a relaxing day on the shores of the Bronx River or the Bronx side of the Long Island Sound.[32]

Giving carefully selected tenants the chance to reside off the urban grid, to escape the "overcrowded apartments of New York . . . from the noisy streets downtown," "to live the amiable, conformist existence of the suburbs," and to "feel they have moved up in the world," Parkchester rapidly filled up. On February 28, 1940, the *Times* reported that the first tenants had moved in the prior week and that "100 families [were] added in a day to the tenant list in the Bronx." Five months later, the paper reported, "more than 3,000 apartments have been leased at Parkchester." And in

September 1940, it was said: "A Fall Rush [was] on for Apartments" as "nearly 5,000 leases [were] signed for living quarters." By that date, when all of the quadrants had been just about completed, the new neighborhood was "draw[ing] 2,400 more families," with "tenants pouring into their apartments . . . at the rate of several hundred a week." Soon thereafter all, 12,273 units were completed and rapidly filled.[33]

Full occupancy was delayed only temporarily in September 1940 when the military draft was instituted. The MLIC "released 1,500 families from moving-in on schedule because the bread winners were going into uniform." The newly inducted were promised apartments when they returned and more than one hundred families came back to the development between 1945 and 1948. These reunited couples evidently contributed substantially to "the advent of the 'war babies' population explosion which became a significant space problem in Parkchester."[34]

The initial moving-in period was a semiorganized mob scene. The MLIC dated the beginnings of "the parade" into the complex to sunrise of February 22, 1940, when "the first moving vans entered Parkchester which before had known only the rumble of tractors and dump truck and loads of steel and brick." The newcomers came in "a steady stream by taxicabs and automobiles" with moving vans right behind them, and "the lobbies were jammed with the furniture." The company identified Barry Crandall, a member of the Parkchester renting staff, and his mother as the first tenants, "installed with their belongings" in 1969 McGraw Avenue. Many years later, Margaret Crandall would recall "the steady stream of tourists who peeked into her ground-floor window to catch a glimpse of the marvel that was rising from the bare ground of the Bronx." Later that first day a small "celebration" took place with food and "other goodies handed out to all comers."

Some of the first arrivals were, however, disappointed that their places were not quite finished when they showed up amid a strike of floor finishers. Management, quick to calm anxious new tenants, offered the dismayed the option of temporary hotel accommodations until the labor dispute was settled or the choice of a different, completed apartment. The management spent in these earliest days some $20,000 in hotel fees.

Subsequent accounts spoke of the "first families moving in on March 1, 1940," 202 strong, even while most of the structures in the unfinished quadrants were still only "outlines in steel," with van drivers not knowing where to go and how to unload. Also reportedly on the scene were newspapermen and women who came along "to question Resident Manager Frank Lowe or anyone else about where to go." Eventually, when other wings of the development were completed, an "information booth was set up as drivers yelled for directions." And once a system was fully in place, if a family from outside of the city arrived during the evening with their "laden van" of clothes and household items, the driver was directed to a "designated area" where a night watchman stood guard. The exhausted "chauffeur" was assisted in obtaining a hotel room for the night.

But even at Parkchester's earliest moment, whether it was February 22 or a week later, with "all the paths . . . not completed and those that were bore slush," as "men and women and little children" walked around "the new paths and looking around somewhat uncertain for it was all new," by midday "curtains began to appear at the apartment windows . . . and as darkness came, the light of the shaded lamps glowing from the long-dark buildings told more surely that domestic life had begun in Parkchester."[35]

For the first two months, however, tenants had a difficult time letting their friends and relatives know how happy they were in the

FIGURE 2.3. Moving into Parkchester, 1940. Courtesy of the Bronx Historical Society.

community. Telephone service was unavailable due to a battle between Local 3 of the Electrical Workers Union and the Telephone Organization of the Bronx over which laboring group had the contract to "pull" the telephone cables essential for the completion of the job for over five hundred families. When negotiations stalled the very month of the grand opening, tenants were warned that the dispute might cause them to be without service for up to a year. Fortunately, in April 1940, cooler heads prevailed and phones were available to those families who requested them.[36]

As the complex filled up and early problems were resolved, Ecker and his associates could step back and reflect on how well their vetting system had performed. The social and economic types of people they had hoped for were occupying the apartments. In July 1940, it was reported that "among the first families" were 163 proprietors, 101 executives, and 220 police officers and firefighters. We may assume that the occupational breakdown here was primarily of male workers. An additional 73 families included men and women who were in the teaching profession and 295 families with members in the employ of the post office and other federal services, while 159 had low-level positions in banks and brokerage firms. Some 252 bread winners were employed in the garment industry where, for example, Kalman Winkler and Julius Horowitz worked, while 197 were also in "paper, printing and advertising lines" and 241 in food, beverage, tobacco, and office-equipment jobs. And 165 Parkchesterites, like Peter Carolan Sr., were employed as skilled laborers. George Grobman, for instance, had been hired to install bathroom fixtures in apartments under construction and was very impressed with the quality of the buildings going up. He also felt that in his prior residence the neighbors were too noisy. He and his wife suspected that those upstairs were roller-skating in their dwelling. The Grobmans wanted a quiet place to raise their children. They took a place at 1969 McGraw Avenue as soon as the development opened. The majority of Parkchester's male residents thus could be found laboring in classic New York blue- and low-white-collar occupations. As one contemporary observer put it: "there are no extremely rich people in Parkchester to be lived up to, nor extremely poor people to be tucked out of sight."[37]

Indeed, at the outset, the management was reticent about making large amounts of work or living space available to those in the medical and dental professions, that particular elite, very-high-white-collar line of work. Apparently to the "astonishment" of Ecker's associates, when Parkchester first went on the market, more than one thousand doctors sent in applications, seemingly both to hang out shingles and to reside in the neighborhood where they would work. The management reasoned that if "so many medical men came in, none of them could hope for a decent living, especially in view of the two existing hospitals within a short distance." After close examination "of the medical needs of the community and of the reputations of the men who wanted to come in," it "was decided to establish a medical center in the administration building with complete medical equipment." Twelve physicians were duly chosen; six were general practitioners and six specialists. Arguably, the neighborhood needed more pediatricians than gerontologists. Eight dentists were accepted. No additional doctors or dentists were allowed to "lease a flat."[38]

Nine years into Parkchester's history, the MLIC was called upon to publicly quantify its economic-class profile. Company third vice president George Grove was summoned to testify in a case involving a dozen Communists on trial in the Bronx. The defendants alleged that juries were chosen only from "the rich, the propertied and the well-to-do," as what they claimed were the affluent residents of Parkchester. In response, Grove enumerated that the Bronx development housed "4,245 white collar and 2,775 manual workers, 624 professional workers, 2,294 service workers, 717 self-employed persons, 415 retired persons and 338 executives who head relatively small companies, living in the 12,242 family project."[39]

Of greater import to the management in those early years was that their "carefully selected families of mechanics and truck drivers or merchants of minor executives of any nationality or religion . . . with healthy young mothers and small children . . . seen everywhere" started early on to come together as a community. Not only were they fitting "into the Bronx as easily as Parkchester's street numbers," but an "in-group feeling" of "back-fence friendliness" within "an integrated group" was evident one year into Parkchester's existence, bolstered by "forty social and athletic groups, a symphony orchestra, [and] two self-supporting newspapers." Parkchester's men and women were known to be "nodding and saying hello to one another in the elevators, [and to be] playing badminton with one another in the parks." No matter their ethnic or religious backgrounds, the fortunate few who had passed the MLIC's investigatory examination were getting along well together.[40]

Flushed with the success of their construction of a mammoth and attractive complex for working- and lower-class families in the Bronx, and buoyed by praise in many quarters, Ecker and the MLIC took their architectural concepts and social engineering policies to the West Coast. By 1941, construction was well underway for large-scale apartment complexes in Los Angeles and San Francisco.[41] And then in 1943, this Bronx idea made its way to Manhattan. Stuyvesant Town—situated due north of the Lower East Side, covering eighteen city blocks between E. 14th Street and E. 20th Street and from Avenue C to the East River—offered thirty-five apartment buildings that looked very much like those of Parkchester and at comparable rental charges to the same economic, social, white ethnic, and religious types of people who had lined up along Westchester Avenue.[42]

In the quarter century to come, some of the original Parkchester tenants who had hustled to secure a spot in the development would have issues with the way their neighborhood had been built and how the MLIC managed its forty thousand residents. Some residents questioned the landlord's decisions over how apartments were allocated. For growing families, there were too few large apartments.[43] By the 1950s, as residential air-conditioning increasingly became a fact of life in New York City's middle-class neighborhoods, Parkchesterites began to feel that they had lost out. The prewar wiring did not allow for this critically important creature comfort. As time went on, the issue of overheated apartments would increasingly be a source of unhappiness. And then there was the annoyance over the many strictures that defined what was deemed proper behavior for tenants and their children. The MLIC doubled down on the regulations on comportment that had already been part of the contracts between it and its occupants back in the Queens project of the 1920s. Parkchester's own security police enforced the many rules, often heavy-handedly, and residents feared eviction due to their own or their children's alleged misbehavior. Nonetheless, more than twenty years into its existence, the MLIC reported that one thousand of the original families still lived in Parkchester and it was estimated "that from 300 to 500 sons or daughters who were in the 1940 lists [had] . . . themselves become second-generation tenants of Parkchester." In 1962 a Louis Harris survey pollster stated that "people who get into Parkchester tend to stay there until the undertaker comes."[44]

Such were the long-range sentiments of Mrs. Anna Batterson, who wrote on the occasion of Parkchester's twenty-fifth anniversary in 1965: "I will be 78 years old in July and hope I will be able to live here until I finish my time on this earth. . . . It seems so safe here. There is no fear of fire, and in the summer when the Oval is so beautiful with all the flowers and the fountain. It is like living on a big estate." This contented resident was no less satisfied that her family surrounded her in the neighborhood. Her son worked for the company in its underwriting department and his daughter and her family, which included a newborn, also had found apartments in the complex. So "now there are four generations of us living in Parkchester." Batterson undeniably would have agreed with the MLIC's boast that "through painstaking effort and efficient management, Parkchester is a clean, progressive community that serves as a model project to answer a great challenge facing our country today—the housing problem."[45]

But there was a dark side to the efforts of Ecker, the master builder and social planner. In a city, and in an era, where many of Gotham's neighborhoods were segregated, the MLIC followed suit. When, in 1939, the "planned community" of Parkchester was described as an "*integrated* residential colony," clearly "integration" meant houses, parks, stores, and playgrounds working well together on behalf of a clientele varied in ethnicity and faith, but exclusively white. This neighborhood of choice was off-limits to African Americans. Through the 1940s and the 1950s, only a few residents questioned that policy. Such were the signs of the times in the pre–civil rights era.[46]

FIGURE 3.1. Parkchester maintenance snow removal. Courtesy of the Bronx Historical Society.

3

FAMILY LIFE IN "STORKCHESTER"

PARKCHESTER RESIDENT MANAGER FRANK LOWE was deeply gratified when, in November 1942, one of the early tenants in the new neighborhood sent him the following complimentary letter: "It has always been our idea to eventually settle down in a small town, away from the clamor and rush of city life. However, without losing any of the benefits of city life, we have found our small town. Except that I don't have to get up at 5:30 to start the furnace or spend all day Sunday painting the porch or mowing the lawn or shoveling snow from the walks during the winter and we hope to settle down here for the next 25 years." Indeed, by that time, contented apartment dwellers had come close to having it all while staying in the city. Not only did the MLIC's crack staff of employees, which included maintenance people, gardeners, snow removal teams, and others, take care of their daily and seasonal needs, but it was possible for a tenant to "satisfy most of his ordinary wants without crossing streets or walking more than a few hundred feet from home." Small towns did not have such ready accommodations. In addition to the main shopping center along Metropolitan Avenue, in the other three quadrants, "small groups of neighborhood shops, drug stores, cigar stores, newspaper stands" had been opened. And the rise of Parkchester had led to "the creation of a new shopping center" just a block or so outside the complex along Starling Avenue. It was a route residents of Parkchester traveled on their way to and from the Castle Hill

Avenue station of the Pelham Bay line, only one stop east of the 177th Street/Parkchester express stop. Such sentiments as those in the account Lowe received were precisely the sort of feelings that he and the home office wished to engender among their more than forty thousand residents.[1]

Perhaps the grandest sign that Parkchester was fully coming of age was the decision of Macy's in 1941 to open its very first branch store on Metropolitan Avenue. It was a major local event as five thousand residents from the neighborhood and "the surrounding communities" turned out for "a preview opening." After a ceremonial ribbon-cutting the "public [was] admitted for a general inspection of the store."[2]

For Macy's, the new venue represented "an effort . . . to embody fundamental Macy's principles in a relatively small 'community store.'" Parkchester was deemed an "attractive community" and the company trusted "that Metropolitan's handling of such a project as the one in Parkchester would mean a project handled to the credit of the city, of the community and of anyone connected with the community." As planned, Macy's-Parkchester, unlike the Herald Square flagship, was pitched to "be closer to the community," with the "customer-store relationship on a more personal basis." Those who headed the department store hoped that the "personal neighborhood-store flavor of Parkchester can be carried back into the parent store." In other words, what would be learned in the East Bronx might be applied to retail merchandising both in midtown Manhattan and eventually elsewhere in the country. Indeed, even during the war, which was soon to cause "handicaps to further unit expansion . . . the Parkchester store was declared to be more than meeting its expectations."[3]

Macy's understood its clientele. To be certain, it conducted, as soon as the store opened, an informal customer survey. Shoppers were stopped and asked questions about their needs. To no one's

FIGURE 3.2. Macy's-Parkchester. Courtesy of the Bronx Historical Society.

surprise, children's clothes, toys, baby furniture, and carriages ranked high on the list of desired items. Parkchester's management team saw their community's demographics the same way. In 1942, the MLIC observed: "many went directly from a honeymoon trip to a new 3 room apartment previously selected and furnished. The largest group of children in Parkchester is the baby carriage group. War has stopped the automobile but not the baby carriage. In Parkchester, it just goes rolling along." By then, the neighborhood already bore the moniker of "Storkchester." Responsive to consumers, in that same year of 1942, Macy's decorated a "baby's room [as] part of a five-room display at Parkchester with Bo-Peep and other wood cuts adorn[ing] the walls. The room [was] pink and blue with harmonizing chintz draperies and rugs."[4]

Some years later, a "one-day sell-out of paper draperies" at Macy's-Parkchester attracted women shoppers en masse in a quest to beautify their living quarters beyond the children's room. The "rush" witnessed crowds buying four thousand pairs of "a new parchmentized paper that puts up greater resistance to sudden showers . . . in a single day."[5]

With Macy's serving as the "big 'traffic builder' for the retail community," elsewhere in the neighborhood's commercial areas, if and when the babies or their parents needed new pairs of shoes, the A.S. Beck Shoe Corporation was also there for them on Metropolitan Avenue. "Similar in design to Beck's Fifth Avenue Shops," the store featured "concealed stock, salon seating arrangements, air conditioning, fluorescent lighting and a soft pastel color scheme." In time, several other name-brand companies established branch outlets in Parkchester. Lerner and Plymouth were available for women's clothing. Singer sold its sewing machines. Horn & Hardart opened a retail outlet. Fanny Farmer and Lofts had their candy stores. Thom McCann competed with Beck for the shoe market. Gold Cross was available for the all-important children's shoe consumers. "Besides these," it was reported, there "are all of the butchers and bakers and candlestick makers . . . that any well-appointed city of 40,000 population would have," even though most of these iconic food emporia were situated on Starling Avenue and other adjacent streets. For refreshments, after a long afternoon of shopping, St. Clair's was there with a restaurant, cocktail lounge, and soda fountain. The Chester House was available for large family functions, like weddings, bar mitzvahs, and certainly many christenings given the young age cohort in Parkchester. It also had a bowling alley. Finally, for matinee or evening entertainment, the Loew's chain built the American, a large theater on East Avenue across Metropolitan Avenue from Macy's that showed first-run movies as did the Palace, located a block south of East Tremont Avenue, and the Circle, situated outside of the southern borders of Parkchester. Although the term "mall" was not then in contemporary parlance, Metropolitan Avenue and Unionport Road's "shopping center" anticipated the commercial and entertainment hubs of suburbia, all within Gotham's city limits.[6]

Parkchester management teams also quickly gained a positive reputation for their care of Storkchester's young charges. In 1943, it was reported that the development had created a seventeen-employee Lost and Found Department. Working year-round, this service was "kept busy receiving articles of clothing, jewelry, toys, tricycles mislaid or dropped by tenants." Ever vigilant, Parkchester policemen or perhaps "cooperating residents," in true small-town spirit, turned over what they found, and the staff was at the ready to find the rightful owners. Sometimes, however, the problem was acute and required immediate resolution, like when "a tearful youngster [was] brought in after wandering away from nurses or from parental care, while a mother gets absorbed in her shopping in the business district." Fortunately for all concerned, Parkchester's Recreation Department usually recognized "the lost one on account of their wide acquaintance with the families in Parkchester and quickly return him to his parents." In a few cases, the youngster was "kept happy in the playground . . . to await a call from the anxious parents."[7]

Putting aside such stressful moments, the recreational staff supervised athletic activity and a full slate of year-round events. Arts and crafts projects, Indian pageants, sports leagues and tournaments, square dances, plays, field trips to museums, and choral groups were integral parts of the programming. Attuned to health emergencies like the polio scares of the 1950s, when rates of infection rose "even faster than the population . . . [at] the height of the baby boom," the staff shut off the outdoor showers in the playground. They were never reopened. Given the directors' sterling reputations, parents were very comfortable sending their children by themselves to the playgrounds. It also helped ensure safety that the configuration of Parkchester limited vehicular traffic. Effectively, these parks constituted an urban apartment village's equivalent of a suburban backyard. While their boys and girls recreated under the watchful eyes of the directors, who knew so many of their charges by name, homemakers could toil without concern in their apartments or choose to join other adults socializing in, or simply enjoying, the quiet beauty of Metropolitan Oval. And the management was determined to maintain, even during wartime, their bucolic ecological setting. For example, the company proudly announced in the early spring of 1942 that "war conditions will not prevent the bloom of masses of spring flowers at Parkchester." It was promised that "coloration will be vivid and changing in Metropolitan Oval. 10,000 violet blue and yellow tulips will nod over 40,000 blue and yellow pansies. The perennial beds in the center park will salute spring with yellow hues of 1,000 narcissi."[8]

Storkchester's youthful demographics were not lost on manufacturers and producers once the postwar "baby boom" era, which began incipiently in Parkchester even during the war, became a national phenomenon. In 1946, the Gerber Products Company tested out "its latest in baby food, chopped apples . . . for the child who is ready to undertake a little chewing" at the neighborhood's Gristede's supermarket. Two years later, Telecoin, Inc., "a chain of self-service laundries," opened its first four outlets in Parkchester. So popular were these "laundry stores" that appointments were required in advance from housewives, and some husbands and their older children too, who wanted to use the fifty-three washing machines that were available every day except Sunday from 8 a.m. to 9 p.m. An estimated sixty-five hundred pounds of laundry were carried daily to the conveniently located operations "in junior's baby's carriage, stroller or toy wagon, or even in a pillow case slung over their shoulders." Reportedly, "the younger set, fugitives from the waiting baby carriages, lined up outside the store . . . keenly interested in watching the laundering process," while their mothers "shop in neighborhood stores or do other chores." Naughty children sometimes opened the machines while they were still in motion, which threatened to flood the store since the swirling action did not stop automatically. A larger problem remained with drying the clothes, including pounds of diapers. Parkchester had "no facilities for drying, and house rules" prohibited "hanging items . . . outside the windows." Remedies ranged "from doing small bundles at a time and visiting the service station several times a week, to using clothes-hanging fixtures that may spread out above the bathtub."[9]

At that point—five years into Parkchester's existence—the MLIC could be more than satisfied that their residents of varying religious and white ethnic backgrounds had come together as a community of cooperative, even friendly, neighbors within their well-planned small town in a large city. Such had not been the case in many of Gotham's neighborhoods during the 1930s where Jews, Italians, and Irish lived in close proximity to one another but did not share common goals or outlooks. Tensions over jobs and differences over interventionism versus isolationism in U.S. foreign policy stoked by anti-Semitic groups like Father Coughlin's Christian Front exacerbated hard feelings that the economic calamity of the Great Depression had deepened. In some places, especially when the Irish confronted the Jews, well-defined no-man's-land boundary lines separated antagonistic groups of youngsters and their parents, as well. In 1939, spates of anti-Jewish harassment and violence in Mott Haven, the very neighborhood that the Carolan family would soon leave behind, had led Father F. C. Campbell of St. Jerome's parish to excoriate anti-Semitism. Father Campbell would become involved in inter-faith work, and men like Msgr. Scanlan would follow in his footsteps within the new neighborhood as a force for religious conviviality.[10]

In Parkchester, no ethnic or religious boundaries existed. As one local newspaper reporter observed: "The Akuskas, the Abbotts, the Breslaus, the Devores, the Gershowitzes and the McCahans"—any New Yorker could recognize the range of white ethnicities enumerated here—were all very content residing with one another. Indeed, in "upset[ting] New York's old pattern of neighborhoods dominated by people of similar national backgrounds," these Irish, Jews, Greeks, Germans, Italians, and all of the other twelve thousand families, no matter their ancestries, were distributed randomly within the four quadrants. Actually, because of the way the MLIC filled up their apartments, without regard for religion or national origin, the community was more ethnically diversified than almost any other place in the city and, certainly, many suburban locales. In 1940, an examination of the names on the mailboxes or doors at 2055 McGraw Avenue would have immediately told Irene and Julius Horowitz that they were among approximately fourteen Jewish families in their building living among fifty-five Christian households. There the Albrechts, Biers, and Friedmans dwelled with the Kerrigans, Eagens, and Giordanos. Almost all of the residents were born and bred New Yorkers who had moved over from older Bronx neighborhoods. Julius Horowitz was a bit of an outlier since he was born in Poland. But then again, so were first-generation Americans Neil and Mary Ludell who came to the U.S. from Scotland, John and Mary McArdle from Ireland, and Edward and Rita Hoffmeister who hailed from Germany. But the "mixing spoon," as it was called, was missing one ingredient. It was racially discriminatory and excluded people of color.[11]

For the Jewish minority, no street was replete with their Yiddish or Hebrew commercial signage or their signature ethnic foods, places where people might buy and sell and informally congregate with their own kind. In this entrepreneurial and culinary culture area, day-to-day life was different from that in iconic Jewish neighborhoods like the Grand Concourse or even in the small enclaves in Park Versailles or Westchester Heights, those East Bronx developments that preceded the building of Parkchester. Ringing the new community, but surely not within it, there were a few old-style kosher butcher shops. Two were situated near one another by the intersection of Archer Street and White Plains Road, east of the complex. Starling Avenue could boast of housing the one kosher delicatessen in the area with a "Hebrew National" sign in the window. But this type of Jewish eatery, so pervasive in other neighborhoods with significant Jewish populations, would not be found on Metropolitan Avenue or Unionport Road or any of the side streets. Other Jewish delicacies, like smoked salmon, pickled herring, and sour and half-sour pickles, also required a walk to one of the Daitch markets either on McGraw Avenue near Starling or south beyond the elevated subway to Westchester Avenue. For those Jews who cared about gelatin-free baked goods, such breads, rolls, and cakes, known to have been produced with concern for dietary laws by virtue of the local Orthodox rabbis' check-ups, were available at Pakula's, also situated on Starling Avenue, and Zaro's, across from the 177th Street subway station. However, both were under non-Jewish ownership and all Parkchesterites shopped there. Some Jewish kids referred to a candy store on Archer Road, around the corner from the West Quadrant playground, as "Sophie's" because the woman behind the counter was known to be Jewish. But she was not the proprietor. Again, over on Starling Avenue near Pakula's, there was a green grocery, Rosemart, known to have a Jewish owner after customers saw a concentration camp tattoo on his arm. Some of the regulars at Rosemart shopped there out of sympathy for what he had endured, even though his prices were higher than those at Gristede's or Food Fair. It was a subtle ethnic preference, though the owner's Jewish name was not on the storefront. At the same time, there were no clothing or haberdashery stores known to be Jewish owned or favored. All told, when Jews went to shop or eat, they largely did so at the same places as did their Gentile neighbors.[12]

Indeed, most Jewish Parkchesterites would not have had it any other way. Though the Horowitz and Winkler families at the YIP and their counterparts at Temple Emanuel desired a robust Jewish community, so many of their co-religionists cared little about strong group identification. The majority had chosen, and had passed the test, to reside in a diverse neighborhood. They did not want to be singled out. Assimilation was not a pressing concern for them.

Jack Slove, the YIP's first financial secretary, picked up on this endemic tentativeness as early as 1942 when he contacted members who had not been attending meetings. He emphasized the need in Parkchester for a "militant Jewish group." For him, militancy did not mean fighting against their neighbors. Rather, Slove specified the need for people "dedicated to their faith in true community spirit." He and other founders wanted a "social center in Parkchester in a refined Jewish environment . . . where young men and women, boys and girls, and small children too, can find a source of recreation and relaxation as well as spiritual and cultural development."[13]

At the same time, elsewhere in Gotham, however, "postwar mobility did not necessarily initiate the immediate erosion of . . . ethnic communities." Put differently, in other neighborhoods, Italian, Irish, and Jewish families availed themselves of new housing opportunities without fundamentally compromising the largely self-imposed residential and social segregation that had sustained ethnic neighborhoods in the first half of the century. But such clearly was not the Parkchester reality within the city. Meanwhile out in Levittown and in comparable suburban locales, families chose what spots in the subdivisions would be ideal for them. Some Gentiles were not happy living among Jews. This sensitivity or prejudice would create in its wake a Jewish section of town. And some Jews "felt themselves out of place among their neighbors." Not so in an apartment environment where occupants could not select their next-door neighbors. Where life in Parkchester resembled, in the best of ways, life in suburbia was the ethos of "getting along with others." From its very start, residents were "terribly eager to be 'nice,' even if they [were] not so already—to live the amiable, conformist existence of the suburbs, to know their neighbors for a change." And as economic conditions improved, lightening families' loads, there was a shared sense that "they ha[d] moved up in the world by finding such a grand place to live."[14]

One very basic, but very indicative, sign of friendship was the open-door policy that evolved among residents in dealing with the bothersome overheating in their apartments during summertime. As previously noted, in the 1940s, air-conditioning was not available in almost any residential area, Parkchester included. A few stores had cooling units that may have led customers to tarry while they slowly made their selections. And it made much sense to sit through a double feature at one of the neighborhood movie houses, which also were air-conditioned. Some fortunate families repaired during July and August to bungalow colonies in the mountains, while those who stayed back in the neighborhood were sure to sit out late into the night in Metropolitan Oval. And by day, many residents were members of the blue-collar Castle Hill Beach Club, located only a short bus ride away—an urban "summer sanctuary" even if it had no beach. After games of handball, a swim, shower, and dances, come evening or late at night, it was back to the apartments that were hot as blazes. To increase cross-ventilation from the all-important floor fans, neighbors, without any directives from management, determined building by building to keep their apartment doors open around the clock. Without any grand statements about cooperation, neighbors simply assisted each other in making life more comfortable for those on their floor during heat waves.

Civility prevailed as Jews became used to living free of tensions with "Christian neighbors"—as Irene Horowitz would refer without a whit of disparagement to those next door—and seemingly vice versa. It was a profound change in attitudes between ethnic group members, even if in the end Jews and Gentiles counted those of their own kind as their closest friends. Indeed, Irene Horowitz would recall a "different neighborhood" where "neighbors got to know one another" and in many instances "became friends." Occasionally, moms took the subway down to Broadway for an evening show, leaving their husbands to mind the youngsters. In 1940, the majority of the kids in the building were preschoolers or in the elementary grades. There were only four teenagers living at 2055 Mc-Graw Avenue. Some families living on the same floor had intercoms with receivers in more than one apartment, making it possible for one parent or a single babysitter to keep track of multiple sets of children.[15]

Sally and John McInerney similarly remembered the conviviality that obtained among the nine families that lived on the second floor at 1552 Unionport Road. Relationships among the four Irish American families, the one Italian family, and the four Jewish families began with their common open-door search for breezes during the summer. These good vibrations continued throughout the year. John recalled pointedly that one New Year's Eve they made sure to stop at each of their floor neighbors' to wish them felicitations for the upcoming year before heading out on the town to a black-tie party. John also recalled friendly competition on the baseball diamond between his Parkchester Christian Association club and Jewish teams. His only regret was that his team "got murdered." He attributed defeat to his opponents bringing in "ringers" (better-skilled ballplayers) from outside the community.[16]

Participation in the patriotic campaigns on the home front during World War II gave Parkchester residents more formal and structured opportunities to cooperate and work together. After December 7, 1941, there was no longer any talk on neighborhood streets about forming a branch of the isolationist and frequently anti-Semitic America First Committee in Parkchester. By contrast, the Parkchester Branch of the British War Relief Society attracted new members. With approximately fourteen hundred residents and more than two hundred employees in the service, the wives, children, and parents whom they left behind were understandably deeply concerned with the war effort and hungered for reports.[17]

Early in 1942, a United Victory Committee of Parkchester was organized to activate "every organization and church in the vicinity" to show "their full support of the United Nations war program." Jack Slove of the YIP was pleased that his organization was invited to participate and emphasized how important it was for his fellow congregants to attend the committee's dances and rallies, which raised funds for the Allies. For him, it was critical "to support the war effort through Young Israel." In May 1942, his fellow congregants who served as air wardens paraded through the neighborhood to demonstrate the array of emergency equipment available in case of a catastrophe on the home front. Perhaps these paramilitary volunteers were clued in to a secret about Parkchester's construction that was neither publicized nor generally known. Beneath all of the buildings, situated below the basement carriage rooms, there was a labyrinth of tunnels designed to serve as bomb shelters in case of enemy attack. The Parkchester air wardens, fifteen hundred volunteers of all backgrounds, helped create a sense of community as they stood guard in the buildings where they lived. When there was a blackout drill, they were the ones to roam through the houses to make sure everyone was on board.[18]

These exercises were a serious matter and specific instructions on how to behave were circulated before the test. The directive stated "all traffic except emergency vehicles will be stopped. All

Parkchester lights—residential and commercial . . . will be extinguished" during the forty-five-minute drill and "no whistles will be blown" to indicate that the drill was over. One other protocol might have caused some additional anxiety among residents: "if during the air test, air raid sirens should be sounded, you will understand that it is an actual air raid alert."[19]

Later on during the war, at a more relaxed moment, a Reliance Civic and Social Association was formed for the expressed "purpose of creating and deepening the neighborly friendships which originated through association in the air warden service." It set out to intensify community interest in "the welfare of neighbors, for the present and the post-war period," which they hoped would come very soon.[20]

Of course, the realities of the conflict were driven home poignantly when neighborhood men died in action. Early in American involvement in the war, fittingly on July 4, 1942, Mr. and Mrs. Everett Kimball unveiled a commemorative wall plaque honoring those in the armed forces. The Kimballs, who lost a son, Richard, in action would be one of fifty-eight gold-star families in the community. So caught up was the neighborhood in the significance of this event that the leaders of the International Building Service Employees Union ordered their striking rank and file to stand down from their protests against the management over "wage, hour and closed shop provisions" on that sorrowful day.[21]

Patriotic Parkchesterites, like most Americans, fully cooperated in following the government's rationing protocols. In fact, in the early summer of 1942, the MLIC instituted a hot-water conservation program that served as a model for the entire city. In order to save fuel oil and coal, the plan called for supplying hot water for only three hours in the morning and evening. There were no reported complaints from tenants. In 1943, a winter season after Parkchester officials contended that "converting its huge central plant to coal" would be "impracticable," and announced that they preferred to just cut oil consumption by one-half, the MLIC changed its mind and voluntarily switched its 171 buildings to coal, saving some eight million gallons of fuel oil until the end of hostilities.[22]

Without management prodding, neighborhood residents, women especially, worked together and enlisted their youngsters to collect waste paper. The neighborhood was praised as "being in the lead" when a ten-ton trailer "filled to capacity . . . delivered [a] load to a nearby paper mill." Collections grew as parents and children made "rounds every day except Sunday to rouse their neighbors to cooperate." In March 1944, the Red Cross was assisted when "a detachment of nine volunteers calling themselves the 'Flying Squadron'" canvassed the community for donations.[23]

Early that same month, the "wives of service men" from the neighborhood formed the United Women's Committee of Parkchester. The initial efforts of the twenty original members were modest, such as the "sponsoring of a child minding service" and the establishment of a "monthly bulletin to be sent to the husbands." The paper was called *Affectionately Yours* and featured "a column on children's activities called 'Dear Pop' . . . along with news comments and gossip about the activities of individual wives." A few weeks later, the organization addressed an issue that struck very close to home when it sponsored a public discussion concerning "the problems of rehabilitation of discharged soldiers and their return to work and normal home life." However, it did not take long for them to turn with ire against a black marketer who was selling meat above regulated prices.[24]

On March 21, 1944, the Office of Price Administration (OPA) hauled Mrs. Minnie Levine into court for "violating price ceilings." She was in the docket because the Parkchester women's committee had identified her as a lawbreaker to the authorities. The defendant claimed that she could not read English and thus was unaware of

FIGURE 3.3. The war effort in Parkchester. Courtesy of the Bronx Historical Society.

the regulations. To ensure that justice be done, the chair of the militant organization was in the hearing room. Mrs. Lorraine Helfond, who was also chair of the United Victory Committee's consumer education committee, told a reporter that "the other women were busy caring for their children but that they would have their Victory Over the Black Market" parade within a few days. The purpose of the neighborhood demonstration, which would find the "crusading housewives" carrying placards, was to demonstrate "to other shopkeepers against several of whom the committee has already filed charges with the OPA that 'it does not pay to chisel in wartime.'"[25]

A sister organization, the Parkchester unit of the American Women's Voluntary Service (AWVS), did comparable work in buoying the spirits of servicemen's families and in helping prepare the community for the postwar period. For example, a "stork shower" gathered clothes "in layette units for distribution to servicemen's children." For older needy youngsters, clothes were sent to summer campers fortunate enough to have been transported away from the city's heat. The unit's canteen service distributed "gift packages to new inductees entering the armed forces and its Business Girl's Unit prepared Easter Duffle bags for overseas servicemen." Proceeds from the AWVS's dances were designated for a "mobile kitchen." Several members of the Parkchester unit's members volunteered for a special training course that the New York Institute for the Blind ran "in preparation for post-war service with blinded servicemen and women." Others took first aid courses that were deemed "one of the most sensational needs on a home front during the war." The Parkchester Women's Club acted similarly when it invited Goodwill Industries to show a documentary, *Victory over Handicaps*, designed to provide members with "guidelines . . . to meeting the normal, the wounded, the disfigured [and] the nervous veteran." Within the neighborhood, efforts also were made to organize child care for those women who went to work to support their families while their husbands were away. House-to-house canvassing was conducted to sell war bonds and stamps. Volunteers set up booths outside of local movie theaters and Macy's soliciting contributions. Their message was "stamps will be helping our government and ourselves." In honoring those who had devoted "an outstanding number of hours in volunteer" work at a unit luncheon in 1944, the *Bronx Home News* reported that Rev. Wayne White and Rabbi Nathan Lublin emphasized the goals of "brotherhood and community harmony," values that the Christians and Jews who labored together evidently shared. The minister and rabbi (whose houses of worship were not identified by the *Home News*) joined hands with a score of other religious and political leaders in a communitywide prayer service that

Msgr. Scanlan organized with the Parkchester Citizens Council outside of Macy's to mourn FDR on a Sunday after the president's death in April 1945.[26]

Four months later, when the Japanese surrender brought an end to hostilities, Parkchester celebrated with a block party that packed "the sidewalks and streets with people." The exuberance of this joyous expression of triumph and relief almost got out of hand when "a neighbor in her excitement and enthusiasm pulled the fire alarm box." As the story goes, she knew that a friend, firefighter Joe Krista, "was on duty and wanted to be part of the celebration. Sure enough, Joe arrived, sitting at the tiller wheel at the back of the ladder truck. Luckily, the false alarm caused no harm." However, among Parkchester's Jews, the realities of what had befallen their brethren in Nazi-occupied territories tempered their happiness as victorious Americans. While the YIP's newsletter was sure to note that "over 1,300,000 Jews fought in the armies of the United Nations," it also reported in the same shortened breath "four million Jews were murdered in Europe during the Nazi siege." Six months after V-E Day, synagogue scribes, like so many American Jews and Gentiles, were not aware of the actual scale of the slaughter—that six million Jews had been murdered during the Holocaust.[27]

Immediately after the war, the United Women's Committee of Parkchester redefined itself as a "consumer group," and with leaders again drawn from all local ethnic and religious groups, had their say about continuing ceiling prices on commodities. It was a government policy that often contributed to the continuation of the black market. The group told the *New York Times* that it wanted the paper to print the standard retail price of commodities to alert consumers about gouging by unethical storekeepers.[28]

Of more enduring consequence, in early postwar days, women activists turned to the question of their children's inadequate school facilities. It was a pressing problem that was only set to intensify as Storkchester's mass of youngsters started to grow up. Within its Manhattan home office, the MLIC's leadership had to have been pleased that these mothers were tackling a problem with Parkchester life that its critics had noted when the development had first opened.

In January 1947, the Emergency Kindergarten Committee of the United Women's Committee of Parkchester rallied at P.S. 102 to protest a decision that the Board of Education had made to lower the age of kindergarten from five and a half to four and a half years without providing space for the additional two hundred or so toddlers who would be attending preschool. Eight hundred mothers turned out for the contentious gathering. If their youngsters would have to attend classes at that more tender age, they asked, where were the facilities for them? The protesters also were unhappy that the central board had determined that advancement to first grade would be annual and not semiannual as in the past, leaving some children in kindergarten for half a year while overcrowding remained a problem. For the *Bronx Home News*, it was clear that the board had not anticipated and planned for the many youngsters that were attending from Parkchester, leaving P.S. 102 and its sister school, P.S. 106, on the opposite outskirts west of the new neighborhood, to run double sessions. On the kindergarten question, the protesters partially achieved their objectives. Two classes were quickly added. Still, one hundred youngsters were left without places within the overcrowded school.[29]

Two and a half years later, in June 1949, with the overcrowding issue clearly unresolved, one thousand parents and pupils from P.S. 102 took to the streets of Parkchester in an "orderly, quiet," but outspoken protest. Carrying signs that read "We Want a House to Learn In'" and "Part-Time Education Means Part-Time Citizens," demonstrators, "including many children in baby carriages," marched from the school on Archer Street and Taylor Avenue, situated right outside of the apartment complex, through the key thoroughfares of Unionport Road and Metropolitan Avenue. The complaint was that there were but forty-nine overcrowded classrooms for the seventy-one classes projected for the coming academic year. Six classes graduating from sixth grade would be replaced by ten entering classes, which would add 125 to 150 pupils to a school bursting with 2,500 students. Seemingly, the parents' association, with the strong backing of P.S. 102's principal, gained the assent of the Board of Education. The group was informed that the Division of Housing had accorded "high priority" to the construction of a new school in the area.[30]

The women's advocacy for better schooling was widely applauded in the neighborhood since it led to "additions for the schools serving the community and also a junior high school"— P.S. 127—"for 2,000 children." But back at the Board of Education, at least one member of the city oversight group, who had thought through "the impact of birthrates on schools," was critical of their stance. For James Marshall, "clamor rather than need" had pushed the Parkchester petitioners to the front. While recognizing that parents had a right to speak their minds, he argued that the board's "proneness to yield" when it was "subjected to a post card barrage from the parents of Public School 102 in the Bronx" privileged Parkchesterites. Marshall was "afraid that there is a temptation to use an audiometer as a measuring device for determining position on the order of priority. . . . Some communities are much more articulate than other communities."[31]

However, Parkchester's "people's voices" were just the type of "outspoken opinion" that Columbia University's Teachers College, the Public Education Association, and others on the Board of Education wanted to hear when less than a year later their "cooperative venture" hatched a "project to promote 'small town traditions' in the New York City school system." "[I]n a big city," they declared, "there is often an invisible barrier between parents and teachers and a need to bring the citizen into the classroom and stimulate local interest." At the same time, cooperating on behalf of their impressionable youngsters, Parkchester mothers were protesting the appearance of "dishonest and misleading" ads for movies shown at the American, Circle, and Palace theaters. These Bronx housewives were described as examples of the "aroused citizenry" dedicated to closely monitoring the motion picture industry. For the MLIC and Parkchester's parent body, it was most satisfying that their section of town was being viewed as an apartment village, which was then seen as an ideal place for children and their doting parents, and that their place in the Bronx was viewed as possessed of the appropriate family values.[32]

FIGURE 4.1. MLIC sign forbidding canines. Courtesy of Getty Images.

"DON'T PICK THE FLOWERS"

Tough-Minded Social Controls and Opposition

T HE APPROVING SMILES AT THE MLIC'S HOME OFFICE
in Manhattan over Parkchester women's activism regard-
ing school space turned to frowns and even anger when the
same mothers and wives turned their abundant energies
against them, protesting the many rules and regulations
that the company imposed upon residents and campaign-
ing against efforts to evict those who allegedly misbehaved.
The insurance company had doubled down on the social-
control strictures that it had promulgated in the 1920–1930s
in Queens—now all Parkchester tenants were presented with
a list of requirements for proper family behavior when they
signed their coveted leases.

According to the rules, there were to be "no bikes with or
without training wheels on the paths, walks or service drives."
The management's safety engineer determined that it "was
essential to ban the vehicles for the safety, comfort and convenience of all the tenants." In keeping with its strict safety
procedures, "public halls, stairwells, elevators" also were not
to be obstructed. The management did not want the wheels
of prams to scratch the walls and floors of their elevators.
Parkchester officials also were quick to remind residents that
"numerous personal articles such as baby carriages, sleds,
overshoes, galoshes and umbrellas . . . have been left in the
corridors," which not only "inconvenienced others" but also

actually was a violation of the New York City Building Code, which mandated that inside corridors had to be "free for emergency purposes." Exceptions were made "for milk bottles put out in the late evening." The place for those many baby carriages was the unlocked basement storage areas. Outside of the buildings, where no one was permitted to set up beach chairs, the place to congregate was the Metropolitan Oval or the smaller parks in each quadrant.

Canine lovers were told that even "man's best friend," no matter how small, could have no place within the confines encompassed by McGraw, Castle Hill, Westchester, and Tremont Avenues. The stricture explicitly stated: "no dogs or other animals shall be kept or harbored in the demised premises." One light-hearted commentator on the ban allowed that, in addition to common household pets, there could be "no pet monkeys, or pet coons. Pet lovers must content themselves with goldfish or the more refined of our feathered friends."[1]

Parkchester also had strict guidelines for how tenants could decorate their apartments. "No shades, venetian blinds, awnings" could be hung without permission. Perhaps as a safety measure, "no cleaning of windows from the outside" was allowed. Residents were formally admonished not to be "careless in disposal of materials in incinerators." They also had to make sure that "the little clothes trees" set up in the apartments to dry clothes would not be "visible from the outside," since their homes "were occasionally inspected to make sure they were properly maintained." And the occupants had to be reasonably quiet. There were to be "no disturbing noises by tenants, servants or employees." All record players, radios—and eventually televisions—and musical instruments were to be played at a low volume. Rugs were to be placed on all floors, again to abate noise.

Notwithstanding this welter of ordinances, the management averred that it was in no way imprisoning its tenants. In 1945, a

MLIC representative told the *Parkchester Press Review* that after five years of good living in the Bronx, "few talk about the fears that they had when they came here that Parkchester would become an institution featured by all sorts of rules, taboos and *verboten* signs." Wild rumors floated around in 1945 that "lights had to be out by 11 p.m. If you got sick, you had to go to the hospital immediately. If you died and happened to be Irish, no wake in the apartment. . . . Singing and other forms of hilarity were prohibited. . . . [Y]our apartment was subject to daily inspection by an alleged Parkchester *Gestapo* [emphasis mine]." Clearly these allegations of Nazi-like behavior so close to the end of World War II angered the company. Years later, Frank Lowe strongly denied that the development was "regimented"; rather it was a community where "neighbors were always ready to help one another."[2]

Still, one memoirist has recalled a strictly controlled and monitored environment. "You were not allowed to change anything. You could not paint a room in some other color. Only management was permitted to do the painting and this was done on a strict schedule of once every three years. If you installed a new fixture, you had to replace the original one when you moved."[3]

Far beyond their instructions to adult tenants, Parkchester's management was very strict about the behavior of potentially rambunctious youngsters. There definitely would be no hanging out on neighborhood street corners. Even small children were not "allowed to congregate or play in front of the buildings, on the grass or planted areas or any other place other than the playground." There, in that designated area, boys and girls were directed to behave properly. On snowy days, while the maintenance crews freed their parents from the obligation to shovel, boys and girls were prohibited from playing in the snow, again except in the playgrounds.

Measures like these to control the play of youths had their own history in New York. Back in immigrant neighborhoods, a genera-

FIGURE 4.2. The Parkchester police. Courtesy of the Bronx Historical Society.

tion or more earlier, Progressives, wary of the streets as incubators of delinquency crimes and fearful of radicalism gaining a foothold among the masses, had convinced city officials to build closely supervised public parks and swimming pools for downtown youngsters. These reformers also believed that these venues were good places to keep the impressionable away from wrongdoers while promoting the values of loyal American citizenship. For the MLIC, the prime concerns were seemingly neither cultural nor ideological but with the physical appearance of the neighborhood—keeping its bucolic setting intact.[4]

The task of keeping Parkchester's children—and sometimes adults—in line was placed in the hands of the MLIC's own security force. The unarmed "Parkchester cops," also known as maintenance patrolmen, monitored the development day and night and kept close tabs on violations of the myriad of rules. A "permanent behavior record" card was kept on every offending youngster. For example, "when a child walks on the grass, picks a flower, marks a fence or indulges in other 'destructive' play an entry is made against the tenant." Similarly, Parkchester management forbade sitting on the stone bases of flagpoles. When an officer approached, "youngsters scattered in all directions" out of the fear that if "arrested" their families would receive a stern letter from the MLIC warning them that future violations might result in their lease not being renewed.[5]

As of 1944, the "dossier" on seven-year-old Robert Simmons Jr. that his parents told the *Herald Tribune* "rivaled police records" included the following misdeeds:

> November 1, 1942, Robert caught on a lawn.
> February 1, 1943, Robert apprehended throwing a snowball.
> June 24, 1943, Robert trampled shrubbery retrieving his ball.
> October 10, 1943, Robert picked a flower in one of the
>   development's gardens.

Always on the case, in response Frank Lowe emphasized that the designated ball fields and playgrounds were the places where "small boys can work off their spirits." He was anxious to "protect the community's 'good families'" and feared that if misbehavior went "unchecked it would transform the section into 'another tenement district.'"[6]

For many families, the misconduct ticket was a worrisome prospect. Peter Carolan has recalled that, as a teenager, he and his friends were just "hanging out in a hallway" when a Parkchester policeman arrived on the scene and instructed the fellows to move on. Some of the guys in his group, but not Peter, "mouthed off" to the cop and all of them had "their names taken." It was widely known that three letters from the management meant trouble for a family. Wary of the policy, Peter and his parents met with the resident manager to plead his innocence and he was acquitted. However, many years later, in 1967, when Peter married and he and his wife wanted their own apartment in Parkchester, his "police record" was still on the books. Ultimately, after an investigation of the young couple's background, they were allowed to live in the neighborhood. In demonstrating that they were law-abiding, it helped that Peter's father-in-law was an NYPD lieutenant.[7]

Many other young men and women who had been, once or perhaps thrice, stopped and recorded were not as fortunate. Their youthful mistakes came back to haunt them as they were denied apartments when they were themselves young marrieds. Such was the unhappy fate of members of the Connor family. When one of their sons at twenty-five years of age and recently married sought out an apartment, "the management told him it remembered an incident years earlier when as an adolescent stunt he had noisily rolled a beer barrel through the center of the complex." His application was denied.[8]

It was also conceivable that good behavior had its rewards. As a five-year-old, Ruby Lukin moved in with her parents and younger sister to 1470 East Avenue the year the community opened. The Lukin family, who previously resided near University Avenue, were a classic early Parkchester family. Louis was a salesman, his wife was a homemaker. Though, while growing up, the well-behaved Ruby may have walked on the out-of-bounds grass, she was never stopped. As a young married, this Brandeis University graduate with a teaching degree and her attorney husband, Stanley Langer, were able to secure an apartment situated off Metropolitan Oval without much difficulty. Not only that, but once this couple "showed that [they] were good tenants" they were able to get an apartment

FIGURE 4.3. Ruby Lukin, for a Parkchester brochure.
Courtesy of the Bronx Historical Society.

for Stanley's parents, who had lived previously on College Avenue east of the Grand Concourse. The MLIC favored extended families residing in their development.[9]

Not all of the rules that were promulgated were easily enforced and identifying minor miscreants challenged the neighborhood authorities. For example, one of eighteen rules that applied to the leases in 1959 stated, "elevators must be operated by adults." Not only was this regulation impossible to monitor but also seemingly contradicted the MLIC's boast back in 1940 that "our elevators are governed by a simplicity of operation which the children can understand. The push-button system which controls them is easily comprehended—almost human." As far as ensuring quiet floor to floor was concerned, the management could never ascertain how many families had full-size rugs in their apartments. And since boys and girls did not carry identification with them, one-time offenders who were not known to the cops, might give a phony name or address. One young man whose father insisted that he always should tell the truth got around an officer's interrogation by giving only his first name. When the Parkchester officer demanded to know his "second" name, the coy boy offered his middle name. That move, which satisfied the authority, could never be used against him in the future, while it still respected his father's admonition. More important than individual efforts to work the system, not all of the regulations were uniformly applied. In fact, an allegation that the management was discriminatory in its enforcement practices led to a widely publicized court case against the MLIC that almost reached the Supreme Court of the United States.[10]

For the Jehovah's Witnesses, who brought the suit, the story of "class legislation and discrimination" against them and "favoring of others" began in 1942 when several of its missionaries were physically barred from preaching to tenants within Parkchester's buildings. Their religious movement was already comfortably on the scene, handing out its literature and attempting to engage residents in conversation. The evangelists averred that in giving "oral testimony" to their faith, with or without a "portable phonograph" to play a religious message, they were "kind and courteous to the persons called upon." The missionaries reported that they "had no difficulty with any of the tenants all of whom were very nice, receiving the literature and making contributions to help the missionary evangelists."

In their view, all was well with their work in Parkchester's buildings until a "guard . . . apprehended a missionary and requested her to discontinue her missionary activity." The officious request became physical when "she was forcibly ushered out of the building by one of the porters." In another incident, "one of the missionaries was stopped by a guard . . . and forcibly taken to the administration office at Parkchester." At that tense moment, and in later encounters, the Jehovah's Witnesses were told that their work "was contrary to the policy of Parkchester to call door to door." Still the work of spreading their "Good News," as they referred to their religious messages, continued for a while, often surreptitiously, as the workers sought "every way to avoid being caught and to evade ejection from the premises."

In August 1944, Chief McGannon, head of the protective division of Parkchester, personally involved himself in the still unresolved conflict. Following a group of Witnesses into one of the buildings, he reportedly informed them that "it would be all right for them to continue" and that his and their legal department would work out a reasonable settlement. But just a month later, McGannon changed his mind, barring them from door to door work, and Parkchester's legal department informed them that they had no right to evangelize in the neighborhood. Even as the missionaries continued to seek entry into buildings and were more often than not rebuffed, the Witnesses brought suit against the MLIC.

The plaintiffs argued that the Parkchester regulation that no one "shall enter any apartment building . . . for the purpose of canvassing or of vending, peddling, or soliciting orders of any merchandise . . . nor for the purpose of soliciting alms, donations or a subscription to any church, religious, charitable or public institution" without the "consent of the management of the development" had not been enforced uniformly and had often been honored in the breach. To make their point, the Witnesses enumerated the variety of nonprofit and profit-making groups whose members regularly walked through the complex without permission and without interference. Daily newspapers had been delivered from the day Parkchester opened with neither question nor official approval.

Every conceivable door-to-door salesperson from Fuller Brush to knife sharpeners to umbrella fixers rang doorbells floor by floor. "From time to time, especially during political campaigns," the Democratic Party and the American Labor Party freely canvassed for votes. The diversity of the other religious organizations that the management countenanced in Parkchester was evidenced by the fundraising activities that the Salvation Army, United Jewish Appeal, and Catholic Charities regularly conducted. And the Witnesses were undoubtedly most troubled that "mendicant nuns, children selling 'chances' for the Catholic Church, ministers and Catholic priests have called upon the tenants of Parkchester for many years." Not only that, the rules against solicitation, which listed more than seventy-five possibly objectionable solicitation activities, was only codified in writing in 1946 amid the imbroglio with the Witnesses. Prior to that time, they alleged "this policy was not stated in writing but was declared orally by the manager of the community to the head of the protective division." Ultimately, they argued that the MLIC's discriminatory actions were a violation of both the federal and state constitutions' protections of freedom of speech and worship.

In response, the MLIC argued that the Jehovah's Witnesses, whom the company's general counsel described as "itinerant salesmen of their literature . . . not noted for their retiring personalities," were banned to "protect the tenants from undesired visits by enforcing a regulation." To prove that they were acting in the best interests of residents, the defendants asserted that the management "went to the trouble and expense of asking its tenants their wishes in the matter." The company alleged that "over 11,000 of the Parkchester tenants indicated that they did not desire the visits," against only twenty-eight who were in favor of the Witnesses. As far as the changing of the rules from private oral to written strictures was concerned, the MLIC fell back on a stipulation in its lease documents that permitted the ownership to change "rules and regulations from time to time . . . for the safety, care and cleanliness of the premises and for securing the comfort, quiet and convenience of all the tenants."

The Witnesses challenged the methodologies used in canvassing the Parkchesterites and pointed out that a petition that they had circulated garnered some 1,736 signatures from people who had "no objection to Jehovah's Witnesses calling . . . door to door." More significantly, the plaintiffs defiantly challenged the many sets of rules that governed life in the neighborhood. The MLIC, they said, "should not be allowed to transform Parkchester village or community into a prison house. The tenants are not vassals who must attorn their constitutional rights to the landlord. . . . The health, welfare and property of the residents of Parkchester are sufficiently protected by the Penal Code provisions against trespassing. . . . It is for the tenants and residents of Parkchester to determine in each case, whether or not they desire to receive such visitors."

The case wound its way through lower courts until the New York State Court of Appeals found in favor of the company. The high court in Albany made a legal distinction between missionary work in the streets, which was protected by the First Amendment, and religious solicitation in the hallways of a privately owned area, granting the "possessory owner" the right to exclude those who were not wanted. The United States Supreme Court denied a request to hear the case. In the end, the victorious MLIC's counsel asserted that the company had rendered "a service to landlords and tenants generally in the interest of quiet, privacy and good management."[11]

The women activists of Parkchester did not comment publicly on the Jehovah Witnesses' suit. But it is evident that they shared some of the religious group's feelings about how controlling Parkchester officials were of tenants, as they too challenged what the management felt were its prerogatives. In the summer of 1947, the United

Women's Committee of Parkchester, which by then claimed a dues-paying membership of "almost two hundred," sprang into action when the MLIC moved to evict seventy-two Parkchester families for alleged nuisances. This was the second time the company had moved against some tenants. Some three years earlier, four hundred tenants were told "their leases would not be renewed" because of "among other things destructive play, automobile parking, rental arrears and the hanging of bed linens out of a window." In many instances, the company and the residents "settled their differences." But seventy-two other residents, with the assistance of the OPA, fought the company in Bronx County Municipal Court to prevent "management from abrogating their leases." After hearing a dozen of the cases, Justice William Lyman was able to convince the MLIC and the tenants "to get together for an adjustment. Other cases were put off for further hearings," which seemingly never took place.[12]

This time around, the most egregious violations, as the company defined them, included "noisy, dangerous and destructive acts, abuse and damage to the landlord's property, unbearable annoyance to other tenants, unsanitary practices, disregard of development or governmental regulations." The problematic behaviors were "noted by 32 uniformed private policemen on the tenants' record." At minimum, they received a curt letter from the management. Other practices that raised management's eyebrows included "vandalism by children, constant parking of cars in open streets and delayed payment of rents." And even as it was concerned about the inability of some renters to pay their monthly bills, the company, in keeping with its middle-income philosophy of long-standing, was also unhappy with those tenants who were making more money than the maximum allowed.[13]

In response, at a meeting that the women called in conjunction with the Bronx Council on Rents and Housing, protesters committed themselves to protecting "the rights and obligations of Parkchester residents." One of their explanations for attacks against fellow Parkchesterites was that the MLIC wanted new tenants who would be obliged to pay higher rents. Their rallying cry was: "No one is safe, you may be next." Early on, Michael Quill, one of the founders of the Transport Workers Union, defending those of his rank-and-file members who lived in the neighborhood, called upon the New York Corporation Counsel to see if the MLIC was in violation of its obligation to the city and asked for removal of its tax exemptions. Quill scoffed "at evictions due to children walking on the lawns or running in the halls or picking flowers."[14]

For Frank Lowe, this protest was nothing more than "a tempest in a teapot." While not backing off from the principle that the MLIC had the right to evict the troublesome, he contended that only a handful of tenants were slated for immediate dismissal. His calculations were that "of the 72, 35 had signed special contracts, 8 had their leases renewed, 5 on a month to month basis and one had moved." For example, those whose violations had been less severe or whose income was far above the norm for residents were notified that their leases would not be renewed but that they were permitted to stay in Parkchester on a month-by-month basis. Those whose status was in question were, however, advised that "they would be well to find housing elsewhere."

These second-chance options troubled the Women's Committee and their friends within and without Parkchester almost as much as the threatened evictions. They harshly criticized the so-called "probationary contracts" which required that accused tenants admit to their violations and "agree to vacate in thirty days if they continue to violate." Reportedly, people actually wrote "confessions" to stay in their apartments. Within this tense atmosphere, "parents complain[ed]: we are on edge now and we're being unfairly treated because a youngster cannot appreciate that his parent's housing is dependent upon their behavior." One woman whose family faced

eviction lamented: "I'm willing to submit to a probationary period ... but how can I get my five year old to do it."

Former Bronx assemblyman Leo Isaacson, who served as counsel for the tenants association, told the local media "parents cannot continually slap their children for walking on the grass, leaving
bicycles in front of the doors or otherwise dirtying the ground."
Isaacson came to the dispute with a reputation as a defender of
working-class people against rapacious landlords. In fact, several
months later, in February 1948, standing as a candidate of the left-
leaning American Labor Party in a special congressional election in
a South Bronx district near Parkchester, he would parlay his position on housing to defeat "a perfect foil." His opponent, Karl Popper,
was "the attorney for the Bronx landlord trade association and as
such handled all the evictions for Bronx landlords during the 1930s."
Isaacson was destined to serve only several months in the House
of Representatives. Come the regular election in November, a fu-
sion candidate backed by both Democrats and Republicans ousted
him from the seat. In any event, when he rose, in 1947, to champion
the issue at hand in Parkchester, he contended that "instead of the
policeman obeying the arbitrary rules we suggest that a child psy-
chologist be called in. Parents could meet with the management
to confer with this expert and a set of rules set up that would be
acceptable to all."[15]

Both neighborhood activists and those whom the MLIC threatened to evict appreciated Isaacson's standing with them. But in 1948,
the vast majority of voters in this religiously mixed, white ethnic
community did not return the favor. Isaacson stood staunchly with
Progressive presidential candidate Henry Wallace. But Parkchester
and other neighborhoods in the borough's 11th Assembly District
went strongly for either Thomas Dewey or Harry S. Truman. Isaacson's candidate garnered but 5 percent of the ballots.[16]

Meanwhile, as the women's activities continued into the fall of 1947, including a rally at the Chester House, Ida Cahn, chair of the Publicity Committee of the United Women's Committee of Parkchester, called upon all of her neighbors to join the protests. Heartened by the reality that, as of October 1, no alleged violator had been removed from the neighborhood, Cahn declared, "not until every tenant in Parkchester is represented through a tenants council will the atmosphere of housing insecurity . . . be eliminated." Stung by bad publicity, Parkchester management backed off from the threatened evictions. In 1947, none of the seventy-two families under investigation was taken to court.[17]

Less than a year later, the women's committee again strongly questioned MLIC policies on a gut issue that was mentioned only in part during the fight against evictions. In July 1948, residents were informed that the management was requesting an increase of "$4 to $7 monthly for their living quarters, beginning October 1." The rationale was that "present rents were established in 1940 based on operating and maintenance costs at that time but since then these costs have risen by about 80%." At that point, the monthly rental for two rooms ranged from $32 to $34; three rooms, $39 to $53; four rooms, $52 to $64; and the few five-room suites went for $63 to $71. Management was quick to reassure tenants that the increase, constituting "on average about 12%," was "voluntary" because rent-control laws protected those who chose not to accommodate the landlord's request. In other words, those who would not "sign up" for new three-year leases at the higher rate "could remain in possession of their suites as statutory tenants under the protection of federal and municipal rent control laws on a month-to-month basis at present rentals."[18]

In response to this plan, the committee said it "was swamped by phone calls" from fellow Parkchesterites "seeking guidance." Committee activists "circulated" around the community, making it clear that neighbors were under no obligation to comply and to reassure people that they were on guard against attempts to pressure them to sign up. The committee publicly questioned, through the local media, whether the proposed increases were at all necessary. The group insisted that "at a time when soaring living costs have strained most budgets to the breaking point, it would be certainly of community interest to learn the statistical basis upon which the proprosed rent schedule has been adopted." For the committee, the way to control the MLIC was through "increased membership" and for those concerned to "organize to protect their interests [against] one of the most powerful lobbies," which was out to eliminate rent controls.[19]

These criticisms seemed to not overly perturb Parkchester management. Five days after the committee called for increased membership, the ownership was "gratified" that eight thousand residents had complied with the rent-increase request. New resident manager Douglas Lowe, who had succeeded his brother when Frank moved up to a higher position within the MLIC, was pleased to report that their offices had to be kept open at night to accommodate those who "wished to sign up." He and his associates also had to have been heartened when a letter writer to the *New York Times* criticized the Parkchester activists for "gang[ing] up on the one landlord." The committee's answer was that "the MLIC is the most powerful landlord in the country and is associated with other such large operations" and that, due to its efforts, "the Federal Rent Advisory Board turned down a blanket 15% increase requested by landlords in New York City." This effective defense of tenants' rights, it was asserted, was achieved due "to combined efforts of tenants associations throughout the city" with whom it had liaised.[20]

Even if in due course 90 percent of Parkchester tenants voluntarily agreed to the increase, some committee members remained on guard against the management. In 1952, when the ownership requested an additional rent increase of 6 percent, some three hundred dissatisfied residents formed an Emergency Rent Committee of Parkchester, which once again held protest meetings at the Chester House. Mrs. Jacob Perlman, the so-called "leaseless leader" of the group and a tenant since 1942, was one of those who had lived in Parkchester on a "statutory basis" since the first increase was suggested. She had no interest in now accommodating the MLIC. Needless to say, she was gratified when many of her neighbors whom, she said, had complied in 1948 "because they feared the threat of dispossession if the rent control laws were relaxed . . . now plan[ned] to become statutory tenants." Calm, however, prevailed at the company's headquarters because in the months since the increase had been proposed more than one-third of the residents had "indicated their willingness to pay the high rent."[21]

Still, throughout its first generation, Parkchester remained a desired residence even if management occasionally had to fend off well-publicized complaints that it was unfair in its handling of apartments. For example, in 1944, a Bronx municipal court stopped the MLIC from compelling Catherine Walsh, "the wife of a soldier and the mother of two children," to give up a Tremont Avenue apartment. Bernard Walsh had been a handyman in Parkchester until his induction into the military in September 1943. By virtue of his being a Parkchester employee, the family had held a two-year lease at a discounted rate. But now the management wanted the apartment for his successor on the job. The court sided completely with the Walsh family, ruling that eviction would cause "considerable hardship" and that Bernard's induction had been "foreseeable" when the lease was signed. The court told the MLIC that if the Walsh family's rent was "inadequate then the landlord may have some other remedy."[22]

Another issue related to military service engendered some pique toward the MLIC right after the war. In 1946, the Veterans of Foreign Wars alleged that the owners had "dodged" their promise to give special priority after V-J Day to those who had served honorably in the military. The MLIC was, it will be recalled, proud that, in its view, preference was being given to veterans. The story the soldiers' organization told was that "families not on the waiting list" were being granted Parkchester residency because they were being displaced by the plan to build the Cross Bronx Expressway. The company did not deny that people in the surrounding areas sometimes were pushed to the front but asserted that "cases of civilian need . . . in fairness . . . deserve consideration." The VFW was unmoved, asserting that powerful city development official Robert Moses said "that no one would be displaced until construction begins." As it turned out, when the massive transportation link was built, thousands of persons in other Bronx neighborhoods were dispossessed. Fully occupied Parkchester would not be an option.[23]

Clearly there were those who perceived Parkchester management as mercenary and uncaring. While there were those who "viewed the rules as a fair price to pay for Parkchester's spotless grounds and hallways," many of their fellow tenants, both activists and those who just were quietly unhappy, deemed the Parkchester police hardheaded enforcers of too many inconsequential rules. Some "irate families" who were threatened with eviction went so far as to characterized the cops' "methods as those of a 'Bronx Gestapo' and 'a reform school.'" But those same security officers did their own part in helping to earn for the neighborhood a reputation as a safe, secure, and untrammeled enclave during a difficult period of widespread street violence in Gotham.[24]

After World War II and well into the 1960s, youth gangs of various competing ethnic and racial stripes victimized fearful residents in other locales throughout the city. This was precisely the era of blight that Leonard Bernstein immortalized in the musical *West Side Story*. His call for racial understanding, though, was largely unheard. In the Bronx alone, between 1949 and 1963 no fewer than seventy gangs

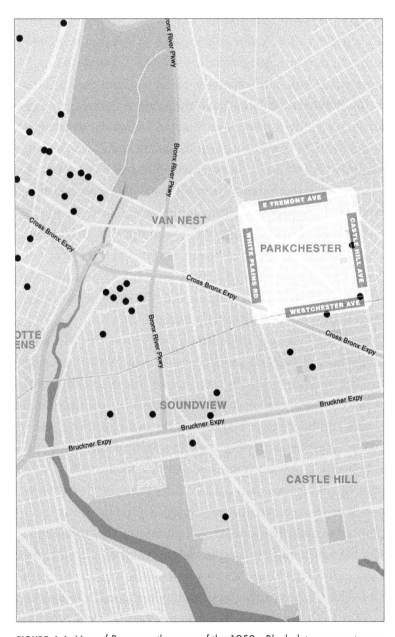

FIGURE 4.4. Map of Bronx youth gangs of the 1950s. Black dots represent gang presence—extant in adjoining neighborhoods but not within Parkchester. Information courtesy of Joe Butera at stonegreasers.com. Map courtesy of the Yeshiva University Office of Communications and Public Affairs.

terrorized the borough's streets. The largest number of organized fighting organizations controlled the area of Morrisania in the South Bronx, where white gangs, like the Knights, conducted turf wars against blacks who had joined the Slickers. Up in the Fordham section, the Baldies rumbled against the Harlem Redwings. Over near Allerton Avenue, in the northern reach of Pelham Parkway, the Duckies fought with fists, knives, and guns against the Parkside Gang and the Wanderers and many other comers. But Parkchester was spared. A retrospective mapping of where these troublemakers hung out shows that, from 1949 to 1963, only three gangs were situated on the outskirts of the new neighborhood. One group of troublemakers, the Golden Guineas, made up of Italian Americans, held sway near Zarega Avenue to the northeast of the Castle Hill Avenue boundary of Parkchester. Another gang controlled turf literally on the other side of the tracks, south of Westchester Avenue.[25]

In 1949, the *New York Times* noted that crime was "virtually nonexistent" in Parkchester "owing in large measure to the special patrol force." For the record, the first recorded crime in the neighborhood took place in November 1940 when two "thugs . . . youths of about 25" held up a stationery store and robbed the owner of $100.[26] But when the security force was fully in place, Chief McGannon—the same man who kept the Jehovah's Witnesses out of Parkchester—reportedly headed up a forty-two-man detail. Under their watch, between 1944 and 1949 there occurred just two burglaries and no more than a few attempted sexual violations involving minors. "Due to their playing a valuable role in curbing juvenile delinquency," McGannon claimed, "less than fifty of the 10,000 boys and girls in the huge project cause all the trouble." Of course, the Parkchester cops could not arrest criminals. They were not peace officers and were unarmed. Serious and dangerous malefactors were turned over to the NYPD.

Indeed, in the evenings, the "regulars" and "specials" divided responsibilities. As McGannon explained: "If Parkchester were laid

out in the city's gridiron pattern it would take six city foot patrolmen to protect the area at all times." Sharing duties, the NYPD
"radio patrol crews keep a close watch on the fringes of the project,"
which was where gang members might be found. Between midnight and 8 a.m., a Parkchester prowl car toured the neighborhood's
inner paths and private streets, the officers wearing uniforms that
closely resembled those of the city police.[27]

Aside from the concerted law enforcement efforts, gangs did not
make their ugly marks in Parkchester because the social pathologies
that gave rise to such violent groups did not trouble this new enclave.
Elsewhere, the frustration of young men—and some young women—
over their, and their parents', inability to secure employment in a
changing labor market, coupled with their sense that African Americans and Latinos were invading their areas of long-standing while
more affluent residents of Gotham happily streamed out of the city
to suburbia, fueled animosities. Gangs provided the disaffected with
common causes, often expressed in rumbles that injured participants and scared bystanders. On the other hand, most Parkchester
families were employed and optimistic about their futures and the
coming years in New York City. They had their privileged enclave,
that "city within a city," within which they could live. And need it be
said again that there was no anger at blacks and Puerto Ricans because the neighborhood was segregated. The Irish and Italians, who
in prior settings had their angry differences, now set them aside and
the Jews, who previously had been set upon, especially by the Irish,
had no trepidations about youthful criminal elements. If anything,
these neighbors, drawn from different religious and white ethnic
groups who had once been in conflict, were becoming friends.[28]

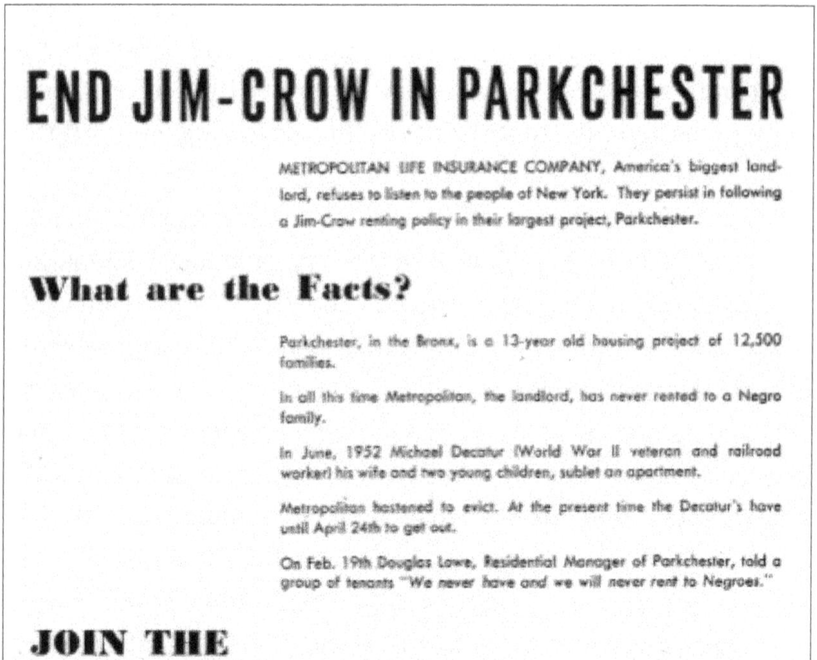

END JIM-CROW IN PARKCHESTER

METROPOLITAN LIFE INSURANCE COMPANY, America's biggest landlord, refuses to listen to the people of New York. They persist in following
a Jim-Crow renting policy in their largest project, Parkchester.

What are the Facts?

Parkchester, in the Bronx, is a 13-year old housing project of 12,500
families.

In all this time Metropolitan, the landlord, has never rented to a Negro
family.

In June, 1952 Michael Decatur (World War II veteran and railroad
worker) his wife and two young children, sublet an apartment.

Metropolitan hastened to evict. At the present time the Decatur's have
until April 24th to get out.

On Feb. 19th Douglas Lowe, Residential Manager of Parkchester, told a
group of tenants "We never have and we will never rent to Negroes."

JOIN THE

MASS PICKET LINE
WEDNESDAY, MARCH 18th, 3 to 6 P.M.
at: Metropolitan Life Insurance Co.

1 MADISON AVENUE   Corner 23rd Street

PROMINENT CITIZENS WILL LEAD THE LINE

Write to: FREDERICK ECKER, Chairman, Metropolitan Life Insurance Co., 1 Madison Avenue, New York City

Auspices: BRONX-WIDE COMMITTEE FOR INTEGRATED HOUSING   953 Southern Blvd., Bronx, N. Y.

FIGURE 5.1. Protest flyer from the Bronx-Wide Committee for Integrated Housing. NAACP Papers, courtesy of the New York Public Library.

"NEGROES AND WHITES DON'T MIX"

THROUGHOUT ITS CLOSE TO THIRTY YEARS OPERATING
Parkchester, the MLIC never conceded that it discriminated
against African Americans. In fact, in 1964, as Frank Lowe concluded a quarter century of work overseeing the neighborhood,
first as its resident manager and then as a highly placed executive in the corporation's Manhattan home office, he asserted
that when the neighborhood was first built, blacks showed no
desire to live there. "It is a most interesting thing," he recalled,
"that in the initial days of renting for Parkchester, Negroes
expressed no interest in living there. To my own knowledge, I
know of no one interested enough even to file an application. In
later years, after the development became fully occupied and
we were burdened by tremendous waiting lists, some interest
developed." Although as late as the mid-1960s, there was nary
an African American in the complex, upon his retirement he
was comfortable saying, "it is a great source of satisfaction that
we now have several Negro families in our community." Truth
be told, Parkchester did not open up its doors substantially
until 1968, when the New York City Commission on Human
Rights directed it to do so. To that point, the MLIC had used its
strict leasing policies and other overt and subtle means to keep
the neighborhood all white.[1]

Frederick Ecker offered a more accurate public expression
of his company's attitude toward race in housing when, in
1943, he opined that "Negroes and whites don't mix. Perhaps
they will, in a hundred years, but they don't now." Casting seg-

regation as driven not by patent, unmitigated racism but rather by dollars-and-cents economics, he explained that "if we brought them into the development it would be to the detriment of the city, too, because it would depress the surrounding property." Those who had followed his company's housing endeavors since the 1920s initiative in Queens would have known that MLIC properties were open to all religions and nationalities but not to all races. And it is again noteworthy that Parkchester's careful design, which did not provide for houses of worship and schools within the complex, was arguably intended to keep the unwanted out of the neighborhood on a daily basis.[2]

Two years earlier, in May 1941, Ecker had made his stance even clearer in a private and contentious meeting with the president of the New York State Conference of the National Association for the Advancement of Colored People (NAACP). James Egert Allen, a public school teacher, tested the company's policy when he sent a letter to Frank Lowe requesting "information concerning Parkchester." He had heard that the development liked educators as tenants. Initially, Lowe responded in a friendly manner indicating, "many [inquires] have come from public school teachers of this city. Feeling that you possess the same interest, we are happy to enclose a folder which contains all the basic facts." In addition, he offered "a guided tour on any weekday" should his group "desire to visit the development." A follow-up letter from Allen, on NAACP stationery, may well have indicated to Ecker that an unwanted African American was seeking an apartment. Still, Ecker invited the putative applicant to visit him at MLIC headquarters.

At that meeting Allen argued that as a "part owner of the company"—a MLIC policy holder—he wanted a place in Parkchester. Ecker replied that admitting blacks was impossible since their presence would pose a risk to the MLIC's investment of over $50 million. Allen's further remonstrations did not avail him at all, and he returned his policy to the Madison Avenue office. He would not see "the inside of Parkchester" until invited to visit a white teacher friend of his one year later.[3]

Such discriminatory declarations and explanations from the management raised only a few eyebrows in the decade before the beginnings of a full-throated civil rights movement. Before the Supreme Court in 1954 abrogated a "separate but equal" understanding of the Constitution, segregation was both the law and the custom of the land. Blacks and whites lived in worlds and neighborhoods apart. South of the Mason-Dixon Line, racial separation in all facets of life, under the rule of Jim Crow laws, was staunchly maintained with little dissent. Meanwhile, up north, in the realm of housing, not only social conventions and economic arguments, but also the force of law and court determinations were used to protect white privilege. All told, "African Americans were unconstitutionally denied the means and the right to integration in middle-class neighborhoods." Following the national color suit, New York City was a very segregated town. Indeed, in the four decades before Parkchester was constructed, the city had an inglorious history of keeping out blacks who could afford to pay the same rental fees as whites from desired accommodations. In the early postwar period, this pattern of discrimination was extended beyond the city's limits. Laws protected segregation and segregationists.[4]

In the first years of the 20th century, aspiring blacks were chased out of the Hell's Kitchen neighborhood on Manhattan's West Side by rioting Irish Americans. Many settled in a neighborhood extending from 90th to 110th Street due south and west of Harlem, where a West Side Improvement Association had been organized to keep African Americans out of the area. Its rationale, according to the black newspaper *New York Age*, reads much in line with Ecker's position of forty years later. Reportedly, its decision was not due to "prejudice against the race" but rather that "their presence in the neighborhood" would cause "the value of property to deteriorate." The restrictionist group's effort failed, as did a few subsequent efforts at segregation in this area of Gotham as it became the iconic black community. Later on, a federal study conducted in 1931 that looked at the question of blacks with the economic wherewithal to reside within predominantly white, relatively comfortable neighborhoods, concluded that while the children of immigrants possessed the "possibility of escape" from tenement life "with improvement of economic status to seek more desirable sections of the city," among "Negroes certain definite racial attitudes favorable to segregation interpose difficulties to . . . breaking physical restrictions in residential areas."[5]

Thus, for example, when Manhattan's Washington Heights was first built up as a neighborhood of large apartment buildings in the 1920s, a Neighborhood Protective Association pressured landlords to sign racially restrictive agreements. Before World War II, in that ethnically contested West Side area the Jews and the Irish did not get along well together and commanded their own separate enclaves. African Americans did not struggle against these competing groups, because they were largely not permitted to mix in the neighborhood. As of 1930, fewer than 1,500 blacks lived in an area that had close to 170,000 whites. Ten years later, in a neighborhood of over 200,000 whites, there were but 2,800 African Americans. Meanwhile, in Long Island City, which included blocks where the MLIC had first built apartments for working- and lower-middle-class families of varying white nationalities and religions, while no explicit statements were made about who was unwelcome, as of 1930 only 212 African Americans resided among 57,000 whites. And over in Unionport, Westchester Heights, and Park Versailles, in the area that would become home to Parkchester, and from whose streets many of its initial residents would migrate, as of 1940, there were almost no blacks at all—just 39 among 51,000 whites.[6]

During the early decades of the twentieth century, there were two beneficent, philanthropist-initiated endeavors that promised, and to some extent delivered, better housing for a limited number of blacks, even as the apartment complexes they constructed effectively kept the races apart. In 1907, two years after he built a mansion on Fifth Avenue for himself and his family, steel industry magnate Henry Phipps created a $1 million fund to build "model tenements" for the poor of the city to be called "Phipps Houses." The first structure, specifically for indigent whites, arose in what is today the Kips Bay section of the eastern part of midtown Manhattan. The second initiative, completed just a few years later on West 63rd Street in what was then called the San Juan Hill area, was almost exclusively for blacks. When the latter houses were opened, social worker Mary White Ovington, who had advocated for the initiative with Phipps, was the only white person in the building. She would stay there for eight months, gathering material for her book *Half a Man*, on the status of blacks in New York. In 1912, a second set of apartment buildings for African Americans was opened on West 64th Street.[7]

A decade and a half later, industrialist John D. Rockefeller sponsored the Paul Laurence Dunbar Apartments, a six-building cooperative housing project just for blacks that rose from 1926–1928 at 149th–150th Streets between Seventh and Eighth Avenue. It was an enclave that boasted parks, playgrounds, gardens, and what we would now call a day care center for working mothers. Residents invested in their own apartments and there even was a Dunbar National Bank on the premises. However, the Harlem initiative foundered at the beginning of the Great Depression. Many in New York suffered financially during the era, but few more than its black residents—many of the handpicked tenants in the Dunbar apartments lost their jobs and were unable to carry the cost of housing. In the 1930s, this "noble experiment" in "the adventure of community building" ended.[8]

Meanwhile, for the most successful African Americans of long-standing in New York, one of the only places to be when other areas in town did not want them was in their own upscale section of Harlem, "Strivers' Row." During the interwar period and even beyond, this enclave of elegant brownstones, praised as "the most aristocratic street in Harlem"—actually a two-block area on 138th–139th Streets between Seventh and Eighth Avenue—was home to African American professionals who had "supposedly arrived." The other elite section of uptown was in Hamilton Heights, west of St. Nicholas Park and due north of the City College of New York (CCNY). After World War II, sections of southeastern Queens like St. Albans, Laurelton, and Springfield Gardens became home to African American "civil servants, teachers, nurses," people with many of the same occupations as the whites who filled up Parkchester. Not only that, but these neighborhoods "contained single-family houses and thus exuded [a] suburban atmosphere," if not a "city within the city," at least a new place for them. Thus, Parkchester would have been an ideal place for these aspiring families especially since so many new suburban locales were off-limits to them.

Put another way, they could have "moved up" literally and vertically to the high-rise apartments in the new Bronx development at a time when places like Levittown would not let them move out to Long Island. Speaking for realtors of that era, and sounding not totally unlike Frederick Ecker, William Levitt, the massive area's developer, commenting on how to remedy overcrowding in old New York City neighborhoods, remarked: "We can solve a housing problem, or we can try to solve a racial problem. But we cannot combine the two." For him too, the combination of racism and economics would keep blacks and whites apart. As of 1960, none of the eighty-two thousand residents in that Nassau County town was black.[9]

Amid this persistent and pervasive discriminatory housing regime, there was an exception to the rule. Beginning in the 1930s in the Morrisania section of the south-central Bronx, only a few miles west of where Parkchester would be built, there was an enclave where landlords actually solicited African Americans to reside in their many unoccupied apartments. Reversing a prior restricted policy, building owners advertised for "select colored families," a definition that has been interpreted to mean "families with light complexions and a securely employed wage earner." In that unique urban setting, blacks and the predominantly Jewish white population lived side by side for a generation. Much of the credit for this integrated environment has been granted to the radical political orientation of the Jews who accepted African Americans as their neighbors. It has been argued effectively that "traditions of trade unionism and political radicalism, heavily influenced by the Communist Party . . . shaped the attitudes of residents of Morrisania and the adjoining communities of Hunts Point and Crotona Park East." This was a place where during the opening of the Depression a "rent revolt" took place over attempts to evict the poor from their homes, which led to "pitched battles between residents, city marshals and the police, involving thousands of people." Critically, "Bronx rent strikers and relief protesters were exposed to the message of militant racial egalitarianism that the Communist Party espoused."

Morrisania's residential policies would not be emulated in Parkchester. Perhaps, when Parkchester was built, some Morrisania blacks who were doing better economically than they had previously might have thought of the new East Bronx neighborhood as a potential further step up. But what is certain is that Ecker and his comrades were not at all interested in taking marching orders from the behaviors of Morrisania landlords and communists. And only a small number of the people who had been admitted to the area—including some with leftist political leanings—showed much interest in fighting for integration. Most Parkchesterites were quiet on the question of discrimination.[10]

As of 1948, there was a new neighborhood in Manhattan, Stuyvesant Town, that would conceivably have been available to working- and lower-middle-class African Americans like those who lived in Morrisania. This new development was located pretty much in the backyard of Ecker's Manhattan office. But here too, in studied segregationist form, the MLIC did its utmost politically and in the courts to deny blacks apartments. Their discriminatory policies were sustained.

In 1943, the State of New York, with the immense assistance of municipal mogul Robert Moses, had granted the MLIC a sweetheart deal to build Stuyvesant Town. Like Parkchester, it was pitched as a community for people of modest means and especially as a reward for returning GIs who could afford the rent in what was also referred to as a "city within a city." Under legislation passed by the New York City Council, the city agreed to purchase the land in a previously blighted area north of the Lower East Side and convey it to the corporation at cost, while the insurance company was granted large tax exemptions for the first quarter century after the project's construction. For Moses, then chairman of the Slum Clearance Committee, this was a great step forward in remaking the city. As one of his associates told the *New York Times*, the Stuyvesant Town precedent would "enable insurance companies to transform sprawling blighted areas . . . into wholesome residential communities." However, to the great detriment of blacks who wanted to be part of this new urban endeavor, the MLIC was given the right to institute its own "tenant selection policy." As one of Ecker's closest lieutenants told a legislative committee, that meant "direct[ly] and explicit[ly] . . . no provisions would be made for African American families." The fact that approximately 40 percent of those evicted from the poor neighborhood to make way for Stuyvesant Town were either black or Latino carried no weight with those in municipal or state power. Discrimination was pitched again as an economic matter and blacks were deemed a bad risk. As Ecker would later explain: "We shall rent apartments to applicants solely on the basis of the standard which must govern a fiduciary's prudent investment in the particular neighborhood in which Stuyvesant Town is located."

Before, during, and after legislation was passed and ratified, black and white civil rights groups widely criticized the community's rental policies, especially since it was in part publicly funded. A 1944 City Council law barring discrimination in future public housing endeavors did not change Stuyvesant Town policies and realities. As protests continued through 1944, Ecker, heeding Moses's advice to head off protests, announced that the company had hatched plans to build "model housing for colored folks in Harlem." Riverton Houses, situated on 135th–138th Streets between Madison Avenue and the Harlem River, was a miniature version of the Parkchester and Stuyvesant Town residential communities and somewhat reminiscent of the Phipps Houses.

Black spokespeople and Harlem residents were of several minds over this initiative, which clearly was in the spirit of the separate and less-than-equal racial policies of the day. Reportedly, "the middle-class Negro[es]" who eventually took up residence in Riverton's twelve hundred up-to-date apartments and "well-kept . . . grounds" were "proud . . . that it is an oasis in the slums in an area that was once one of the worst slum neighborhoods in the city," even if the development turned out to house only blacks—a segregated enclave. For sociologist Kenneth Clark, however, "the residents of Riverton are as much prisoners of the ghetto as their neighbors in the rat-infested tenements across the street or in the low-income public housing on the other side." As he perceived these tenants, "their very attempt to exist in isolated defiance inevitably involves them in the total system of the ghetto . . . [which] is all-encompassing, a psychological as well as a physical reality." Author and social critic

James Baldwin concurred: the folks in Riverton "know that they are there because white people do not think they are good enough to live anywhere else." To think otherwise and to "imagine" that their placement in better housing "protects him against the common pain, demoralization and danger is self deluded."[11]

Meanwhile, back at Stuyvesant Town, in 1947, just as the complex was about to open, three African American army veterans, led by former Captain Joseph R. Dorsey and with the sponsorship of the NAACP and the American Jewish Congress, took on the MLIC for the right of blacks to be granted apartments. After negotiations with Ecker's associates failed to change the MLIC's position, Dorsey and his backers turned to the court system for relief. In its defense, the company asserted that if it had "any objections to Negro tenants as such, it would not have embarked upon the construction of Riverton." Besides which, the company had received one hundred thousand applications for only nine thousand spots in Stuyvesant Town. In addition, it alleged that admission of blacks would "make it impossible or substantially more difficult to attract and retain other tenants . . . and thereby endanger the economic success of the enterprise." Ultimately, the case found its way to the New York County Supreme Court, which sided with the company. Ruling that Stuyvesant Town was a "private project," Judge Felix C. Benvenga allowed that while "it may well be that from a sociological point of view a policy of exclusion . . . is not only undesirable but unwise . . . the wisdom of the policy is not for the court" to decide. The New York State Court of Appeals affirmed that ruling. Such were the social, economic, and definitive legal barriers to integration during that era.[12]

However, if the courts would not do the right thing, a small group of white tenants moved to circumvent the MLIC's policies. In the summer of 1949, they invited a few black families to stay as "unpaying guests" in their apartments. To sublet for a fee would be a

clear violation of their leases. In one case, Jesse Kessler, a union organizer, acting very likely in the radical egalitarian spirit of Morrisania, turned over his apartment to a black Harlem resident while he
and his family were on summer vacation. In a more celebrated instance, born seemingly out of similar political motivations, Dr. Lee
Lorch, a mathematics professor at CCNY, let a black in when he set
off to teach at Penn State University after he was denied tenure and
promotion at the New York City school. The backstory that eventually became front-page news was that the professor contended that
his activism in Stuyvesant Town did not sit well with colleagues, especially since he was reputed to have Communist leanings. Even at
CCNY, renowned for its history of radical activity among students
and faculty alike, the "Red Scare" of the day apparently permeated
the halls. Eventually, Penn State also dismissed Lorch, arguably for
similar political reasons. In any event, over the next two years or
so, a battle royale ensued as the MLIC sought several times to evict
these troublemaking tenants and the City Council passed legislation outlawing discrimination in publicly funded housing, retroac-
tively including Stuyvesant Town. The MLIC yielded partially and
admitted a handful of black aspirants while it continued to assert
its "right to select tenants of its own choice." As of 1960, even with
favorable legislation on the books, Stuyvesant Town had forty-seven
blacks, just 0.2 percent of the 22,045 residents in the neighborhood.
With sixteen Latinos added to the mix, the total percentage of minorities was a mere 0.3 percent. The protesters were now winning
almost all their legislative battles, but the MLIC still found multiple
ways of circumventing the new laws.[13]

Opening the doors for blacks in Parkchester was an even more
difficult task. To begin with, the Bronx enclave was privately owned
and the civil rights legislation of the 1940s and early 1950s thus did
not apply there. Second, as a fully occupied development with virtually no turnover of residents, it was easy for the MLIC to simply say,

"No vacancies." A collateral barrier was the company's unwritten yet well-known policy to let relatives of persons already in Parkchester jump the long waiting list whenever apartments became available. It was no secret around St. Helena's and St. Raymond's parishes that the Lowe brothers were quick to find room for the parents and siblings of Catholic clergy if Msgr. Scanlan put in a call. It was said matter-of-factly, if hyperbolically, that "there were more relatives of priests in Parkchester than anyplace else in the city." There was even some talk of the Lowes making apartments available for a rectory in the heart of Parkchester.[14]

It is not known if YIP lay leadership was aware of the special treatment accorded the families of Catholic clergy. But it is certain that they were perturbed when, late in 1958, management did not immediately provide their new rabbi, Maurice L. Schwartz, with an apartment when he was called to the neighborhood. Inveterate letter writer Charles Rubinstein, who represented a small congregational committee, appealed to Douglas Lowe on behalf of their spiritual leader and, while he was at it, put in a request for a larger apartment for another Jewish family, the Gitelmans. Lowe's circumlocutory assurance that both petitions were "receiving proper consideration" although "the limitations placed upon both requests limit us in our efforts to be of further assistance but you may be certain that when we can again be of help, we will notify them promptly" did not satisfy the synagogue group. However, a few months later, an apartment was indeed found for the rabbi and his family on West Avenue, a two-block walk from the shul. YIP lore has it that some politically connected congregants brought their influence to bear upon Lowe. In 1960, the Gitelman family got their coveted five-room apartment at 1555 Unionport Road.[15]

But whatever difficulties Jews may have faced in jumping the line for themselves, or for their leaders, such concerns never led to large-scale public controversy and in no way approximated the problems African Americans faced in trying to break through concretized barriers.[16] Given this long-enduring state of affairs, beginning in 1949 and extending into the early 1950s, some white advocates for integration within and without the neighborhood and blacks, who obviously lived outside of Parkchester, pushed back against the tradition of segregation. When Bronx protestors made their voices heard, they modeled their efforts after what their comrades had tried to do in their sister community downtown. Perhaps they also affirmed what integration had meant to those who lived in Morrisania. Not only that, but some of Stuyvesant Town's activist tenants actually came uptown to rally those interested in the cause of fair housing practices. However, their efforts were unsuccessful.

The first public challenge came from the Parkchester Chapter of the Civil Rights Congress, which met at the Chester House in May 1949 to "demand . . . that the next vacant apartment be rented to a Negro family." Among the speakers who denounced "the infamous practices of discrimination in housing . . . a blot on this nation's ideals" was Paul Ross, chairman of the Town and Village Committee to End Discrimination in Stuyvesant Town.[17]

Moving beyond words of protest, in the spring of 1950 the Parkchester Committee to End Housing Discrimination was formed. Its first effort was a petition drive to demonstrate that residents of the community were in favor of blacks living among them. The findings gave the integrationists some hope that rank-and-file Parkchesterites were willing to "welcome" blacks. Polling conducted in the West Quadrant revealed 58 percent "favored admission of Negroes to the project on a full equality basis." The Committee was quick to note that these affirmative respondents included both those who were willing to sign a petition in support of open housing and those who were unwilling to lend their names publicly "because of fear of repercussions." However, the latter cohort surely could not be counted upon to take action against the MLIC. Meanwhile, 30 percent "issued a flat 'no'" when queried, while 12 percent had not made up their minds.[18]

Subsequently, the group began issuing a community newspaper called *Good Neighbors* "to help in this fight for democratic principles." To further raise awareness of their cause, it "organized special children's programs." To encourage interracial harmony, some of the leaders "published and distributed literature" about the cause, held meetings with sympathetic "housing experts," and even "sponsored a special art exhibit featuring the work of leading Negro artists." None of these expressions of tenant opinion or interest impressed the MLIC.[19]

The protest turned much more dramatic in July 1952, when Mrs. Priscilla Simon, a member of the Committee, emulating the provocative personal stance that the Kesslers and Lee Lorch had taken downtown, sublet her apartment to an African American family, Michael and Sophie Decatur and their two children. Management reportedly "immediately placed a 24 hour guard outside the Decatur's door in hopes of intimidating the neighbors as well as the Decaturs." But when an estimated group of "hundreds of tenants protested the action," the guards were withdrawn.[20]

Turning simultaneously to the court system, where the MLIC clearly had an advantage, the management moved to evict the family. As a suit against Simon for "illegal" actions "barred by the terms of their original lease" moved through the municipal and then the state court system, the left-leaning Bronx-Wide Committee for Integrated Housing and the borough's branches of the NAACP and the Urban League joined the Parkchester Committee in championing the cause. Taking heart from what Simon and the Decaturs were doing, some nearby black residents who had been displaced from their homes due to urban-renewal slum-clearance initiatives submitted applications for admission to Parkchester. When nothing came of their efforts, they went out into the streets with leaflets and picketed the MLIC offices in Manhattan.[21]

In January 1953, the Parkchester Committee to End Housing Discrimination held a one-day conference at the Hunts Point Palace. Reportedly, 150 attendees from all over the Bronx heard speakers like the famous ballplayer Jackie Robinson and actor Sidney Poitier, along with lawyers who represented both the Stuyvesant Town protesters and the Decaturs, demand that the MLIC "state publicly that it was in favor of equal rights for all." Co-sponsors of the rally, which included the chairman of the Committee to End Discrimination in Levittown, signed on to the Parkchester Committee's assertion that "discrimination and segregation in housing impose a steady drain upon the economic, social and psychological resources of the community." It was explicitly pointed out "this is not Metropolitan's first experience with Negro tenancy." Claiming victory in the struggle downtown, it was said that "only a short time ago this great quasi-public insurable company was compelled by the sheer force of public opinion to accept a token number of Negro families in Stuyvesant Town. We propose to extend this breakthrough to Parkchester" and beyond. For those who attended this gathering, the fight over Parkchester was clearly more than just a Bronx neighborhood problem.

Out of this meeting, the Bronx-Wide Committee determined to take the fight directly to the MLIC. A window of opportunity opened late in January when a judge granted the Decaturs a three-month stay on his decision. For the activists, the time was ripe to intensify communal advocacy. A Continuation Committee called upon all Bronxites "to speak about this un-American discrimination in your club or trade union, in your church or synagogue to your friends and neighbors." All were asked to write directly to Ecker to demand "in the interest of simple justice to terminate [the MLIC's] discriminatory policy." In the beginning of February, a press conference was held at the Decaturs' apartment to personalize in front of the media the exploitation of a "war veteran." Michael Decatur's story was projected much like the Dorsey case in Stuyvesant Town. A few days later, Bronx-Wide Committee member Oliver Eastman, president of the Bronx NAACP, advocated a boycott of the MLIC until "we remove from our own life every vestige of the pernicious doctrine of white supremacy."

With the time growing short before a final court decision, the Bronx-Wide Committee organized for March 19 what it called a "Big Action," the picketing of the MLIC's Manhattan headquarters. Their flyer promoting the event informed would-be participants that as late as February 19, Douglas Lowe reportedly "told a group of tenants; '[we] never have and we will never rent to Negroes.'" Lowe's quick denial of having made that inflammatory statement did little to mollify activists. He had insisted that the question of admitting minorities was an "academic one" since "we are loaded to the gunnels up there and unless we have more rapid turnover it will be years before we can accommodate anyone." Two days after the protest, the Committee was successful in having a local television station—WPIX—broadcast a "Meet the Decatur Family" show. Supporters were implored to "tune in, notify your membership, arrange parties, see and hear the people who are making history."

On April 19, the Parkchester Committee to End Housing Discrimination staged a testimonial dinner and reception in honor of the Decaturs. Messages from leading black and white politicians who supported the cause were read. Earlier in the campaign, the Parkchester group had published a flyer, apparently for voters' future reference, containing the names of government officials who had responded favorably toward or who had failed to back their fight. The highlight of the event that the organizers said "jammed" eight hundred "neighbors and friends" into the New Terrace Gardens on Boston Post Road was the performance of "original songs lampooning Parkchester to the tune of 'The Mikado,' written and sung by Parkchester residents." In satirizing restrictionist policies, the lyrics exclaimed: "If you are brown or black or pink or any other hue, except the shade of lily-white, that list [to be excluded] will include you."[22]

On May 19, 1953, the court rendered a final decision in favor of the MLIC and the company moved to immediately evict the family. As a last-ditch effort to stop the move, or even more likely as a final demonstration that their supporters hatched to publicize what they deemed as a travesty, Sophie Decatur, another black woman—Shirley Sheppard—and five white friends appeared at the MLIC's downtown headquarters demanding to see Frank Lowe. After keeping the group waiting in his anteroom for five and a half hours, Lowe and his attorney Alfred B. Carb "emphatically denied that discrimination was involved," asserting "this is a simple case of unlawful occupancy." The eviction would take place as scheduled.

After another hour of fruitless discussion, the women "pulled from their purses chains of stainless steel," wrapped the chains around their waists, and fastened the restraints around chairs. They pledged to remain "until we get a concrete policy [change] from Metropolitan Life on the Parkchester Development." The standoff between the sit-in protesters and Lowe continued until three in the morning, when the defiant and now exhausted protesters had to admit "it was physically impossible to stay any longer."[23]

At 11 the next morning, city marshals battered down the apartment on Metropolitan Avenue where the Decaturs and some fifty supporters from Parkchester and elsewhere had barricaded themselves. "The First Negro Family" in Parkchester was evicted and their belongings were loaded into a moving van but not before two white sympathizers, William Friedman and Irving Roy, who had come into the neighborhood from outside, were arrested for assault and obstruction.[24]

Though dispossessed and forced to live temporarily "with a Bronx family not in Parkchester," Sophie Decatur promised to continue the fight for integration. She told the *New York Amsterdam News* that Lowe had offered her "a six week stay of eviction if I would sign a statement that I would move out 'quietly.' . . . I told them that if they would guarantee to move a Negro family in to the next empty Parkchester apartment I would go 'quietly.' Otherwise I would just be accepting their jim crow [*sic*] policies."[25]

In the aftermath of the dramatic confrontation in Parkchester over the Decaturs, the New York State Committee on Discrimination in Housing (NYSCDH), organized by civil rights groups amid the Stuyvesant Town integration campaign, met with Frank Lowe.[26] The Committee members, concerned that "irresponsible groups"—those with seemingly Communist leanings who had come into the neighborhood to protest—were undermining the cause of integration within Parkchester, got no satisfaction from him. The MLIC executive stuck to the company line that "sooner or later" Parkchester would be integrated, but he would not be pushed to act by tenant activists. Moreover, he complained that the MLIC was "tired of being singled out" for criticism since, in his estimation, his company had done more for African Americans "than any other insurance company."[27]

Ten months later, in March 1954, the MLIC was again pressed for change. A new combine of activists, the Intergroup Committee for Integration in Parkchester, composed of a dozen Catholic and Jewish groups and several civil rights defense organizations, urged the company to end its discriminatory "tenant selection policies." While tacitly and tactically acknowledging that the laws then on the books did not compel Parkchester to desegregate, the advocates called upon the company to join the "pattern in our most enlightened communities" through ending discrimination in their operation of "the largest privately-owned housing project in the world on an all-white basis."[28]

Several days later, "eight of the most responsible human relations agencies in New York City" brought together by the NYSCDH met with Frank Lowe. But neither the bad publicity nor the sit-down nor a stinging editorial that the liberal *New York Post* published just five days before the meeting altered the MLIC's unyielding stance. Calling its attitude a "Metropolitan Disgrace," the newspaper accused the company of "practicing white supremacy in the Bronx." The MLIC, it asserted, was lobbying Washington to "hold off public housing" in favor of "privately funded low cost housing" and then kept blacks out. For the *Post*, "if minority groups can have no hope for nonsegregated housing under the auspices of private industry, where do they go. This squeeze play can permanently condemn millions of Americans to second class citizenship." Moreover, "the claim that it is the law is a lame one. That is what the folks in Mississippi say about 'separate but equal.'"[29]

Unmoved to change policy and still able to stall integration with the power of law on its side, the MLIC continued to keep out people whom its own internal office notations referred to euphemistically as "not the Parkchester type." That meant that rental agents were told to turn away applicants who "lived on a street in the Bronx that had been poor for a very long time." In practice, for example, in June 1954, when a female Harlem resident wrote in about the availability of space in Parkchester and followed up with a phone call, the agent evaded her questions about the complex's policies toward integration. The practiced response was that "there were no Negro residents in Parkchester and that the large backlog of requests made it likely that the project would not accept new applications."[30]

Unwilling to abandon the cause, in September 1954, the Intergroup Committee organized a "Symposium on Inter-Group Living" at the Concourse Plaza Hotel. Its meeting notice, entitled "Parkchester: Barrier to Democracy," observed that just two months earlier, the United States Supreme Court in the monumental *Brown v. the Board of Education of Topeka, Kansas* decision had "condemned . . . the evil of segregation in education." Taking heart from that fundamental turn in jurisprudence, the public was urged to give "expression to . . . feelings on whether it is a healthy attitude to prevent any minority from living with other groups purely and solely because of race" by making their views known to the MLIC and the media.[31]

Immediately after the symposium, committee leaders turned to New York City Mayor Robert F. Wagner for an "audience at an early date to discuss the problem." To this point, notwithstanding the prior three years of protests, both confrontational and civil, City Hall had been silent on the issue. In fact, a day after the Intergroup Committee's letter arrived at His Honor's desk, an assistant to the mayor inquired of one of his colleagues: "What is our position on this?" A month later, Wagner's people got back to the committee members, advising them that the city was prepared to host a conference in early November 1954 with the civil rights advocates and the MLIC. The mayor sent a far-from-confrontational letter to Frank Lowe advising him that City Hall had "received a number of communications requesting . . . a conference with you for certain individuals and groups interested in the alleged admission policy at your development in Parkchester."[32]

Later in September, City Hall received a number of similarly worded letters from both residents of Parkchester and other New Yorkers, some of whom identified themselves as members of the Intergroup Committee, calling upon Wagner to take a strong stand in support of desegregation. The writers asserted that, with the Supreme Court decision, a new era in civil rights had begun nationally and it was time, as one missive argued, "to put an end to our [city's] disgrace." Several concerned constituents noted that the meeting at the Concourse Plaza Hotel had moved them to articulate their feelings. One communicator noted, much like James Egert Allen had argued before Ecker some years earlier, that there were "a large number of Negro policy holders and I think it is unjust when the Metropolitan refuses to rent to Negroes."[33]

In response, Assistant to the Mayor Stanley H. Lowell sent each one of these writers the identical letter, which noted that representatives of the insurance company had been called to a City Hall meeting, just like the committee had requested. However, Wagner's deputy was also quick to add: "I am certain you are aware that there is no legal power available to the Mayor in connection with this problem." Indeed, His Honor did not use his bully pulpit to effect any meaningful policy change. A private meeting, and not a public conference, was held on November 5, 1954. The gathering was so private that it received no media coverage from either New York's general or black press. And ten days later, an internal mayoral memo indicated that there would be no follow-up: "no point in a further meeting." The MLIC had held its ground and carried the day.[34]

Amid these early 1950s struggles over segregation in Parkchester, one highly consequential municipal business leader, with close personal and professional ties to many of the involved leaders and organizations, was publicly silent as the battles moved from the neighborhood to the MLIC's corporate headquarters and on to City Hall. Through all the contretemps, Robert W. Dowling stayed apart from the fray. Apparently, he did not pressure any of the disputants to alter their views nor did they attempt to prevail upon him to take a stance. At first glance, given his background and interests, the housing discrimination issue should have engaged Dowling's attention.

This millionaire real estate developer was, to begin with, a close friend of Frederick Ecker and an essential part of that handpicked inner circle that designed, financed, and built the company's model East Bronx community. In fact, in 1938, it was Dowling who had surveyed the property on behalf of his colleagues before determining that the Catholic Protectorate was ideal for their massive construction initiative. He closed the deal at the cost of approximately $5 million. In the years that followed, Dowling was very proud of his efforts as he was positively characterized as a "romantic metropolitanite" who believed that cities should "grow up rather than out." For him, cities were "so basic to our country's existence that they must be the safest of investments."

Simultaneously, Dowling was a leader "in many civic endeavors" under multiple city and state administrations. For example, in 1947, Mayor William O'Dwyer appointed him president of the Citizens Budget Group, which, among other important tasks, "reorganize[ed] the Police, Fire, Sanitation, Corrections and Public Works Departments." As an entertainment entrepreneur, Dowling was also a name to be reckoned with on and off Broadway since he owned seven playhouses in the city. He was also deeply connected politically. In 1951, he helped future mayor Wagner become Manhattan borough president on his way to Gracie Mansion. Seemingly in return, Wagner appointed him to the honorific post of "cultural executive" of New York City. In 1954, he was a key figure in Averell Harriman's election as governor. Two years later, he headed a businessmen's committee designed to promote Harriman's projected run for the presidency.

As much as Dowling was part of Gotham's and Albany's power elite and the city's best social circles, he was also applauded for his concern for the poor and disadvantaged. Given what would transpire in Parkchester, it is noteworthy that he was acclaimed "for his concern for improving the economic and social status of the Negro." Dowling made his feelings evident when he chose "'The Roots are Deep,' a rather daring play about racial prejudice for presentation at the Fulton Theater." It was also known that "one of his secretaries at his penthouse office at 25 Broad Street is a Negro." In early 1950s

America and New York, this was a statement in its own right about where he stood on the race question.

Even more significantly, at the precise time that Parkchester roiled over rental policies, Dowling was serving as national president of the National Urban League. After his tenure concluded, he would remain an honorary trustee until his death in 1973. In other words, from 1950 to 1956, he was a prime figure in an organization that "advocated for equal economic opportunity for African Americans." From that rostrum, Dowling would heap praise on companies like International Harvester, which in 1954 committed to ensuring that "all people of the South, Negro and white, would enjoy the same opportunities for employment." Yet Dowling was silent on the MLIC's Parkchester rental policies.[35]

Several factors may begin to explain Dowling's public reticence. First, Dowling was unquestionably a lifelong friend of Ecker's, and he also knew both Frank and Douglas Lowe quite well, and thus may have been predisposed to accept the MLIC's position that there simply was no room in Parkchester for applicants of all races. Second, although Dowling undoubtedly respected the motives and actions of the NAACP and the Intergroup Committee, other organizations tainted with the brush of radicalism and even Communism had taken part in the protests. This taint, so conspicuous in the early 1950s, may have deterred him from identifying with the case. Most likely, however, Dowling did not stand up for fair housing because the reality was that the MLIC's privately owned housing development had the law on its side. Such indeed was the opinion of the courts and ultimately the view of Mayor Wagner when His Honor was approached to take a stand. Given this legal barrier, the National Urban League, perhaps with Dowling in the lead, focused instead on improving the lot of blacks where legislation supported their cause.

The National Urban League was then engaged primarily on ensuring that laws dating to 1941 that mandated fair employment opportunities for all people would be enforced. From the perspective of the African Americans who served with and under Dowling, a white business leader like him, whether or not he spoke out on other civil rights concerns, was widely seen as useful not only for the financial contributions he made to their organizations; he and his well-heeled colleagues were also deemed instrumental in making sure that doors to previously segregated places of employment that had been opened would remain ajar for qualified black candidates. No one asked for more from these supporters. Indeed, Kenneth Clark would subsequently characterize the Urban League's "strategy of law and maneuver" just that way. The organization temperamentally would "work within the existing systems of constitutional society and democratic capitalism, achieving gains by patient hard work, and by tough, relentless pressure on those who hold political and economic power, working with whites where practical." Moreover, for what it was worth, the MLIC had a good record and was proud of its behavior in training and hiring employees without regard to color. It was a position that had to have been known to the National Urban League, which monitored employment practices. Thus, they may well have determined that, when it came to the Parkchester case, it was efficacious to stand down. Fighting housing discrimination would wait for another day in the slow evolution of the civil rights struggle in the United States.[36]

In the meantime, the MLIC's tried and true—or false—answers about their efforts to admit blacks into Parkchester became somewhat more difficult to sustain in 1957, when the New York City Council passed, over the objections of real estate interests, the Sharkey-Brown-Isaacs Bill, which "barred racial discrimination in the sale or rental of private housing." Feeling that now they finally had the power of legislation on their side in dealing with a private development, the Bronx Branch of the NAACP moved to seek out African Americans who were anxious to find better housing to test out the law. One plan was to have a black couple go to Parkchester and request an application and "if refused they should be followed by a white couple." If the latter couple were favorably received, it would be proof positive that racial discrimination was still the MLIC's policy and theoretically legal action would be initiated. Another stratagem was to call upon other white civic organizations "to send representatives to greet Negro applicants" when they showed up with their completed applications in hand to smooth their way in. Meanwhile, the Bronx NAACP demanded from the MLIC that it do more than just take "token" families in minimal compliance with the law "so that their policy be to give Negro applicants first preference to make up for Parkchester's history." However, the civil rights group was unable to rouse widespread public support for this position.

In March 1960, the Executive Committee of the Bronx Branch of the NAACP reported a "lack of interest in the community" and deemed it appropriate that "letters be sent to the churches, PTAs and civic and fraternal organizations to promote interest in housing problems." Unfortunately for the NAACP, it was unable to rally people like those who protested the ouster of the Decaturs some seven years earlier or those who, for some moments, stood with the Intergroup Committee at a time when the law was not on their side. Meanwhile, the MLIC had long in place the potent strategy of using "full occupancy" as a weapon against integration. When questioned in public hearings about what precisely were its policies on race, Frank Lowe "would not come out specifically for anti-discrimination legislation, but said his company found non-discriminatory policies created 'no unusual problems, tensions or difficulties.'"[37]

As a result, until late in the 1960s, Parkchester remained a virtually all-white preserve. John Dearie, who as an adult would be a major figure in advocating for tenant rights in the neighborhood, remembered that growing up he almost "never saw a black in the neighborhood except for an African American employee" whom he frequently would see from his window "walking to his job in a drug store." Dearie's contemporary, Sara Wyner, recalled "the only black person I knew personally was our cleaning lady Martha who came once a week." Her friendly conversations with this domestic worker during her lunch breaks constituted "the sum total of my experience with black people or as they were called then, 'Negroes' or 'colored,' until I was a teenager" and enrolled at the integrated High School of Music and Art. In retrospect, Wyner has noted the cruel irony that "we sang out with enthusiasm in the P.S. 106 auditorium in the early 1950s . . . 'you can get good milk from a brown-skinned cow, the color of your skin doesn't matter, anyhow.' Oh, how we believed it, yet if we looked around the assembly, there was not a black or brown face to be seen."[38]

Another Parkchester child of the 1950s, Peter Carolan, noted another significant neighborhood venue where blacks were never around. After spirited games of basketball with and against Jewish players in the West Quadrant playground, Carolan would go off to the local candy store on White Plains Road, a block west of Parkchester. There he would see black youngsters of his age, but he never played with them in the development's designated recreational areas in daylight hours. Rather, the athletic fields and courts were the places where, more often than not, white Christians— primarily Irish Catholics—and Jews met up with each other on a daily basis. However, though they played together, competition and cooperation in games and sports between young men and a few young women of different faiths rarely extended to great friendships outside of fenced-off precincts. After all, most of the Catholic youngsters attended St. Helena's or St. Raymond's parochial schools, while most Jews went to one of the public schools. On the other hand, while there were some Christian bullies in the community who sometimes pushed around more callow Jewish boys, religious epithets generally were not an integral part of playground trash talk. Hard fouls might lead to fights but only occasionally did athletic battles lead to "Christ-killer'" canards. Such were the ground rules of the era.[39]

Robert "Lefty" Krain, also a neighborhood boy of that early Parkchester period, who helped organize an all-Jewish basketball squad made up of classmates from P.S. 106 called the Vikings, re-called a prevailing "get along" attitude. He and his teammates played "very competitive games" devoid of any ethnic ten-sions when they squared off against teams of Irish youngsters in Parkchester's recreational leagues or when they matched up every Saturday morning in pick-up games in the playgrounds or at St. Helena's or St. Raymond's gymnasiums. The Vikings were known as a Jewish team only when they represented Temple Emanuel in a dif-ferent, Jewish community league that included clubs from around New York and New Jersey. Meanwhile, another of the Jewish fellows, Robert M. Lewis, who earned street recognition as a "ringer," also played for the Shamrocks, a St. Helena's team that competed in the Catholic Youth Organization's loops. But, significantly, he estab-lished no enduring friendships with the Irish fellows after the final whistles blew.[40]

Peter Quinn, that proud St. Raymond's boy, believes that when all was said and done "we lived separately together." Of course, as a "Bronxite" dwelling in the largest Jewish city in the world, he did pick up a "familiarity with Yiddish," acquiring words like "schlepp" and "kibitz" and learning "the difference between a smuck [*sic*] and a mensch." But he "had no Jewish friends . . . and no acquaintance with Jewish girls." At the same time, he asserted strongly that there were no so-called "Irish pogromists" like those whom Jews feared in other neighborhoods. As a Jewish girl in the neighborhood during the same era, Sara Wyner is only partially accepting of Quinn's—

and for that matter Krain's—estimation of the tenor of this deci-
sive interethnic relationship within Parkchester's streets and gyms.
While agreeing that she "was brought up in a neighborhood which
was dominated by two very different cultures: the Irish and the
Jews" and was never victimized by concerted attacks, in describing
her "love/hate relationship . . . with the Celts of the Bronx," she has
remembered "during grade school and junior high school running
away from tough Irish boys on Halloween. They would fill socks
with chalk and run after us, and if they caught up, hit us hard with
the socks and yell 'Halloween'! I think I remember being afraid of
them not only because of the humiliation and pain of a rock-like,
chalky sock but because I was Jewish." For her, it was a memorable
moment in time where she was made aware of religious difference.
Meanwhile Quinn, who seemingly tried his utmost to stay out of
nasty mixes, recalled that there were more fights in the St. Raymond's schoolyard, "where the weak were bullied and tough Irish
battled it out with tough Italians," than attacks against Jews after
school. However, amid all of this interethnic interaction of varying
sorts, feelings about blacks were not expressed because they were
not part of the ongoing athletic-social scene.[41]

Similarly, the women's group advocacy in the neighborhood
that succeeded in expanding educational space and opportunities for Parkchester's youngsters did not avail black boys and girls
who lived outside the community. Roberta Stern, who in the late
1950s was a student in one of the first classes at P.S. 127, remembered that when she started junior high school "there was a rumor
going around that there were three black teenagers in the school.
But during the three years that I was there, I never did see them."
However, there is also evidence that the visibility of young blacks
at night was of some concern to those omnipresent Parkchester
police, who would question these outsiders about what they were
doing in the neighborhood after dark. John McInerney recalled that

after a night of bowling in the Chester House a black employee was rudely directed to go directly to the subway.[42]

As an unintended consequence of how it ran its trains, the New York City subway system also limited white contacts with blacks and Latinos. From 1946 on, East 177th Street/Parkchester was an express stop. During rush hours, the train skipped over stations in the Soundview section of the borough before stopping at Hunts Point. And then five more stations were skipped before the train opened its doors for passengers at 138th Street/Third Avenue. From 125th Street in Harlem, the next station, it was only four local stops until the train reached Yorkville. Effectively, Parkchester passengers avoided, or had at most limited contact with, those stations in the poorest sections of the Bronx, where racial minority groups lived.[43]

Many Parkchester residents of the era also had no interaction with African Americans when they stepped out of the neighborhood during summertime to frequent the Castle Hill Beach Club. Since opening its doors in 1928, this recreational site, predominately for Jews but also for "many Catholics, Protestants . . . and people of other nationalities," did not have a single black member. In the summer of 1953, at almost the same time that the segregation issue was first raised about Parkchester, Anita Brown, a bold African American woman, challenged the club's unwritten, but clearly evident, policy when she applied for membership. Rejected, she turned to the New York State Commission against Discrimination (SCAD). Seemingly, she had the law on her side since by then such racist behavior within public accommodations had been outlawed. When investigators confronted the club's managers, they defended themselves with arguments that were very similar to those the MLIC was then using successfully. First, they contended that "admission of a Negro . . . would result in a violent reaction by the white members . . . and the disturbance may be of such a proportion that it would get out of control." Beneath the physical threat was an equally potent economic one—that "if a black person were allowed membership . . . whites would abandon the club in droves." In other words, as Frederick Ecker might have put it, blacks and whites don't mix and forced mixing would be at the expense of the ownership's fiduciary obligations.

Perhaps more importantly, from a strictly legal standpoint, the club argued that the public accommodations laws did not apply to it as a private entity. The owners explained that they had gone "private" surely not to keep out African Americans but to exclude "troublemakers," thieves, and vandals. As one long-time member expressed it: "A strange element of people came in from all over the country . . . broke lockers every day and started to steal stuff." Concerned management claimed that it simply wanted a more controlled environment. Though the race question was not necessarily on members' minds when they swam and socialized in the club, those from Parkchester could well understand the meaning of social controls in a private entity. In response, Brown's attorney argued that the club's "members only policy was inconsistent with how it presented itself to the public and a smoke screen used to hide its racially discriminatory policy."

Unable to convince the State Commission against Discrimination that their operation was a private club, the defendants went beyond the specter of racial violence to evoke a very different but very present trepidation of the early 1950s. The Communism card was again played. This allegation was raised during precisely the same time period where in Stuyvesant Town, and in nearby Parkchester too, the idea that Communist troublemakers played a role in desegregation efforts was at least implied. It certainly was on the mind of the major civil rights organizations that their efforts would be tarred as radical. In the Castle Hill case, the attorney for the club alleged at a SCAD hearing that Brown was part of "a conspiracy amongst people with ulterior motives whose credibility . . . cannot be taken under any assent by people of ordinary intelligence." Brown was framed as linked to a group committed to "the destruction . . . of private beach clubs and other things under our capitalist system." Wary of this instigator's intentions, Brown was barred not because of her race but because of her "preaching or advertising different Communistic ideas."

The SCAD did not accept any of the club's arguments and directed the ownership to open its door. The State Supreme Court affirmed the decision. However, more than a decade would elapse before the club was desegregated. Reportedly, the Commission "lacked the personnel and resources to ensure full compliance." The club worked around the ruling by changing its membership procedures to require an existing member to sponsor a newcomer. And perhaps as significant, unlike the courageous Anita Brown, throughout the 1950s other blacks in the vicinity did not test the policies of a club that did not want them. The Castle Hill Beach Club would not be integrated until the mid-1960s, amid a new era of civil rights activism over discrimination in public accommodations and, certainly, housing.[44]

In the early 1960s, during those halcyon days of protests down south against racist policies involving voting rights and schooling, advocates against discrimination in New York redoubled their efforts to desegregate housing in the city. But as before, MLIC management stonewalled activists' efforts. In July 1963, the NAACP demanded that Ecker and his company articulate "an across-the-board pledge . . . that there will be a change in this No-Negro pattern" in both its downtown and Bronx developments. The civil rights group charged with reference to Parkchester that thirty-eight thousand people lived there but not one was black. African Americans, it was asserted, were directed to Riverton. If no change was "forthcoming then there will be dramatic demonstrations" at MLIC properties "to enlighten the residents of projects and the public about a situation that must be changed." This threatened protest garnered a front-page headline from the *New York World Telegram and Sun*: "NAACP to Turn Fire on Bias in Apartments."[45]

The MLIC's rejoinder, alleging that apartments had indeed been offered to black families in Parkchester but due to the long waiting list the applicants ended up elsewhere, did not mollify the NAACP. With the pressure on and a demonstration in sight, Ecker and his associates agreed to sit down with the NAACP under the auspices of the New York City Commission on Human Rights.

Out of those meetings, perhaps under the advice of counsel, the MLIC "reaffirmed its long-established policy of non-discrimination in the fields of housing employment and investment." It asserted that "no bona fide applicant is denied housing . . . because of race creed or color." Management, in short, admitted to no wrongdoing in the past and seemed to suggest that it intended to carry on as before the recent protests. While NAACP leader Roy Wilkins walked away from the deliberations with the belief that a "major breakthrough" had been achieved, Parkchester management still retained much discretion in filling its apartments. While an MILC official told Wilkins that "we are ready to go down the line on this. If a Negro is a qualified tenant and there is a vacancy for him, he will get an apartment," the definition of "qualification" and the determination of vacancies remained with the insurance firm. When the MLIC failed in the months that followed to act on their pledge of integration, the NAACP was once again at Frank Lowe's office demanding swifter action.[46]

This time, late in 1963, Lowe would not indicate how many black families had recently been admitted to Parkchester, but he did submit that the problem lay with the lack of applications forthcoming from such families. That position comported well with the aforementioned recollection he would offer two years later, that when Parkchester opened back in 1940 African Americans did not request apartments. (Frank Lowe would be the foremost defender of company policy until September 1965, when he retired. Ecker had died in March 1964.) He also more than intimated that it was the MLIC's longstanding policy not to solicit potential residents. In response, the Urban League's Operation Open City, which used volunteer "scouts" to check out accommodations citywide, publicized in the *Amsterdam News* the availability of apartments in the supposedly desegregated neighborhood. That move increased the number of black New Yorkers who aspired to live in the East Bronx neighborhood. Then, using a tactic reminiscent of the one used by the Bronx NAACP a decade earlier, these soft-spoken, yet determined advocates employed white "checkers" and volunteer white attorneys to follow up when a African American applicant was turned away from an apartment advertised as available. If a white applicant was not denied the same housing place, Operation Open City would first press the landlord to explain the discrepancy; if negotiations failed, the advocates would next turn to the City Commission on Human Rights. To help the cause, Open City developed a detailed list of "Instructions for Homeseekers and Checkers" that emphasized the need for participants to initially "keep careful records of the time, place, date, and person spoken to in answering an advertisement" and after the staged encounter "to compare notes immediately . . . [and] if there was any evasion [used] towards the seeker" to formulate a complaint. Still, according to Betty Hoeber, who directed Operation Open City, ultimately the problem with the law against discrimination lay with enforcement. "It's a do-it-yourself law," she explained. "The individual has to bring an air-tight case to the commission and the process of getting the evidence can be terribly mortifying."[47]

Thus, for all of their efforts, as late as May 1968, complainants would contend "that only 25 Negroes and Puerto Ricans have ever been rented apartments since [Parkchester's] opening" and "all of these rentals occurred since 1963," even though there was an estimated "average of more than 400 vacancies a year."⁴⁸

One of the fortunate few was Mildred Hall, who along with her auto mechanic husband, Gilbert, and their young daughter, Valerie, was granted an apartment at 1541 Metropolitan Avenue in 1967. Mildred knew all about the Open City campaign as she was a long-term and successful fund-raiser for the Urban League. In that role, she approached and got to know well the city's major political figures and other well-heeled New Yorkers, including, most significantly, Robert W. Dowling. Fifteen years after his presidency ended, Dowling was still on the board of the Urban League and always responded favorably to Hall's appeals for funds in support of the organization. When Mildred sought to move her family out of the Morrisania section of the Bronx, she thus turned to Dowling for assistance. He responded affirmatively, probably leaned on the MLIC's officials, and quietly, without fanfare, as was Dowling's style, the Hall family was accepted. For Frank and Douglas Lowe, doing their friend a favor did not change the scene in Parkchester. But once ensconced, Mildred was not a docile tenant. Rather, she would play an active role in community leadership for decades thereafter. She was also prepared from the start of her family's life in Parkchester to help fellow minorities enter the neighborhood, that is if only the MLIC would yield. However, a year after the Halls entered Parkchester, the Urban League was still struggling to open the complex to a significant number of black tenants.⁴⁹

It remained for the City Commission on Human Rights; after two years of fruitless "extensive negotiations," to charge the MLIC in May 1968 with the "deliberate, intentional and systematic" exclusion of blacks and Latinos from the neighborhood. As for the oft-repeated contention that the unwanted did not really desire to be in Parkchester, the Commission explained that "as a result of the [company's] past exclusion of Negroes and Puerto Ricans from its 'white' properties," they "knew that applying would be "futile, embarrassing or degrading." Moreover, it was contended that Riverton "was run as a 'black property' to which Negroes were encouraged to apply while being discouraged from applying" to Parkchester and for that matter, the MLIC's downtown properties. True to form, the MLIC's response to the charges was that, in tenant selection, no discrimination was taking place and that such had been its "firm policy long . . . followed in all phases of the company's activities." The company claimed that in Parkchester's twenty-eight years of operation only 279 applications had been submitted by blacks and Latinos, and that if virtually all had been turned down, they "were rejected on economic bases not racial ones."[50]

But faced with the threat that if the Commission's complaints were sustained in subsequent court proceedings that its officers might face not only minor fines that could be chalked up to the cost of doing business as usual, but a year in jail, the MLIC agreed in July 1968 to make substantive policy changes. Soon thereafter, however, it became apparent that there were battles still to be won as, rhetoric aside, the management continued to drag its feet. The Urban League's Housing Division reported that the first black families who renewed their applications, having sought accommodations for "up to four years," were stymied as before by a "run around." Such was the unhappy reality when five black families met in the Open City offices at the end of July and dialed up Parkchester "to test the new agreement." As the Parkchester staff reportedly awaited "new rules" from the home office, communications did not go well.[51]

Mr. and Mrs. John Fisher told the *New York Times*, for example, that their application had been filed some four years earlier and to date they "had heard nothing." Presently, they lived in a two-room apartment in Brooklyn and with Mrs. Fisher pregnant they "needed a larger space." When a rental agent answered the phone,

John Fisher informed her that "he was black and had read of the Metropolitan's agreement." In response, Fisher was asked whether he had filed a written application. When he answered, "I've written to you and have been in for an interview," the agent replied, "You will hear from us." When asked if there were vacancies to be had, the representative of Parkchester declared, "I really have no idea." Dejected, John Fisher told a reporter: "It's really the same reaction that they had been giving. . . . It's really brilliant diplomacy."

Barbara Nell also felt that nothing had changed when she, her husband, and three-year-old son wanted to move out of a different Bronx neighborhood to Parkchester. She heard from a different agent: "We know of no change. Things are just the same as they were as far as we're concerned." Two other dismayed applicants were informed that their files had been misplaced. And yet another couple, whose application had been on file since 1966, were told that there was no definite time frame for their admission to Parkchester. One clerk told them brusquely: "I don't know. That depends on turnover, sir. We don't specify any time."[52]

Finally, in the late summer and early fall of 1968, the MLIC made policy changes that would promote integration. Still under pressure from the Commission, the management agreed to inform Riverton residents of "opportunities" in Parkchester and that those who now applied "would be considered simultaneously" with those people on the existing waiting list "without regard to race." The MLIC also agreed to "end its practice of giving preference to relatives of tenants, which often enabled them to avoid the 3 to 5 years of waiting."

Despite its hand having been forced by a direct, unequivocal government command, the MLIC put the best possible face on the decision. At the start of August 1968, hewing still to the company line, an unchastened MLIC told its employees that with the "*aid* of [Chairman William] Booth, they have developed new approaches designed to *encourage* fuller participation of Negroes and Puerto Ricans . . . since there has been a *reluctance* on the part of qualified persons from minority groups to apply [emphases mine]." At the same time, management made clear as before that "while Met encourages qualified minorities to express their interest, it is not possible to promise immediate results because all apartments are under lease." But apparently with the new protocols in place, accommodations were soon found because thirty-five non-white families started moving into Parkchester beginning in August and 140 others were "being processed."[53]

FIGURE 6.1. Leadership of the Parkchester Branch of the NAACP (far left: Beverly Roberts; second to left: Beatrice Franklin), circa 1990s. Courtesy of Beatrice Franklin.

A MIXED RECEPTION

EXCEPT FOR THE VERY EARLY SURVEY THAT THE Parkchester Committee to End Housing Discrimination undertook in 1950, the attitudes of neighborhood tenants toward integration were never formally assessed. And no polling, no matter how sophisticated, can delve into what respondents might have said to those closest to them in private at their dinner tables. What is certain is that through all of the decade and a half of struggles to open up the community to people of color, from the Decatur confrontation in 1952–1953 to the civil rights organizations' successful petitioning of the government in the 1960s, the overwhelming majority of Parkchester residents were not heard from. They sat on the sidelines and neither actively supported nor vocally opposed integration efforts. And remember, the street protests against the MLIC in the early 1950s occurred miles away from Parkchester at the company's Manhattan offices, while NAACP and Urban League efforts were largely court-based or quiet appearances at rental offices. It is thus unknown whether these initiatives fully captured the attention of or even interested the men and women who sat every day on the benches of Metropolitan Oval and routinely discussed the pressing issues of the day, including the turmoil over race both down south and elsewhere in their home city. Still, one attempt to both gauge, and perhaps change, the attitudes of people on the question of race within the Jewish community took place on a memorable evening early in the 1960s.

At one Young Israel of Parkchester Friday Night Forum, the Horowitzes' now grown son, Michael, a civil rights activist, attempted to raise the consciousness of his parent's fellow congregants. From the social hall pulpit, he challenged his listeners, asking if "in our carefully made up community, one third Jewish, one third Catholic, one third Protestant"—his religious-affiliation demographics were off—"do you think it might be possible for us to add one or two Negro families without destroying community stability?" His remarks were met with silence and some "nervous shuffling of feet," except for Rabbi Schwartz, who praised his "idealism" while ducking his imperative. Michael Horowitz would go on to teach law in the first integrated law school class in Mississippi. Reflecting many decades later on the non-reaction of his community's elders to his "telling them how to live their lives," he has come to believe that his fellow Jews were not racists, but rather "good people" who simply were comfortable with the status quo and not in personal touch with the ongoing national debate. Irene Horowitz would recall that his assigned topic was "my community . . . meaning Parkchester"; her committed son, however, declared that the "whole world is my community" at a time when "things are changing."[1]

Similarly, many years later, YIP members Ruby Lukin and her husband, Stanley Langer, who may well have been in the audience when Michael Horowitz challenged his fellow Jews, wondered to themselves why they did not take an activist stance against the segregation in their neighborhood turf. After all, as a secondary school student Ruby had connected with a black sorority at Evander Childs High School and at Brandeis University was a charter member of the school's NAACP branch, at a time when only a handful of African American students were enrolled at the Massachusetts college. Stanley had made a far more public statement on where he stood on the question of racial equality when, as student body president of DeWitt Clinton High School, he publicly declared "high school students could no longer remain silent when it came to prejudice and discrimination." Under his leadership, the student General Organization "voted to petition the New York State Legislature to enact laws that would do away with racial, religious, and regional discrimination in New York colleges and universities that were tax exempt." Under Stanley's prodding a number of other schools joined the fight. Ruby, reflecting on those days in Parkchester when they were newly married, said: "We never had a conversation about 'how come we are living in Parkchester, there are no minorities here.' . . . When you think about it, you could be liberal in your thinking but that was the world . . . it was segregated. It wasn't like anyone I spoke to at that time was raising the banner."[2]

Actually, in the years immediately after Horowitz's provocative speech, the ever-popular Friday Night Forum occasionally considered the issue of "civil rights," especially when the synagogue partnered with the Parkchester branch of the B'nai B'rith. The integration question in Parkchester was perhaps on participants' minds when, in January 1965, the issue at the rostrum was "How Can We Improve Our Changing Community." And Horowitz came back in December 1967 to talk again about "American Jews and American Negroes." But more often than not, the Forum's topics focused on issues like the fate of Israel. More than once, local Jewish and Christian politicians used the event to emphasize their devotion to the cause of the Jewish state. And increasingly concerns were articulated about the fate of oppressed Soviet Jews as that international issue moved front and center among their co-religionists in the United States. Particularly for the strictly Orthodox rabbi of the congregation, the most pressing issue of intergroup relations was how closely he should work with the Catholic clergy in interreligious dialogue. He was very reticent even during the era of reconciliation after Vatican II. On the question of race, he privately expressed the hope that the cohort of blacks who might enter Parkchester in the long run would be much like the first African Americans whom he got to know in the neighborhood, people anxious "to improve their lot." But Rabbi Schwartz never preached in favor of, or against integration, from his pulpit. That was not his homiletic style.[3]

But over at St. Raymond's Church one noteworthy Sunday in 1960, a young priest, John C. Flynn, committed to the growing vision of social-action Catholicism, "challenged a packed house at 12 o'clock Mass to embrace the example of the 'Negro Protestant minister' Martin Luther King and see his struggle for equality in the light of the gospels." Reportedly, this departure from traditional homilies, which generally emphasized the quest for eternal salvation, was met in the pews with some approving smiles but also with "horrified . . . gasps" and glances. Like many in the YIP crowd, a substantial share of Catholic parishioners did not see support for civil rights as part of their churches' "agenda."[4]

Several years later, Father Flynn pushed the issue of race directly and far more provocatively into St. Raymond's life when, in the days before segregation ended in Parkchester, he sought to blend minority students from a Montessori school in the South Bronx with whom he was working, with the predominantly Irish pupils in the parish's own Montessori school. From the pews, one disapproving congregant told his priest, "If you love them so much, why don't you go live with them." Eventually, Flynn would do just that, spending three years in the barrios of Caracas, Venezuela, among the poor before returning to ministries in the South Bronx. Before leaving for his mission of mercy in South America, he helped soothe the process of integration in at least one neighborhood dwelling. As the story goes, when the first black family moved into a particular building, Flynn walked over to the apartment of one of his parishioners and requested that the white family "be godparents to the new resident who was converting to his wife's Catholic religion."[5]

Notwithstanding Flynn's prodding of his Catholic flock and Horo-witz's appeal to his fellow Jews, Parkchester's white residents were largely disengaged personally from debate over racial change in their neighborhood. Their silence or equanimity may have had much to do with the aforementioned ways the Urban League and the NAACP went about striving to open up the neighborhood. Unquestionably, the Urban League, which has been characterized as not so much a "protest organization but much more one of advocacy assistance and legal action," and which placed its faith in "institutionalized . . . activism" stayed clear of intentionally raising hackles.[6] Accordingly, there were no street protests in Parkchester, no marches or sit-ins to raise resident consciousness or trepidations. The threatened "demonstration," in the works in the summer of 1963 before the agreement that Roy Wilkins called "a major breakthrough," never took place. Thus, there was no visible strife about racial matters in their neighborhood. Yet when that original concordat was reached, a local newspaper picked up an undercurrent of fear and perhaps prejudice.

Early in August 1963, the *Bronx Press Review*, which generally reported neighborhood news without significant comment, argued in an editorial entitled "New Neighbors in Parkchester" that while "residents in the majority will continue their flawless record of a quarter century of amity and quiet," it had heard to its dismay "'interpretations' and excitable comments on the agreement." The paper did not identify who was "disseminating" what it deemed troublesome words and thoughts. In its view, "extravagant speculations and prejudgments are to be avoided," for the newcomers "once being processed as tenants with due regard for all, will turn out to be nothing less than good neighbors." In the editorial's view, "25 years of good neighborly common sense and morality are on the line." For the editorial's author or authors, the long-existing get-along attitude among Parkchester's white ethnic and religious groups was worthy of extension to African Americans and Latinos. Of course, the moment of decision was not yet at hand. Five more years would pass before these new neighbors would arrive in significant numbers in Parkchester.[7]

At that latter point, in 1968, it is entirely likely that many of his neighbors shared the opinion of Charles Tripodo, a worker for the Board of Elections, who had lived in the development since it opened. A few months after the MLIC's final concession, he told the *New York Times* that his fear was "not of a few Negro neighbors but that once integration begins whites will start to flee in large numbers." He worried that his community would share the troubling fate of "projects that became all black after integration began." Such was then the unhappy case of racial patterns, for example, in Brownsville, Brooklyn. In that neighborhood, when public projects that were ostensibly constructed for people of all races attracted increasingly large numbers of blacks, whites left. A section of Gotham that in 1957 was two-thirds white became in just five years three-quarters black and Latino. Parkchesterites were reassured, to some extent, that where they lived was not a *project* and it was certainly not public. And, of course, the development had long-standing rules over admission, even if management would now not discriminate against minorities or privilege white families who had relatives already in the development. Still, Tripodo hoped that where he moved "stays as nice as it has always been. We just don't want another ghetto."[8]

No polling was done at the time to ascertain how Parkchester's twelve thousand or so white families felt about the first handfuls of blacks moving in, with more on the way. Besides which, as one reporter suggested, "Parkchester people are not blunt. . . . They are not loud about their politics. Used to living among friends, they are circumspect and a bit suspicious with strangers." But a study of residents' attitudes in Parkchester's sister community, Stuyvesant Town, in December 1967 may offer an inkling into attitudes in the East Bronx neighborhood. Downtown people of similar social and religious backgrounds and economic standing in an overwhelmingly segregated complex preferred by a 58–42 percent margin to have their community "more integrated racially" as opposed to "remain[ing] almost entirely white." When queried further about the "most reasonable and desirable percentage of Negroes and Puerto Ricans residents" they would like to see in the neighborhood, the majority felt that the best figure would be between 15 and 25 percent non-whites. However, residents drew a clear line when it came to the economic class of blacks and Puerto Ricans they would comfortably accept. By a majority of 70–30 percent, present tenants objected to "low-income families being accepted into Stuyvesant Town under some kind of government rent-supplement program," even "assuming continued care in the screening of applicants."[9]

This local study cohered with some national trends. Back in 1942, when Parkchester was just two years old and Stuyvesant Town was still on the drawing boards, a coast-to-coast survey found that more than eight out of ten white Americans wanted blacks to live in their own segregated parts of the country's cities. But during the period 1958–1978, the percentage of whites who were determined to move if any blacks settled in their neighborhood dropped from 44 to 14 percent. And, on the crucial question of whether "it would make any difference . . . if a Negro with the same income and education . . . moved into their block," 85 percent indicated that they were accepting of that prospect. Back in 1942, only 36 percent felt that way. Thus, if Parkchester's tenants thought at all similarly, African Americans of economic station comparable to theirs would be accepted in the area.[10]

There was perhaps, however, a segment of Parkchesterites who strongly objected to integration. Apparently, 8.5 percent of Parkchester's vote in the 1968 presidential election went in favor of arch-segregationist George Wallace, more than all but one other assembly district in the Bronx. It is not known if these people acted on their views and quickly fled the neighborhood. The sources are not there to chart their life decisions.[11]

However, dealing with future race problems would not be the MLIC's concern. In September 1968, they sold their "city within a city" to the Harry Helmsley real estate syndicate for $90 million. The selling price was "23 million more than Parkchester had cost Metropolitan to build, a price believed to be the highest ever paid for a single piece of property." In explaining their decision, the MLIC emphasized unequivocally that "the reasons for selling were strictly financial" and "not determined by rent control, racial problems and other such factors." In fact, when a reporter from *Time* magazine got wind of the possibility of a sale and questioned its motivation, a set of talking points had been developed at the home office. An internal memo suggested that the public be informed that due to "a number of inquiries from real estate interests ... within the last year ... it was decided that a sale of the property to a qualified purchaser at an attractive price would be in the best interests of the Company and its policyholders." Funds accruing from this transaction "could be invested more advantageously in fields other than directly-owned property."[12]

Upon assuming ownership, Helmsley pledged to abide by the City Commission on Human Rights rulings. Indeed, in December 1968, "12 apartments out of an available 39 were rented to non-whites."[13] However, some evidence indicates that at least during the first years of the new management's tenure, some degree of white privilege still prevailed. For example, among the first black residents in Parkchester were James and Beatrice Kibler, who moved from 206 East 175th Street, two blocks from Grand Concourse, to 2150 East Tremont Avenue. In many respects, they were a classic Parkchester couple. He was a subway system track worker and later a supervisor for the Transit Authority. She worked for the telephone company. Where they differed from the white family that previously had resided in their two-bedroom apartment was that they were obliged, to their dismay, to pay $125 a month for the same accommodations, $40 more than the prior occupants.[14]

In 1973, twenty-two-year-old African American Beverly Roberts, a manager and buyer in the fashion industry, and her husband, who owned a yellow medallion taxi, applied for an apartment. Her interest in living in the neighborhood dated back to her days as a student in the nearby James Monroe High School in the Soundview section, where as a member of an extracurricular dance group, she went for exercise classes in what she saw as "a beautiful area," even if she recalled Parkchester cops sometimes following her through the still-segregated neighborhood. Newly married, Parkchester was for her and her husband "the place to be." After her husband tendered their application, they received notification within two weeks that they had been accepted, and they found a two-bedroom apartment much to their liking. However, two other black couples who came to the rental office at the same time were told that there was a "two-to-three-year waiting list," the old saw. Beverly Roberts attributed her family's success to the fact that her husband was white even if, after their initial application was in and the vetting crew came to investigate their lifestyle in their old neighborhood, it was clear that they were an interracial couple. Apparently, the prior rules had been bent appreciably but not totally broken.[15]

Meanwhile, among the first African Americans to take advantage of the desegregation of the neighborhood were individuals who most certainly could not be toyed with. These were people who had participated in the struggle for effective change. Most notably, Harlem-born Lady Anne Dunbar had moved as a teenager to the South Bronx where, ironically, one of her first jobs, while attending college, was as a clerk for the MLIC. A self-described "community activist," she worked for Operation Open City. Immediately after the Helmsley group took over, she submitted her application, passed the social worker's home evaluation, and in January 1969, Dunbar, her four-year-old son, Chris, and her mother moved into 1940 East Tremont Avenue. The Dunbars were the second black family in the building. They were preceded just a few days earlier by postman Clarence Gantt and his wife, Rosetta, a hairdresser, who came over from the Hunts Point section of the Bronx on the advice of relatives who were the initial African Americans in a different building in Parkchester.

While Rosetta Gantt remembered "acceptance" from her white neighbors—some even "knocked on [their] door to welcome [them]"—Lady Anne Dunbar has recalled a mixed reception from her fellow tenants. One man on her floor was very troubled sharing an elevator with her, while his wife was not. On the other hand, "an elderly Irish woman" who lived several floors above her was pleased to often invite her mother upstairs for afternoon "spiked tea." A more significant sign of acceptance took place their first summer in Parkchester when people on their floor continued the neighborhood tradition of dealing with the heat by opening their doors for cross-ventilation. Lady Anne Dunbar would live at 1940 East Tremont Avenue for the next half century and, as an adult, her son would take an apartment in the same building.

Once ensconced in the new neighborhood and still the community activist, in April 1975, Dunbar became the first president of the Parkchester branch of the NAACP. The impetus for launching an NAACP branch in a now integrated neighborhood was threefold. First, its founders wanted to promote harmonious relations with the white majority. Though there was no organized resistance to combat, Dunbar knew from her own experiences of some white discontent with the reality of integration. Others could report unwelcome notes posted on black tenants' doors and comparable nastiness. Slamming of elevator doors in the faces of new black residents was one common way unhappy whites reacted to their new neighbors. Beverly Roberts, on the other hand, felt entirely comfortable in her apartment. She recalled that as "a model tenant with a model family," including a four-year-old son, who "came for a better life" just like so many others who had come early in the development's history, she had no personal difficulties in her building and "eventually [everyone] fell in love with us." However, she had a sense as she walked through the once-segregated streets that some old-time residents would stare at her "as if to say, What is she doing here?" In sum, while whites made no moves to stop blacks from settling in the neighborhood, many were not comfortable actually living among minorities.

Given these complex street and hallway realities, Dunbar initially wanted to call the neighborhood group "Whites and Blacks Together," but Dr. Stewart Adler, a white resident, convinced her of the advantages of joining the renowned national civil rights organization. Adler would become the branch's second president.

The second rationale for Parkchester NAACP was the need for the black minority to create a sense of community for themselves, within the still majority-white neighborhood. The newcomers were spread all over the development while, as of 1970, only 1.5 percent of the community's some forty thousand residents were black. For example, hospital employee Sarah Alleyne, whom the Urban League helped secure a place in Parkchester in 1969, was initially the only African American in her building at 1560 Metropolitan Avenue. Given the option of moving from her small space in a rooming house in Washington Heights to either Peter Cooper Village, which was the upscale section of Stuyvesant Town, or the Bronx, she opted for Parkchester because of its "gorgeous beauty." But upon settling in, she felt a sense of loneliness. Looking for friendship in the new neighborhood among folks with whom she could easily interact, Alleyne developed a close relationship with the four other blacks who entered Parkchester at precisely the same time she did, also thanks to the work of Operation Open City. The Parkchester NAACP did its part in facilitating more formal friendship circles. Finally, with an organization up and running, the NAACP developed a power base to ensure black voices were heard in the neighborhood. Lady Anne Dunbar was destined, over the succeeding decades, to be an outspoken advocate for Parkchester residents of all races and backgrounds.[16]

Sitting across from Dunbar at subsequent NAACP meetings was Beatrice Franklin. Though not as much the community activist, she and her husband, John, were among the African Americans who had kept close tabs on the process of desegregation. Not very long after Parkchester opened its gates to people of color, they moved forward with their application. As of 1970, Beatrice worked in the personnel advisory service of the New York Telephone Company where, among her duties, she assisted blacks and Latinos in filing their applications with the new ownership corporation. In 1975, one year after they moved from Harlem to West 180th Street in the Bronx, where they were not happy, they put in an application for Parkchester.

The Franklins, who would live at 1501 Metropolitan Avenue for the next forty years, recalled a strong degree of cooperation between themselves, a middle-aged black couple, and the predominantly elderly white building occupants. In 1977, newcomers and old-timers joined together in a neighborhood watch group at a time when criminality had become a major concern of all Parkchesterites.[17]

It remained for Franklin Graham, an official with the City Commission on Human Rights, to ameliorate the pains of housing discrimination that Harold and Dorothy Jackman had felt elsewhere in the city and facilitate their entry into a now-integrated Parkchester community. In 1968, during their first year of marriage, Dorothy, a legal assistant, and Harold, a well-positioned law enforcement officer who served in the New York State Special Investigations Bureau, lived on Mapes Avenue in the Crotona Park section of the Bronx. Unhappy with the decline of their neighborhood, they applied for apartments first in the Inwood section of Manhattan and then on Newbold Avenue, just a block south of Parkchester. In both instances, they put down a $100 deposit only to have rental agents subsequently turn them away because they were black. The prideful couple was ready to punish these offenders, but Graham, Harold's close friend, advised them that Parkchester, which his office had just recently helped desegregate, would be a better place to reside. Instead of continuing their good fight, Harold and Dorothy took Graham's recommendation. In January 1970, after the usual interview process, they took a one-bedroom apartment at 18 Metropolitan Oval. They were the second black family in the building.

Much like Lady Anne Dunbar and, for that matter, Beverly Roberts, the Jackmans received a very cool welcome from the whites in the building. Dorothy had her own nasty elevator encounter when a door was slammed in her face and the antagonist spewed some racial epithets at her. She was told to "go back to Harlem where you came from." Her response was: "I never lived in Harlem and besides which I pay more rent than you." Dorothy also sensed the discomfit of other young mothers when she took her son, Harold Jr., to the playground. But after her then eighteen-month-old boy got into a fight with a white kid who rubbed his face expecting to remove his color from his cheeks, a confrontation that the mothers broke up, the two kids became fast friends and so did the mothers. In fact, the white family sponsored the Jackmans as members of the Castle Hill Beach Club, that long-time whites-only preserve. Yet there was apparently a complex ambivalence in that white household over race. The family had moved to Mamaroneck in the mid-1970s, much to the dismay of the wife, because of her Parkchester-born husband's "unhappiness that the old neighborhood was changing so rapidly." Regardless of his viewpoint, the families continued their relationship for several years. As it would turn out, notwithstanding how they and other African American families were received, in the years to come, as residents of every race and background struggled with increasing crime and social pathologies in the neighborhood, Harold Jackman's law enforcement expertise would be useful to all in keeping the peace in Parkchester.[18]

FIGURE 7.1. Leaders of the Unity Day Rally II, November 1977 (left to right: Mildred Hall, John Dearie, John C. McEllicott). Courtesy of John Dearie.

7

"MRS. HELMSLEY SHOULD BE FORCED TO DO HER TIME IN PARKCHESTER"

MSGR. THOMAS DERIVAN SERVED WITH GREAT distinction as pastor of St. Helena's Church for forty-two years (1972–2014). An iconic figure in the neighborhood, he was on the scene during some of Parkchester's most challenging decades. He recalled that the times of trouble began when, in 1968, the MLIC sold the complex to the Helmsley-Spear corporation. The real estate giant would own and operate the neighborhood until the late 1990s. When asked in 2017 for a sense of how his parishioners and other Parkchester-ites felt about life and living conditions during the Helmsleys' tenure, he replied knowingly but with some sadness: "Many people felt that Mrs. Helmsley should be forced to do her time [in prison] in Parkchester." In 1989–1990, multimillionaire luxury hotel owner Leona Helmsley, who had been tarred with the unflattering sobriquet "Queen of Mean," served eighteen months in federal prison for tax evasion. Mrs. Helmsley was the titular boss of the family's East Bronx property, even though the word on the street was that a variety of relatives and operatives of the newly established Parkchester Management Corporation were in charge of the development. But the dislike for her and husband Harry's tenure at the helm of Parkchester led to expressions of *schadenfraude* in response to her incarceration.[1]

Harry Helmsley came to this residential endeavor amid a career that would make him "one of the nation's largest and most diverse real state entrepreneurs." He would possess, or own a financial piece in, "just about every type of real estate–office buildings, apartment buildings, warehouses and vacant land" in New York City. At the very moment that his Helmsley-Spear company took over Parkchester, his group was managing one of Gotham's greatest landmarks—the Empire State Building. Still, he told the press "there is a certain glamor to buying a city within a city," immediately adopting the MLIC's longest-standing tag line. His plans for the neighborhood would falter, however, due to a series of strategic mistakes of his own doing, some greed to be sure, along with social and economic factors in the city that he could not control but perhaps he might have anticipated.[2]

Helmsley's grand plan was to find ways to circumvent what he saw as the onerous rent-control laws in New York City that limited realtors' returns on investments. In 1964, during his valedictory interview, Frank Lowe had made clear that "Parkchester would have been an even better investment for the Metropolitan Life Insurance Company if World War II had not brought rent control and ever rising taxes had not followed." Back in the early 1940s, the municipal government, cognizant of how landlords had capitalized on the housing shortage during World War I, had strictly capped the amounts that could be charged on apartments of all sorts. Almost a quarter century later, Parkchester only "yielded $14.9 million in rents annually, the top rent was kept on a three-bedroom apartment to a bargain of $165 a month even while taxes and operating costs have soared." The new owner's initial solution, which was announced immediately after he took over the property, was to attempt to raise rents by appealing to the State of New York for a "hardship increase" under rent-control strictures. His argument was that Parkchester, at present rent levels, would not provide the

company with a "6% return on . . . investment plus 2% for deprecia-
tion." With the hardship proviso in hand, his next step would be to
put in new wiring, which would allow another increase. From day
one of Helmsley's tenure in the Bronx, he was off on the wrong foot
with Parkchester's residents; especially those who had been in the
neighborhood for more than a generation.[3]

Although some senior tenants may have recalled the turmoil
of the late 1940s and early 1950s over voluntary rent hikes that
called several neighborhood rent committees into action against
the MLIC, Ecker and the Lowes had still earned much street credibility as "paternalistic landlords" of an extremely well-kept-up
community. As one veteran Parkchesterite told a reporter: "Good
old Metropolitan, when they went it was like losing an old friend."
Gerald Doyle, the editor of the *Bronx Press Review*, who had lived
in the neighborhood since 1944, explained his neighbors' attitudes
this way: "The thing about these people is that they have grown
old calling an insurance company 'Mother Metropolitan' will take
care of us." Now there was great uncertainty in the streets and anxiety that the community's "golden age was passing." While no one
could object to Helmsley's desire to rewire the buildings, since an
improved infrastructure—most importantly, air-conditioning—
was surely warranted, what about the concomitant rent hikes? And
what would come next from a management team that was tarred
early on as so "secretive that it makes you think something funny is
going on." Indeed, fear of the future would characterize community
life throughout the Helmsley era.[4]

Parkchester residents were also not amused early on when, in
July 1969, during the first summer of Helmsley management, the
new owners moved again to maximize profits by transferring $1.2
million in security deposits into non-interest-bearing accounts.
Under the MLIC, tenants were obliged to place funds in escrow to
protect the landlord against damage to the apartments or for com-

pensation in the event a lease was broken. In return, the company paid back 4 percent interest—or $8–10 a year—on the bank deposits. Now this appreciable sum of money accrued from some twelve thousand families would remain in the bank. It was a new financial outlet that was willing to lend money to Helmsley without requiring that he post collateral—to the mutual benefit of the lender and the businessman and at the expense of Parkchesterites. State attorney-general Louis J. Lefkowitz brought suit against this agreement, which he charged was a "quid pro quo . . . for mercenary considerations . . . that deprived and defrauded" the tenants. Helmsley, however, won the round in New York State Supreme Court when the justice found that the owner had no obligation to hold security deposits in an interest-carrying account. Still, Judge Joseph A. Sarafite did comment that his decision "does not invite judicial applause." On Parkchester's streets, it was again clear that the prior state of affairs was over.[5]

The worries of many long-term tenants about the future of their neighborhood were magnified exponentially two years into Helmsley's tenure when he announced plans to transform Parkchester into a condominium community. As early as November 1968, there was "speculation" that the "hardship increment" was only the beginning and that "a cooperative or condominium arrangement may be undertaken." When the plan was fleshed out late in 1972, under which the North Quadrant, with its four thousand apartments, would be converted to condominiums as the first step in transforming the entire area, aggrieved tenants immediately felt that Helmsley-Spear was seeking a "windfall" at their expense. The word on the street was that the new ownership was looking to "escape from the squeeze of rent-control and rising maintenance costs," and the residents way of living would be endangered as a result.[6]

To counteract negative perceptions of these efforts, the new owners sought to project themselves as both the heirs to the best of the MLIC's housing history and policies while in command of up-to-date strategies that would benefit all. Early on, residents had to have been reassured that the economic and social backgrounds of apartment applicants would still be closely monitored because the new owners continued the MLIC vetting system. The Helmsley group sent their own teams of investigators to the homes of potential renters. In a further effort to fulfill Helmsley's expressed "hopes that the excellent landlord-tenant relationship will be continued," the company ran a full-page ad in the *Bronx Press Review* in March 1973, informing readers, "Now You Can Own a Piece of Parkchester!!" with "all tax benefits of home ownership." It asserted that "the established security and community of pride of PARKCHESTER will be insured forever through this condominium ownership plan," much like their predecessors, thirty-three years earlier, had "pioneered a better way of life for thousands of families in this beautiful section of the East Bronx." The promotional piece described "a secure established community, complete with shopping within the PARKCHESTER community, houses of worship nearby, public and parochial schools within walking distance, attractive parks and grounds and express transportation to and from Manhattan." It was hoped that this marketing effort would attract people from all over the Bronx, and possibly elsewhere, to "come and visit" and eventually stay as stakeholders in the community.[7]

Helmsley also frequently reassured families who lived in Parkchester that no nefarious attempts would be undertaken to force out those who would not buy into the condominium project. In its official notice of transfer to the office of the state attorney general, which had to approve the conversion prospectus, and in subsequent court documents and comments to newspaper reporters, the syndicate reiterated that "it voluntarily agreed not to evict non-purchasing tenants whose apartments were rent-controlled." Opponents of the realtor would repeatedly point out that this concession was hardly a "voluntary" accommodation. Rather, it was made in return for permission from Lefkowitz's office for the "sale of individual apartments without the voted approval of 35 percent of any building," which was then a discretionary administrative requirement. The 35 percent requirement would be a major point of contention as the Helmsley era proceeded.

In the meantime, for those who lived in the three hundred non-rent-controlled units of the North Quadrant, whose apartments might be sold once their present leases ran out, the management tendered a significantly lower insider price, with an additional 10 percent discount if the tenant "paid cash in full." Such emoluments may have well determined the decision of some of the families who signed agreements in the first two weeks of the conversion opportunity early in 1973.[8]

Patrick and Carol Hanley were among the first Parkchester residents to enthusiastically participate in the new housing system. In many ways, they resembled the families of the community's past. The young couple, both in their early thirties and employees of General Motors Corporation, where they were reportedly "paid well," moved into 1598 Unionport Road right after their marriage in 1968. Ensconced in their apartment under the existing rent-control laws, they paid their landlord $124 in monthly rent "with free water, gas, electricity and—to hear them tell it—great service." But they were attracted to the idea of owning their own digs and to the tax break and they wanted additional space "for the baby they hope to adopt." They were Storkchester parents in the making, albeit of a later date. So they bought a four-room decontrolled apartment for $16,800 that would also cost them an estimated $200 a month in mortgage payments and carrying charges. Optimistic about the neighborhood's future, they believed "it's not such a big step for a young couple. We look upon it as a bit of forced savings. You might say we're rolling the dice." For Patrick Hanley, having decided to put down deep roots in the neighborhood, there was no gamble on the question of whether his family could live there harmoniously with blacks and Latinos over the long haul. He believed that the switch to condominiums would head off any racial tensions that might arise from a Parkchester that was now finally integrated: "if someone moves next door or down-stairs or upstairs, he'll take care of what he owns. People don't de-stroy what they own. I'd be awfully surprised if it didn't work out that way." The Hanleys were prepared to get along well with their neigh-bors. The family would figuratively, and perhaps literally, continue to adopt Parkchester's tenants' summertime open-door policy.[9]

The Helmsley people had to have been gratified with the public views of an insider interested in staying long-term in the neigh-borhood. Still, the company was destined for a long struggle in its bid to convert the remaining apartments and to stop those who wanted to abort their efforts. A major demographic problem for the realtor was that the Hanleys were actually an exceptional family. They were different from the many young couples of their genera-tion who had no interest in Helmsley's offers since they were on the way out of Parkchester.

By the early 1970s, the children of Storkchester had grown up. The simply actuarial fact was that a boy or girl who, for example, was born the first year of the development's existence had long reached his or her majority. As adults, with perhaps growing families of their own, they possessed many warm memories of their youngest years in the neighborhood. These were "the teenage children of the 50's" who had performed the "bunny hop, twist, stroll and lindy" at dances at St. Helena's or St. Raymond's. But they also knew about its inadequacies. There were only 550 three-bedroom apartments in the entire development as opposed to 7,000 one-bedroom and 4,000 two-bedroom suites. There was a long waiting list to deal with if an expanding family wanted to upgrade their residence. Practic-ing Catholic as well as observant Orthodox Jewish families tended to have large families. The MLIC preferred to reserve the larger accommodations for families with both boys and girls. Otherwise, the managements' view was that two kids of the same sex could readily share a bedroom. Bunk beds were a common sight. Some of those awaiting the three-bedroom offer that often never came accommodated children of both sexes in the same bedrooms by building wood partitions—a violation of another of Parkchester's rules.

Julius and Irene Horowitz had the parental master bedroom in their McGraw Avenue place. Michael and his younger brother, Bernard, shared the second bedroom while their sister, Rivka, put up with sleeping for years on a day bed. Hank de Cillia considered himself quite fortunate to have his own bedroom in his family's apartment at 1590 Metropolitan Avenue. His parents, Kay and Harry, who settled in the neighborhood in 1941, three years before he was born, slept on a foldout bed in the living room. In this three-generational household, his older sister and his grandmother used one bedroom. And he, describing himself as "the prince, had his own bedroom." Donald Dwyer shared his bedroom with his two brothers in their three-bedroom apartment at 1504 Metropolitan Avenue. His sister had her own room, as did their parents. They all shared one bathroom. As a teenager, Donald cut down on his wait for a shower in the morning by walking across the hall and using the facilities of a kindly neighbor. Sometimes, the dentist and his wife on the sixth floor offered him breakfast after he toweled off. While such situations were tolerable for children and for their parents who might recall how they themselves had lived back in the 1920s–1930s, the now mature products of the 1940s baby boom wanted more room for their own families. Owning a condominium in Parkchester would not have addressed that desire.[10]

Then there was the annual annoyance of the absence of air-conditioning. It must be noted, once again, that when Parkchester was constructed, although commercial buildings were increasingly air-cooled, apartment air-conditioning was "out of reach of most citizens." It was the preserve of "primarily luxury [residential] buildings." However, "by the 1960s, most city residents had at least limited access to air-conditioning in their home, at work, or in a publicly accessible space." But in Parkchester, the best residents could do was to access those cooled–off public places like stores or movies. Back home, in ultimately futile efforts to counteract "the heat [that] invaded the halls and . . . living space [and] would hang around like an unwanted sweaty guest," it was imperative to "close . . . blinds and draperies to keep out the sun's heat" and "turn off all unnecessary appliances." Dwellers might also purchase a Hunter window fan, which promised to cool "several rooms at once" with its "two speed, intake and exhaust . . . electrically reversible motor," even though it was officially prohibited under the MLIC's management. Some families tested the rules, and their fates, even further, installing small, and not very noisy, air-conditioning units in bedrooms. One family, in which the father had a heart condition and the five fans in the three-bedroom apartment were deemed in-sufficient, prevailed upon a friendly Parkchester maintenance man to secretly upgrade the wiring for their single apartment without blowing the fuses in the basement electrical box. They positioned a 5,000 BTU tube two feet from the window. A few other families acquired similar devices and hid their efforts behind darkened win-dow coverings, out of sight of the management.[11]

For most other families, opening doors to neighbors across the hall for cross-ventilation surely had its place in strengthening the social fabric of the buildings. Still, conviviality did not overcome heat. Here too there was an age-group divide. First-wave Parkches-terites, who may have slept out on tenement fire escapes and in public parks when they were young, generally put up with this great inconvenience. In fact, when in the 1950s the MLIC had floated the idea of rewiring the development, which would have made air-conditioning possible, but at the cost of a significant rise in rents, tenants had voted down the plan. The new group of first-generation residents, blacks and Latinos who previously had lived in city projects like those in Harlem and the South Bronx where in many instances there also was no air-conditioning, largely felt the same way as their predecessors. Second-generation Parkchester people, on the other hand, may have pledged as youths to do better for their own families when they had the chance. As grown-ups, they looked at other places to reside within and beyond the city. And many of them had the economic wherewithal to make a move away from the now old neighborhood with its deficient prewar wiring.[12]

In other words, as of the early 1970s, many thirty-something men and women whose "fathers were blue-collar workers, sales people, clerks who rarely had a college education" had risen to become "college-trained accountants and junior executives who take Florida vacations and buy color television sets." In the words of one newspaper report, "unlike its parents, Parkchester's second generation thinks that there is a better world beyond Parkchester and is learning where to look." While there were still accounts of third- and even fourth-generation Parkchester families in the area, the generational momentum was away from the East Bronx. If young adults raised in the neighborhood had to make a down payment on where their families would live for the next decades, it would be on a house or a co-op or a condominium in suburbia or in another Gotham neighborhood and not in Helmsley's Parkchester. Such was the case with the family that had snuck in air-conditioning for their ailing father. One son who became an attorney lived with his wife in the neighborhood for several years immediately after they were married. But when they were expecting their first child, they bought a house in the Pelham Bay section of the North Bronx. Later on, they moved to Long Island. A second college-educated brother who became a New York State Supreme Court clerk was drawn to Rockland County when he married. The third brother did not have a housing issue as he became a Catholic priest and lived in church housing. He eventually rose to become a monsignor, serving a flock in Westchester County. Given this pattern of out-migration of the children of Parkchester, it was said that moving vans were a ubiquitous sight in the neighborhood. Reportedly, "the 7 Santini Brothers were everywhere." The management had to find other types of tenants.[13]

Within the neighborhood's Jewish population, there was a youth brain drain underway out of the Young Israel of Parkchester in the direction of Riverdale. Among the first young upwardly mobile professionals to make the move to the community in the northwest corner of the Bronx was the fellow who as a clever boy had outwitted a Parkchester cop by giving only his first and middle names when stopped for a rules violation. As early as 1968, now a graduate of the University of Chicago and on the road to becoming an internationally renowned economist, Joel Stern had the financial wherewithal and the desire to live in an upscale Jewish community. Still tied strongly to his Orthodox moorings, Stern was the first to lend substantial financial support to the creation of the Young Israel of Riverdale. It was the synagogue his cousins, who were both college professors and YIP alumni too, would soon attend. One brother moved in 1970, the other in 1973. In May 1973, Ruby and Stanley Langer, in search of a four-bedroom residence for their large family, and uninterested in Stanley commuting from Long Island or Westchester to his law office in Manhattan, also chose Riverdale. Their presence influenced a second chain migration from the YIP to another congregation in their new habitat, the Hebrew Institute of Riverdale. Through their relocation to the Northwest Bronx, the Langers effectively went from being one of the few younger couples in their erstwhile synagogue to senior leaders of this new Riverdale shul. Years later, Rabbi Maurice L. Schwartz would comment ruefully, but also with a degree of pride, that Riverdale had benefitted from the talent and commitment of children whom he and his lay leaders had trained. But in the 1970s, the home congregation was troubled by its declining membership base. One sure sign that times had changed, and not for the better, was a post in the June 1973 synagogue bulletin "for the first time in its history" requesting volunteers for "Jewry Duty"—manning the daily minyan. Orthodox synagogues require ten men in attendance to conduct services. This basic congregational need was not being met due to, among other reasons, "our regulars moving from Parkchester."[14]

These Orthodox Jews and other migrants who were drawn away from the neighborhood may have been worried about their parents' situations under the new management but were not outspoken in their criticism of how life was changing in a community that had, it was said, "grown old."

It remained mostly for elderly residents to deal with their fears and the realities of what was afoot. The 1970 census revealed that 28 percent of the neighborhood's population was now sixty-five years of age or older and 7 percent over seventy-five, both double the Bronx and citywide averages. And many of these Parkchesterites of long-standing simply did not trust Helmsley-Spear's promises and intentions. For those who were worried, even reassuring words from the *Bronx Press Review* that the condominium project was "no cause for alarm" and that "all we really want to say, and underline, is that groundless fears will be harmful to everyone" fell on deaf ears. Though the disaffected understood that the management could not forcibly evict them, they saw themselves "at the mercy of a man who knows the sooner he can get me the hell out, the sooner he can sell my apartment." They foresaw a multitude of ways by which Helmsley-Spear could intentionally fail to uphold Parkchester's sterling reputation for keeping the buildings and grounds in excellent condition, thus making life uncomfortable. They were worried that when one of the "old geezers" across the hall passed on, after

Helmsley's operatives "rub[bed] their hands" in joy as they emptied the residence, how concerned the realtor would be about who might next occupy the old-timer's apartment?[15]

At the same time, these older white tenants, who had never openly opposed integration and who generally were accepting of the first African Americans, also started to wonder whether the latest newcomers would "abide by the rules" that had governed their and their children's lives. The optimists believed that even if whites eventually would become the minority in Parkchester, since "unofficial figures indicate[d] that at least 40% of the [outside] buyers were black and Puerto Rican," the majority of those who now opted for the neighborhood were much like they had been thirty or more years earlier. They were solid families seeking better places to live and willing to put up with no air-conditioning and few bedrooms. Mrs. Jeanette Thompson, who in 1974 was "a 23-year-old black mother of a small son and wife of a postal worker," told a reporter, "We came here because it's a clean, decent place to live. I come and go and people say hello. Today in the elevator, an old gent tipped his hat. Took it off completely. That really shook me up." This family fit Parkchester's prior population profile in all regards except for race.[16]

Maretta and Joe Krista were among the long-time white residents who were not overly perturbed with the changing neighborhood's racial composition. They would recall that "when our white community first became integrated, we were concerned. We didn't know how we would interact with these newcomers. But for the most part our fears were unfounded." They "remember[ed] passing the playground one day and thinking how strange it was to see almost all little black faces. But the laughter and sounds of children at play sounded exactly the same as when our children played there. There was no difference."[17]

But then there were those like Harry and Sallie Brown, who bought a three-bedroom apartment in 1975—quintessential

Parkchesterites, distinctive only because they were black. Both employees of the post office, the Browns initially felt the sting of their white neighbors' negative stereotyping. In time, Harry would rise to become the postmaster in suburban Hartsdale, New York and became a leader of Parkchester tenants. Interestingly enough, they had relocated from the all-black Phipps Houses to Parkchester due to its physical beauty only to find that some of Sallie's fellow white residents presumed when they saw her in the building that she was a cleaning woman. Nonetheless, they remained "optimistic" about their future in the neighborhood, including their belief that air-conditioning would eventually come their way. Years would pass before that creature comfort would serve their summertime needs, even as the Browns would reside at 1541 Metropolitan Avenue for more than forty years.[18]

That same year, a twenty-five-year-old Latino man, who was destined to play an important role in the later history of Parkchester, rented an apartment for himself and his bride at 1548 Unionport Road. Future Bronx borough president Fernando Ferrer grew up in a five-story walk-up tenement on Fox Street in the depressed Hunts Point section of the borough. Already a high achiever, with his feet firmly planted in city work and politics, when he and his wife-to-be looked for their first apartment, the East Bronx development attracted them. For Fernando, the well-kept-up Parkchester carried a cachet of "luxury" and some friends of the same ethnic background were already living there. It was a "good place for a young married couple." He also knew that the once restricted neighborhood was now wide open for people of his background. He had worked for the same City Commission on Human Rights that had forced the end of segregation. His intended spouse, Aramia, who hailed from a solid middle-class Latino family that owned a private home in the Wakefield section of the Northeast Bronx, would not countenance residing where he had been raised. Her family most definitely agreed.

Ferrer recalled a "mixed reception" from his new, majority-white neighbors. He did not expect "a welcome wagon ... but if there was bias, it was infinitesimally less than elsewhere in the city." His fellow tenants were "laid back" and "everyone walked to the subway to-gether and on the way home stopped for pastry delicacies at Zaro's Bake Shop" on the corner of Hugh J. Grant Circle across the street from the elevated train station.

However, the Ferrers stayed in Parkchester for no more than two years. While they loved sitting out at Metropolitan Oval with a coffee in hand on a bright afternoon, they found the summers in their hot apartment to be "incredible." Fernando Ferrer recalled, "if my wife turned on the air-blower while a toaster and television were set on, a fuse would be blown." He also remembered, "winters were not so great either" due to the drafty casement windows in the apartment. This upwardly mobile couple, like many of their second-generation Parkchester counterparts who also wanted air-conditioned homes, would look elsewhere for just the right accommodations.[19]

Meanwhile, as the Thompsons, Browns, and other black and Latino families set roots in Parkchester, the pessimists among the white population, including many who would not necessarily say a discouraging word publicly to their new neighbors, were hardly so sanguine about the effects of a changed racial balance. They checked their retirement savings accounts to determine whether they might follow their children and move out. Their fears were not lost upon at least one "older black man" who, in 1974, told that same newspaper reporter who spoke with the upbeat Mrs. Thompson that he hoped that whites would not flee an incoming rush of African Americans. If that eventuated, he thought that he too would seek to move on. "If condominiums win," he said, "blacks will come in en masse, and I'm going to have to pick up and go the way I've been running away from ghetto neighborhoods all my life." While long-term white Parkches-terites who now shared their concerns with one another and with reporters might have remembered the MLIC's racial priorities as re-gressive and wrong, Helmsley was attacked as having but one prior-ity, maximizing his profits at their expense.[20]

And then, notwithstanding Helmsley's good or bad acts and their fantasies about what the future might be like, there was a difficult-to-quantify but palpable concern among many of Parkchester's aging first generation about the entire idea of apartment ownership. Throughout their lives, these tenants had been comfortable pay-ing rent to landlords and letting them worry about property values while providing adequate services. The MLIC had managed their residential lives so very well. They only hoped that Helmsley would step up and do likewise. Even if a condominium was a good deal, a buy-in was "foreign to them." This was the response of the parents of Parkchester-born Phillip Schneider when he suggested that they "invest in a home" by purchasing their three-bedroom apartment at 1945 McGraw Avenue. Banking on the "status quo" as renters, they would hope for the best and continue to live with people who shared their social values, including the small number of "mature, middle class black adults" who then lived in their building in the early 1970s.[21]

As that decade began, a new neighborhood was emerging, situ-ated just a few miles north-east of Parkchester, that promised to both recreate and indeed improve upon some of the best of the now-old development's early history. It attracted two generations of Parkchesterites. Remarkably, the same week that the *Bronx Press Review* reported on the sale to the Helmsley group, it took note that "the first tenants and public officials gathered for the dedication of Co-op City." According to the newspaper, there were now two "Cit-ies Within the City," as the headline read. As for Helmsley, he had a stiff competitor in his backyard.[22]

Co-op City boasted thirty-five large buildings. Some were as tall as thirty-three stories, spaced across three hundred acres of land—almost three times the size of Parkchester—with room for approximately fifty thousand people, ten thousand more than the older East Bronx area, with many three-bedroom apartments and even some townhouses. It was pitched for, among others, "salesmen and civil servants, accountants and bakers"—working- and lower-middle-class folks like those who always had flocked to Parkchester. They too could reside in a bucolic environment in close proximity to Manhattan via express buses with parks, lawns, trees, and play-grounds. Its street scenes were also reminiscent of Parkchester's. It had its own houses of worship, shopping center, movie houses, restaurants, and bowling alleys. A thirty-five–man security force patrolled the complex and enforced an 11 p.m. curfew on unhappy teenagers during the week, midnight on weekends. Miscreants were ticketed with "Community Complaints" for loitering. Most crucially, their homes were blessed with air-conditioning.[23]

For elementary school teacher Selma Pickei and her husband, Pascal, who worked as a claims adjuster for the New York State Labor Department, Co-op City offered the Parkchester couple the chance to move out of their cramped one-bedroom apartment on Unionport Road to a three-bedroom suite with a terrace in the new complex without a major increase in their cost of living. They took up residence in their air-conditioned flat in 1970, sparing them what Selma would describe as the tortures of their "incinerator apartment" where they had lived since their marriage in 1948.[24]

Lenore and Morton Greenwald felt much like the Pickeis about the summer heat in Parkchester and had the same desire for more space for their family. In fact, they were ready to leave the commu-nity of Lenore's youth as early as 1965, when they tendered one of the first applications for a place in Co-op City, almost a half-decade before the complex opened. They were intrigued that this com-munity under construction promised to be "similar to Parkchester" and they had no interest in a suburban home with all its commut-ing hassles. They had come to feel cramped in their two-bedroom apartment on Wood Road and wanted both their son and daughter, who were approaching their teenage years, to have their own rooms. They had had enough of relying on "cross-ventilation" fans and open doors during summer time. And attorney Morton and then homemaker Lenore had enough money in the bank to put down $7,500 to become stakeholders in Co-op City, while handling their townhouse's $102 monthly maintenance fee ($24 more than their Parkchester rent). Co-op City proved, in the end, to be less than an ideal neighborhood, as it suffered from its own management problems. From the mid-1970s through the 1980s, like so many places in Gotham, it also suffered from the scourges of crime and illicit drugs. But when it opened, it promised to be a sure and safe residential alternative to Parkchester. If anything, quipped Judy Cohen, who migrated with her husband and two children from Metropolitan Avenue in 1969, "it was a move from one womb to another womb." Or, put another way, "from familiar surroundings to the same sort of environment, still living in the city in a large development."[25]

While some of their neighbors had Co-op City in their sights, other Parkchester residents who liked the way things had been before the Helmsley era, but were neither willing nor able to move, decided to support new groups of activists who arose to take on the new owners. Perhaps for the oldest leaders and backers of the Parkchester Defense Fund and the Parkchester Tenants Association, memories of what neighborhood protesters had done a generation earlier in fighting against Mother Metropolitan's rent-hike moves fueled the struggle against Helmsley. In all events, as early as the fall-winter of 1972–1973, these organizations, though they had somewhat different missions, complemented each other in vigorously challenging the condominium plan and confronting other issues that troubled their fellow residents.

Even as the Helmsley group, with approval from the state attorney general's office, made ready to begin apartment sales, the

Parkchester Defense Fund was working to stop the initiative in its tracks. Under the leadership of a Parkchester resident, John J. Whalen, district leader of the Community Democratic Club, two lawsuits were filed seriatim to invalidate the realtor's efforts. The first legal action, filed in March 1973, contended that Lefkowitz's office had been negligent in its oversight of the Parkchester Management Corporation's application. It alleged that many of the details required for approval were overlooked, such as "the profits it expects to make from the sale of the condominium units, the income tax effects of ownership, the proposed budget for the first year of operation for the Parkchester North Quadrant," not to mention that there was "no engineer's report on elevators and wiring." In public statements about the case, the Defense Fund also expressed its concern that the management would retain almost complete control over the development, including both renters and owners alike, in contravention of the law. Accusing the Albany office of acting in an "arbitrary and capricious manner" by denying them the chance to be heard before a quick and poorly deliberated approval was granted, the Defense Fund called "for the offering to be viewed, annulled and vacated."[26]

Two months later, the Parkchester Defense Fund legal team attacked the Helmsley syndicate directly in the courts, contending that "the literature submitted to tenants and prospective buyers contain[ed] misrepresentations [and] fail[ed] to state material facts" and that the prices for the condominium apartments had been set far in excess of market value "by the selling agent," who was conspiratorially affiliated with Helmsley-Spear. Even the MLIC, by then seemingly five years out of the picture, was named in the suit for its alleged failure "to disclose the terms of the mortgage or mortgages between the company and the purchaser."[27]

In mounting its campaign to "maintain Parkchester as a rental community at fair rentals," the Defense Fund turned to the people whom they sought to serve for both moral and financial support. At the outset of their struggle, the advocates set out to recruit two tenants from each floor to spread the word about the pending cases and request a $10 per family contribution for the cause. In June 1973, the fund organized a rally that reportedly attracted twelve hundred residents; they heard speaker after speaker offer "words of encouragement [and] some warnings" about how "it would be in the interest of the landlord to make things uncomfortable to rental tenants towards pushing them out," and they listened to a "call for participation in efforts . . . to upset the Condominium offering." However, this last-ditch effort to stop the North Quadrant transformation ultimately failed in the courts. While the Defense Fund secured a restraining order against further condo sales from the Civil Court, that victory was short-lived. The same week of the rally, the State Supreme Court determined that the "plaintiff's charges of fraud, deceit and misrepresentation . . . framed in conclusionary terms" was not compelling. After that ruling, sales of apartments resumed.[28]

Eleven months later, the hopes of the Parkchester Defense Fund were further dashed when the Appellate Division of the New York State Supreme Court found again in favor of the Helmsley group. In rendering its decision, the justices additionally ruled that "the Attorney General's office could not refuse to consider the owner's condominium offering plans for the rest of the development as well." The door was open for Helmsley to turn the rest of Parkchester into condos.[29]

Meanwhile, stopping, or at least slowing down, the conversion of the remainder of Parkchester would become a major objective of the Parkchester Tenants Association in its struggle against the Helmsley group, which would last close to a decade. When the organization was founded in 1972 under the leadership of attorney John Dearie, the condominium problem had been but one of several closely related community issues that galvanized the advocacy group. Dearie explained at the Parkchester Defense Fund's rally that while both groups were "working in common in opposition to the single most influential real estate operator in the country . . . the scope of the Defense Fund focuses total attention on the fight against the Condominium Plan." His association, by contrast, "works for tenant rights in all other fields," especially with the quality-of-life concerns of the aging, often frightened long-term Parkchesterites.[30]

John Dearie was known within the four quadrants as a "real Parkchester boy" who had made good. A second-generation resident whose family had moved into a two-bedroom apartment at 1735 Purdy Street in 1941, Dearie first gained local attention as an outstanding athlete on the concrete courts of the North Quadrant. After garnering All-City honors at Manhattan Prep, he went on to play basketball and study hard at the University of Notre Dame. After earning a law degree, he secured a "prestige job . . . at the United Nation's Secretariat." However, unlike so many high-achieving children of blue-collar workers—his dad was a plumber—Dearie did not exit the old neighborhood as a young adult. His older sister did. She was married at twenty-one and by age twenty-six had seven children. "Crowded out" of the Bronx community of two- and three-bedroom apartments, she would raise her brood in a house in Cleveland. But John, whom the *New York Times* described as "tall, articulate, movie-star handsome" would stay and become perhaps Parkchester's most eligible bachelor, while representing the aging community. Some of his friends, many of whom now resided in Rockland County or in Pearl River, New Jersey, said he remained "out of love for Parkchester." Others said that "it's politics he loves."[31]

The Parkchester Tenants Association's first major effort to establish itself as a presence in the neighborhood took place on November 19, 1972, when the organization staged a "Unity Day" march, rally, and candlelight procession at the North Quadrant ball field.

To bring out a substantial crowd, the association designated captains to talk up the event in each of the buildings in the complex and enlisted the support of all of the churches and synagogues that served Parkchester. Local politicians, from the Bronx borough president to the local city councilmen and assemblymen, also joined Dearie on the rostrum. In promoting the meeting, Dearie had proclaimed in a full-page advertisement that the present moment was "the most critical period in the 32 year history of our community," requiring that "our unified voices [be] heard by government agencies, legislative bodies, police departments and the management whose policy decisions touch each of us directly. We must loudly say 'stop' to the onslaught of legislative and administrative decisions which have been made with seeming disregard for rent controlled tenants like ourselves."

At the rally, which attracted four thousand people of all races and creeds, including both long-time and newly arrived residents, the legal and political actions said to have benefitted Helmsley-Spear at residents' expense were strongly criticized. The most pressing financial threat that had to be addressed was the maximum base rent law that had gone into effect three years earlier. It permitted "annual rent increases of up to 7.5% in rent controlled apartments." Until then, rents could be raised only "for such things as increased services, capital improvements, increased labor costs and 'hardship'"—the ploy the Helmsleys had used when they first took over. Now, it appeared that the new landlord could double down on attempts to squeeze financially long-term Parkchesterites. The maximum base law had to be repealed. Great concern was also expressed about the potential impact of the vacancy decontrol law passed in 1971, which allowed landlords to hike rents every time there was a turnover in occupancy. That measure too had to be rolled back. Meanwhile, in thinking about where the syndicate's future condominium plans would take Parkchester, Dearie and his associates chose not to further challenge the North Quadrant conversion effort that had been upheld. Rather, their demand was that all proposed future transformations require a minimum of 51 percent of tenant approval.[32]

There was an additional fundamental problem that exercised the audience which could not be laid directly at the feet of the Helmsley group. Criminality was increasingly victimizing Parkchesterites, or at least there was a palpable fear in the neighborhood that it was becoming crime-ridden. Parkchester, of course, had never been entirely free of crime. In prior decades, attacks on residents had received front-page coverage in the local weekly newspaper. And in the MLIC's last years, there already was a sense on the streets that the 43rd Precinct was undermanned and thus providing inadequate protection. The problem apparently was that the NYPD defined Parkchester as a "low–crime area," resulting in officers frequently being shifted to other places "in times of emergency" and never being shifted back. In response to this concern, in June 1967, after "conferences with the highest police officials," initiated by some unidentified residents, "new schedules [and] new police patrols were activated to strengthen the uniformed force" at the 4–3.[33]

In October 1968, however, right before the Helmsley-Spear takeover, the newly formed 43rd Precinct Community Council wrote to the mayor complaining about "the rising crime rate, the inadequate amount of police protection and the increasing narcotics problem." At a public meeting, protesters expressed their "alarm and fear that our community has deteriorated due to the crime rate. What is now a stable community is in the process of becoming a ghetto."[34]

The problem of crime in Parkchester, opined the 4–3's Lt. Jack Seltzer in 1969, was caused not so much by troublemakers from within the neighborhood as by ones from outside it. "It's very difficult for a poor guy to rob a poor guy," the officer explained. "So they come here, snatch a purse and knock down some elderly person and they make a quick escape. You cannot tell someone who was robbed that the crime rate is lower in Parkchester than elsewhere." However, viewpoints like his, that "crime is everywhere but under control in Parkchester," did not reassure those who felt increasingly vulnerable and frustrated.[35]

Police statistics published in July 1970 verified the impression that while Parkchester was not nearly as crime-ridden as Hunts Point, which suffered 950 violent crimes in May 1970, or close-by Morrisania, with its 945 attacks against life and property, its 43rd Precinct, which included parts of Soundview, was a significant problem area, rife with troublemakers of all sorts.[36]

In September 1972, with the city still unresponsive to Parkchester's needs and fears, the municipality was slapped with a "'show cause' order action demanding that the Police Department fulfill statutes ordering private residential communities be accorded the same protection that is given others." Parkchester assemblyman Anthony J. Mercorella, a driving force behind this legal move, claimed that for seven years he had protested the 43rd Precinct's "being depleted of manpower for the benefit of Manhattan."[37]

Back at the rally, leaders and attendees called for more regular city policemen and auxiliary cops to patrol the neighborhood's streets and for the Helmsley group to finance locks for the front doors of all buildings and the installation of intercom systems. To improve security and quality of life for both old and young, the Parkchester Tenants Association also called for the conversion of carriage rooms into recreational centers in each quadrant. These facilities would provide safe spaces for the aging who might not want to venture far from their homes for social activities, indoor athletic areas useful for wintertime sports, and, more generally, for keeping an eye on the neighborhood's young people. Long a trademark Parkchester amenity, carriage rooms were not nearly as important as they had once been. Clearly, Storkchester's days had passed.[38]

Three weeks after the rally, the Parkchester Tenants Association sent petitions with twenty-three thousand signatures to the State Police Commission, the City Council, the state legislature, the NYPD, and, of course, to Helmsley's Parkchester Management Corporation, reiterating demands for "rental legislation reform, improved security and youth and senior citizen centers."[39]

A week later, Dearie refocused attention on the North Quadrant condominium plan. He did not question its legality. Rather he deemed the business initiative "over priced," unworthy of the investment by wise renters. He asserted that "it attempts to sell a 32 year old apartment without wiring for air-conditioning, without central locked-door security systems without services for painting, internal appliance repairs or replacement." He reminded the community of how far the neighborhood would be drawn from the arms of Mother Metropolitan.[40]

Beginning in March 1973, Dearie was able to take the cause of Parkchester's residents directly into the legislative chambers in Albany when he was chosen as assemblyman in a special election. The incumbent, Anthony Mercorella, had been appointed to the City Council seat occupied previously by Mario Merola, who in turn became Bronx district attorney. Early on in his tenure, in May 1973, Dearie made himself heard when he charged that a "conspiracy between the real estate lobby and State legislative leadership" was undermining the rights of his constituents. He was specifically outraged that a bill "requiring 51 percent of tenants to approve before a condominium plan could be instituted" had been held up in Assembly committee rooms. That was the same minimum share of residents the Unity Rally had demanded be on board for the Helmsley initiative to move forward in any given building. Undeterred, in 1974, Dearie joined forces with liberal Manhattan Republican state senator Roy Goodman in successfully pushing through the so-called Goodman-Dearie Bill. The law, in effect until 1977, "required

35 percent of tenants in occupancy to buy their apartments in order to have a plan declared effective." In due course, "requirements for eviction plans [were] stiffened to 51% while non-eviction conversion minimums [were] set at 15%." With Dearie in Albany, the battle over the fate of Parkchester's three still-renting quadrants had been joined with the power of state legislation.[41]

Even as the Helmsley group would continue to battle throughout the 1970s to secure the share of buyers necessary to transform the rest of the complex, as "the fears among rental tenants, plus their political strength" was difficult to surmount, the city's daunting problems undermined the attractiveness of the entire real estate endeavor.[42] By mid-decade, much of the Bronx and many other areas in Gotham were no longer deemed desirable places to live, especially for the elderly. The fears that had been expressed at the Unity Day Rally in November 1972 had become magnified in a city spiraling into decline. For the Bronx, in particular, patterns of physical destruction and social despair reached their human nadir in July 1977 when, during a regionwide blackout, marauding gangs of youths, angrily characterized by some as "jackal packs" or "vultures," decimated much of the businesses along the once-fashionable expanse of the Grand Concourse and other, less classy areas of the borough. Three months later, adding rhetorical insult to real and terrifying injury, President Jimmy Carter made a surprise visit to Charlotte Street near the southern end of the Grand Concourse, which the media described as an example "of some of the country's worst urban blight . . . a decaying remnant . . . through blocks of rubble that looked like the result of wartime bombing." The reputation of the so-called South Bronx, which now included in the popular mind much of the Central and West Bronx, took another body blow only five days after Carter's appearance. During a World Series game at Yankee Stadium, broadcast coast to coast, acerbic sports commentator Howard Cosell looked out beyond the bleachers, saw a building ablaze, and declared to his audience, "The Bronx is burning." Cosell's pronouncement further etched into the national consciousness the feeling that the city of his birth was a metropolis of broken promises.[43]

A series of interrelated problems and circumstances had conspired to plague the city. Gotham's long and prosperous history as a light manufacturing center ended as the garment trades, printing industry, and other businesses migrated out of the heavily unionized and tax-laden metropolis to the Sun Belt in search of higher profits—a first step, in many cases, toward leaving the country entirely. New York lost these firms' tax revenues and thousands of workers, predominantly African American and Latino, saw their jobs disappear. With unemployment rates cresting, the city's already overburdened welfare system was further encumbered.

Making matters worse, the apartments that these unemployed workers lived in fell into grave disrepair as landlords, many of who chafed under the same rent controls that the MLIC and then Helmsley-Spear had railed about, saw little profitability in maintaining their aging, deteriorating properties. Some owners tried to find a way out of their financial holes by taking advantage of the 1971 decontrol law, the ill-advised legislation that Parkchesterites had complained about during their Unity Day rally. In afflicted neighborhoods, as increasingly transient populations moved in and out, rents were hiked with each turnover. Some landlords abandoned their buildings to avoid real estate taxes; on the way out, the most unscrupulous were complicit in torching their properties to collect on insurance. In this environment, despair over unemployment and rage over poor quality of life, especially among black and Latino youths, contributed to a spike in illicit drug use and sales and a concomitant rise in violent crime. Many of the victims were the elderly who either remained attached psychologically to, or were economically unable to leave, deteriorating neighborhoods.

Given the city's financial woes and the unwillingness of the federal government to bail out Gotham, essential services were seriously cut back. Most importantly for the vulnerable, now fewer police patrolled their mean streets.[44]

Parkchester was spared the worst of the storms that hammered the borough and city. One indication of how the neighborhood was doing was a remark that Bronx borough president Robert Abrams made in November 1976, when he was interviewed for a *New York Times* article on "how many elderly in the Bronx spend their time in terror of crime." He and an unidentified police spokesman together characterized Parkchester, along with Riverdale, Co-op City, and several other locales, as places that were "not snake-pits for the elderly" even though now aluminum gates protected store windows after closing and tenants put extra locks on their apartment doors. A month later, a government study group of Bronx neighborhoods provided a map whose legend clearly indicated that Parkchester was among the borough's "sound" and "fair to good" residential areas. However, the illustration also showed that "deteriorating" and "dilapidated" sections of the Bronx could be found not far to the east and south of Parkchester, including Morrisania, that once hopeful community. Moreover, an accompanying narrative also pointed to Parkchester's tenuous geographical locus, stating chillingly that "if the housing loss continues at the present rate, we estimate that the entire housing stock of the South Bronx ... will not last beyond fifteen years.[45]

Indicative of Parkchester's relative safety, amid the grievous problems all around, was the scene there during the calamitous 1977 summer blackout. According to the *Bronx Press Review*, "while some parts of the borough were reeking with smoke and covered with looters ... the community came through the trial by darkness admirably, with only two stores windows broken." There was "no rampaging, no looting. The total darkness pervaded in a hush. ... Neighbors who had never spoken to one another acted in friendship and cooperation lending matches and the use of flashlights, escorting others, offering help in the anonymity of the night." The only fire in Parkchester that evening was accidental, apparently caused by a candle. The paper also praised the Helmsley group for "the prompt action given by the development's corps of service personnel. Parkchester service men toured the community in radio cars and moved out to meet emergencies." Ben Lafiosca, president of the Parkchester Management Corporation, returned the compliment, stating that "the tenants acted beautifully." Evidently, an enduring sense of community still prevailed during an uncommon moment of tension.[46]

Indeed, many Parkchesterites sincerely believed that the troublemakers who plagued their community came from without rather from within their ranks. Speaking with a reporter in 1980, pub owner Kevin Burke declared that "most of the people moving into the neighborhood are willing to work for their piece of the dream just like the rest of us." He blamed "the relentless encroachment of the South Bronx" for the predators spawned by its hopelessness and decay. For him, "it was not a question of blacks and whites but of haves and have nots, of economic despair and the crime it breeds." Nonetheless, he and his wife made plans to relocate with their children to Westchester.[47]

Around 1980, as well, African American schoolteacher Camille Redmond, uncomfortable with the "problems of the Bronxdale projects" in the nearby Bruckner Boulevard area, relocated with her two teenage children to Parkchester. She "got a good deal" on a one-bedroom apartment that was previously owned by a white family—the father, in the armed services, had been shifted to another part of the country. Much like Parkchesterites of prior generations, Redmond avoided having to cope with the "horrible heat" in their building by spending July and August in a bungalow in Middletown, New York.[48]

Board of Education office administrator Geraldine "Geri" Flowers and her husband, Edwin, a foreman at the Barracini Candy Company, had a similar story to tell about why Parkchester was for them. Until 1976, the African American couple and their two children lived in a two-bedroom apartment on 156th Street in Morrisania's Melrose Housing Projects. Concerned that the neighborhood was "getting rough and [that] it was no place to raise their children" who were becoming teenagers, they felt fortunate to secure a three-bedroom apartment at 1718 Purdy Street near St. Raymond's Church, in what they described as an "upgrade" to a relatively secure neighborhood.[49]

Parkchester management strongly concurred with the impression that the sources of the area's problems emanated "from the surrounding areas" and that it was impossible for "a city of 40,000 without walls to keep the outsiders from coming in." In its view, newspaper accounts of criminality in the vicinity of the complex mistakenly claimed that the trouble was taking place on the streets of Parkchester, where its security force complemented the NYPD. The company asserted that "if anything happens outside the complex, the media refers to it as being in Parkchester because we are a separate city in a big city."[50]

Still, the reality or prospect of crime invading their neighborhood, remained a prime concern of aging Parkchester residents. Not only were they easy targets, but the very topography of Parkchester, one of the elements that had made it so attractive two generations earlier, was now seen as "tailor-made for criminals." As a spokesman for the police of the 43rd Precinct explained in 1980: "A lot of the problem is the way the development was laid out. Parkchester is becoming part of a world that its designers never dreamed of." The planned community featured a "maze-like world of banked and landscaped path, playgrounds and terraces that provided hiding places for muggers as they prepared to pounce." This, of course, was long before surveillance cameras would become a common sight in many New York neighborhoods.[51]

In response to the threat, some senior citizens, harkening back to a tradition of activism that had years earlier been part of the fabric of neighborhood life, made their feelings about the criminality around them known in public forums. In April 1978, "70 elderly residents" descended on the Bronx Family Court to make sure that one youthful offender, a recidivist with a rap sheet of some dozen offenses against people and property, was "kept off the streets." To do otherwise, said Doris Mirsky, aged sixty-eight, would "make emotional—if not physical—cripples of us all."[52]

But it was the Parkchester Tenants Association's neighborhood patrol that would systematize tenant defense both to the benefit of residents and ironically also to Helmsley-Spear, for whom the reputation of Parkchester was so financially crucial. Supported by a second Unity Day gathering in November 1977, that attracted hundreds of residents who "marched and rallied . . . to prevent the spread of the Bronx's deterioration to their homes," the patrol aimed to station guards "in the front and rear entrances of each building from 7 P.M. to 10 P.M." The unarmed volunteers were not supposed to take on "intruders," but just provide a deterrent presence. The patrol leaders also agreed with the management that "education classes" were warranted for all new occupants about Parkchester's rules. Concerned residents now set aside their prior feelings about the Parkchester cops' oppressive oversight of their youngsters when the neighborhood was new and reminisced about the good old days, when MLIC management strictly enforced regulations.[53]

In July 1979, with crime continuing to distress the community, the tenant patrol organized with the help of Rabbi Seymour Schwartz of Beth Jacob Congregation, a "Thursday Night Community Walk." Starting out in the early evening at Metropolitan Oval, with a different community leader as grand marshal each week, the group determined "to get people out of their homes and back into the habit of walking freely through the streets." And they sought "to encourage neighbors to walk together and get to know one another."[54]

Soon thereafter, measures were taken under the auspices of the Neighborhood Emergency Telephone System (NETS) and a group of allied Bronx social service agencies to protect Parkchester's elderly during the day. Young people employed in the Summer Youth Employment Program were enlisted to patrol "assigned regular 'beat[s]'" and report any irregularities back to the NETS through street-based phone extensions set up throughout the complex. These youths were also made available to escort senior citizens who needed assistance in shopping or other daily errands.[55]

The following spring, the Parkchester Tenants Association and the Helmsley group took another step together to improve security when "Operation Light Up replaced incandescent bulbs with high pressure sodium lights" throughout the development, especially in areas around apartment buildings where troublemakers might congregate. Harold Jackman headed up the operation, earning a reputation, certainly in the Metropolitan Oval area, as a vigilant protector of his neighbors. Several years later, the NETS inaugurated a "back-lock program in conjunction with [its] mobile patrol cart," designed to check the rear of buildings in all quadrants and to report problems to Parkchester management.[56]

Despite all of these efforts, a persistent sense of instability severely hampered condominium sales. As late as December 1984, more than ten years into the Helmsley group's efforts to find buyers for apartments in the North Quadrant, only one-half of some four thousand available residences had been sold. The rest remained rentals or were kept unoccupied in anticipation of future sales. Making matters worse, the word on the confused Parkchester street was that "while the property is still beautifully maintained, with the floral display in the Oval drawing crowds every spring" and the "bodegas and discount stores [that] have replaced some of the older businesses" had not undermined the neighborhood scene because the new owners were as "hard working" as their predecessors, "when Helmsley couldn't sell the apartments, he just opened it up to anyone—welfare recipients, people who had been thrown out from some other place—and drove people out." Finally, "none of the infrastructure improvements" that had been promised when the condominium plan was initially tendered had been effectuated. Opponents of Helmsley's attempts to gain permission to transform the rest of Parkchester were quick to point out that glaring deficiency. Nonetheless, by 1983, six years after the Goodman-Dearie law had run its course, and with momentum gaining in Albany and City Hall toward approving condominium plans all over New York due to massive real estate lobbying efforts, Helmsley gained permission to transform the remaining eighty-three hundred apartments within the three other quadrants—so-called Parkchester South—requiring the sale of only 15 percent of apartments to have "the non-eviction plan declared effective by the State Attorney General's office." The Helmsley group would meet that minimal goal. But the matter of selling the reminder of the properties would pose a continuing dilemma.[57]

A survey of resident attitudes that the Parkchester Tenants Association conducted in 1984 offered an indication of the difficulties the management still faced. Only 4 percent of Parkchester renters at the time expressed interest in buying their apartments. Within that minuscule group, those who had moved in recently—between 1971 and 1984—into rent-stabilized apartments predominated. The longest-term occupants, grateful as always with rent control, were content to pay their low monthly fee. A few indicated that they might change their minds, but only if "improvements" were made to their forty-four-year-old buildings.[58]

The prospects for bringing in outsiders willing and able to buy condominiums received a boost in March 1983 when the New

York City Chamber of Commerce and Industry listed Parkchester as among sixty-one "neighborhoods as good communities for executives and their families." Through the distribution of a twenty-nine-minute film and various booklets, the Chamber, dedicated to promoting the best Gotham had to offer, sought to offset "the images of New York based largely on such things as photographs of the South Bronx ... [that] have colored the thinking of many ... executives that some have simply refused transfers to the city," opting instead for settling in suburbs. The highlighted enclaves were selected "on the basis of school and housing quality, parks, shopping and other amenities." In making the choices, "some neighborhoods were eliminated because they were too expensive for middle management, while others were eliminated because they were looked upon as too rundown." Significantly, "such integrated neighborhoods like Parkchester" and Co-Op City were "emphasized as good places to live," along, of course, with the very upscale Riverdale. In reaction to this promotional endeavor, the director of marketing at Merrill Lynch Relocation Services cautioned that "New York City has a reputation that I think is going to be difficult to overcome, whether justified or not."[59]

Two years later, in October 1986, the neighborhood received only mixed reviews in a *New York Times* evaluation headlined "If You're Thinking of Living in Parkchester." The article allowed that "residents say ... it [is] a special enclave within the city that surrounds it." As always, reporters picked up on neighborhood interviewees' ambivalence about the status of the development. John Dearie, ever the Parkchester advocate, asserted, "it's as good a model of a integrated community as exists anywhere in the city." But the survey also stated that the neighborhood's "transition from youth to middle age has been troubled." Security concerns were identified as a paramount issue, along with the deterioration of the neighborhood's infrastructure and the unending problem of no air-conditioning.[60]

As before, concerning the crime issue, responsibility was still attributed by some to the situation in the city as a whole. For example, in 1985, a local historian, whose teenage son had volunteered for the NETS, argued that "most of the vandalism reflects trends of the 1980s—graffiti, broken elevator windows, broken entrance door locks and garbage-laden lawns. In most cases, it is not residents renting tenants or condominium owners who vandalize but passers-by who account for most of the destruction. These transients do not care how dirty or disheveled they leave our neighborhood, because they don't live in it."[61]

Others, however, laid the problem squarely at the doorstep of the Helmsley group. Tenants were outraged when, in 1986, the company fired thirty-nine private security guards and hired employees of the Burns Guards in their stead. The move smacked of betrayal; some five years earlier, Dearie had reached out to the estimable Harold Jackman to apply his background as an instructor for the New York State Police to dramatically upgrade the training and status of the Parkchester cops. Parkchester management had agreed to fund Jackman's efforts, seemingly demonstrating Helmsley's commitment to public safety, no matter the cost. In 1981, Jackman had established an academy to educate both old-time officers and newcomers to the force in their roles as "peace officers." Through a four-to-six-month program that he developed and ran, students were exposed to "the state penal code, criminal procedure etc." Upon its completion, they could now carry guns. Reflecting on his efforts, Jackman indicated how his carefully selected pupils learned that "there was much more to police work than just saying, 'Get off the grass.'" Parkchesterites were now grappling with real and present security concerns, and the residents had to be properly protected. But Jackman's well-prepared officers now were to be replaced.[62]

For Dearie and the Parkchester Tenants Association, Helmsley's move meant that the "condominium issue [had] utterly given way to the management amok problem." The petition that he quickly circulated, signed by twenty-one neighborhood religious and political leaders, asserted that "the benefits of full-time trained and supervised patrol outweigh the part time, minimally trained personnel hired by a business firm such as Burns." The problem, he argued, was that the new security people were "light-years away in terms of understanding of the community, the buildings, the interconnecting mazes." Msgr. Philip Mulcahy of St. Helena's, head of the Parkchester Crime and Safety Committee, readily concurred, stating that "the only problem with the [prior] security force was that it did not have enough men. I don't know what's going to happen with the Burns guards because they don't even know the neighborhood." Not only that, in the opinion of the protestors, from a purely legal perspective, "the dismissal represents a cut in service which is prohibited under rent-stabilization and rent-control guidelines." They emphasized that the prospectus filed with the office of the state attorney general that was necessary for approval of the condominium plan specifically stated that there would be a "security staff directly employed as in-house employees rather than this new contract service with an outside company."

The management's response—that the change in personnel was "purely a business decision" due to its "seeking to get out of the security business" because of "increasing concern about insurance liability"—did little to calm tenants. If anything, it brought back to the fore the fears Helmsley-Spear's takeover had initially sparked among Parkchesterites. In pursuit of a greater profit margin, their way of living would be endangered. Dearie likely spoke for many others in the community when he turned his ire directly at the Helmsley family and declared, "They may know something about the East Side where they live, but they know nothing of Parkchester." Never one to back away from a struggle against the powerful landlords, in June 1986, Dearie and an assortment of other community leaders marched on the Helmsley-Spear headquarters in Manhattan. When the full-time security guards were reinstated a month later, Dearie declared their success "an unmistakable community victory."[63]

While the Parkchester Tenants Association continued to vex the management over its failures to contribute adequately to guarding the neighborhood and other quality-of-life concerns, in 1987, a second, even more aggressive group, the First Parkchester Coalition, went to court seeking to halt "any future sales of condominiums" in the South Quadrant. This rival organization had first made its feelings known in 1980 when it proclaimed that Dearie and his associates were not adequately addressing the need for what it called "a desperate effort" to cut down crime in the area. One of the Coalition's proposed solutions was to have a "trained attack dog" patrol different sections of the complex every night to scare off potential criminals. The Coalition allied itself with the Guardian Angels, a citywide activist civilian defense group. Aiming directly at Parkchester's management and using the alleged deterioration of the property as a wedge, the group initiated a $300 million class-action suit charging that Helmsley-Spear had "misrepresented the condition of the plumbing and electrical systems in its offering plan." Helen Brandt, head of the organization, contended that an engineer's statement that "replacement of the hot and cold-water circulation piping is 'a necessity'" had been concealed, an egregious act in a housing complex which, she said, had suffered from "a couple of thousand pipe breaks over the past five years." It was further alleged that vacant apartments had been sold as condos without the new owners being informed that there was a plumbing problem, which in turn had led to "an infestation of vermin." In filing the suit in federal court under the Racketeer Influence Corrupt Organizations Law, which grants successful plaintiffs triple damages, the protesters, in effect, accused the management of criminal activity. Though the coalition's legal endeavor did not succeed, the publicity around the case did damage to the management's reputation and its efforts to sell apartments.[64]

The fiftieth anniversary of Parkchester in 1990 gave the Helmsley group an opportunity to push back against these criticisms and challenges by emphasizing in a promotional brochure that no matter the readily apparent infrastructure problems, the company had fulfilled one of the basic mandates that the Human Rights Commission had set out for it a generation earlier. "Diversity" was the theme of the brochure, which was distributed widely. It was noted that, much as in Parkchester's early history, resident leaders were engaged in a variety of lower-middle-class occupations. The resident members of Parkchester South's board of managers included an engineer, two union leaders, a teacher, an accountant, and a woman who worked in her family's printing business. Up north, their counterparts included two schoolteachers, a civil service employee, three social workers, a medical laboratory supervisor, a retired hospital worker, a medical technician, and a lawyer—an economic profile still very reminiscent of Parkchester's first generation of occupants. The president of that northern group was Urban League fundraiser Mildred Hall, possibly the first African American to make her way into the neighborhood with Robert W. Dowling's help. Underscoring the diversity of the neighborhood's most concerned citizens, Hall's counterpart to the south was educator turned business woman Margaret Walsh, an Irish American who had lived in the community since 1943. In a sense, she represented the elderly white population.[65]

The anniversary brochure trumpeted the fact that not only could Parkchester's African Americans, many by now residents of long-standing, have their concerns addressed by their duly elected peers, so could the neighborhood's newest ethnic and racial groups. As one Helmsley representative quoted in the brochure observed, "The latest wave of newcomers are Indians, Asians, Pakistanis and other

Orientals . . . a mosaic" of different peoples living together with "just about a non-racial situation." Such were the words of Amit Sikdar, executive vice president of Parkchester and Helmsley's man on the scene, who was himself of Indian descent. He allowed that "there have been some adjustment problems especially with the Asians, but they are not problems that we have to address." In his view, members of the most recent wave of new Parkchester residents were getting along quite well with their neighbors.[66]

In May 1992, the *New York Times* published a second "If You Are Thinking of Living" evaluation of the neighborhood. Much as it had six years earlier, the community received mixed reviews. As always, it was home to "many civil servants—teachers, postal employees, social workers and the like." Sticking up for the place where she had lived for close to fifty years, board member Margaret Walsh told the paper that "there are many places in New York City where you can't find three trees close together. Here we see robins in spring and watch the leaves turn color in the fall." African American new-comer Barbara Terry, a television producer who had relocated from Harlem just three months earlier, spoke about "how she grew up nearby and always saw Parkchester [as] the garden spot of the Bronx." She pointed out that "when I was a child . . . they [the MLIC] would not sell to anyone who wasn't white. Now the neighborhood is integrated, multi-cultural and exciting." However, she made clear that she "would like to have her two-bedroom apartment air-conditioned." One of the longest-standing complaints about the complex had endured.

The *Times* article also praised the quality of education that youngsters were receiving in the area's public schools, reporting that Christopher Columbus High School, one of the neighborhood's two public secondary schools, "was designated by the State Depart-ment of Education as one of 12 New York City Schools that work." The school's principal proudly declared that of the some three thousand pupils enrolled at Columbus, "all but 100 read at or above grade level." For him, it was "really an accomplishment" since "sixty percent of our students report that English is not their first language. We have more than 30 different language groups, including Ethiopians, Russians, Bengals, Koreans."

Four years earlier, P.S. 106 had been similarly singled out for praise by the *Times*: "76 percent of the graduating students are reading at grade level . . . compared with 61.3 percent city wide." Many of these youngsters' families hailed from places like Bangladesh, Puerto Rico, Ghana, Ecuador, the Dominican Republic, Cambodia, Vietnam, Yemen, Cuba, and the Soviet Union. English was their second language. Meanwhile, for PTA president Gail Bond, formerly of the South Bronx, "one reason she and her three children moved in with her mother was to be in the zone for P.S. 106." All told, Parkchester's student educational achievement had not diminished even as the school, which had "no minority students . . . 20 years ago," now was "40 percent black, 41 percent identified as Hispanic, 7 percent Asian and 11 percent white."

However, the newspaper account also underscored that "Parkchester is not immune from the problems of the surrounding areas. Phone booths are marred by graffiti and many building fronts have been painted brown to hide the graffiti. . . . A recent rash of push-in robberies and a January murder have made elderly residents feel insecure."[67]

The many unhappy residents of Parkchester sadly concurred with the newspaper's analysis. For sure, they knew from their own experience what was always right about their neighborhood, but they also felt strongly that the Helmsley group, in its constant search for higher profits at both renters' and condominium owners' expense, had let the neighborhood's infrastructure badly deteriorate. For critics, worries about the future of the community were now more than ever justified.

In May 1994, a spokeswoman for the city's Department of Housing Preservation and Development reported that "688 violations had been cited at the Parkchester complex since 1985, most of them in the last year." The *New York Times*, touring twelve apartments in four buildings, found "water leaks of varying severity in all the units . . . broken pipes, holes in the walls and toilets not working." The Montalvo family complained about "raw sewage" that filled the "hallways and their foyer when it rains." Fabric store clerk Merna Wright, a forty-eight-year-old immigrant from Antigua, believed that her "American dream" had been fulfilled in 1987 when she bought in at the cost of $36,000. But now she alleged that her dream had been betrayed by managerial indifference and outright malevolence. In her "dank apartment . . . mold and mildew cover[ed] her walls and the paint [was] peeling. All her possessions, save a sofa and some knickknacks, [were] in the middle of the room covered with plastic sheets."[68]

Bengali immigrant Jannat Hussain felt trapped in the apartment that she owned with her father and sister. She told a local newspaper, "If only we had the money, we would have left long ago." Instead, they were stuck when, in 1992, "their apartment was flooded when hot water pipes in the wall burst. They lost a TV, a VCR and a toaster" and their cabinets were ruined. Besides having to replace these appliances, they were obliged to pay for annual paint jobs to walls that were frequently damaged. Residents throughout Parkchester concurred that "the entire electrical system must be rewired" to keep appliances from blowing outdated fuses and to permit air-conditioning.[69]

Even when Parkchester's management instituted a mini-improvement at the behest of the municipal government, the effort almost literally blew up in their faces. Beginning in 1994, as part of a "city conservation program," the development began "replacing old toilets with water-saving models." All went well until a bowl "ruptured, spraying pieces of porcelain" all over Violeta Rivera's bathroom, injuring her thumb. Subsequently, a ten-year-old boy was allegedly "traumatized" by a similar occurrence. In two lawsuits filed in Bronx Supreme Court, an attorney referred to these "shrapnel-like explosions" as part of an "epidemic of exploding toilets," and alleged that no adequate warning had been provided to tenants about this "very dangerous and life-threatening situation." The plaintiffs did not prevail, while consultants disagreed over whether it was "too much water pressure" or a "design defect in the bowl" that had caused the incidents.[70]

Several years later, Ken Patton, a real estate dean at New York University and a former chief operating officer for the Helmsley organization, commented dispassionately on how and where the corporation had gone wrong—they had "made a critical mistake in keeping a large number of apartments vacant in preparation for sale.... [W]hen the real estate market faltered," right after the fiftieth anniversary in 1990, "the owners were left with vacant apartments and with the condo charges to pay. Instead of investing in the property, the sponsor looked to cut expenses further to reduce losses."[71]

To many of the two thousand Parkchesterites who packed St. Raymond's Church auditorium in May 1994, and at subsequent protest meetings at other local houses of worship, Patton's chronology of mismanagement was way off. What they saw around themselves was the culmination of malfeasance that dated back to the 1980s. While the overwhelming share of their vitriol was directed at the Helmsley sponsors, who still owned "fifty percent of the complex," the elected members of the condominium boards also absorbed criticism from both renters and their fellow unit owners. They were perceived as incapable of pressuring Helmsley to do the right thing.

For Abu Shakoor, elected to the Parkchester South board in 1989, three years after he and his wife bought their condominium, the fact was "there was resentment [of Helmsley] both within and without the board." There was verbal "fighting within the board," frequent complaints about Sikdar, and letters sent directly to the Helmsley Manhattan offices demanding they open their financial coffers for infrastructure improvements. Shakoor, the first immigrant from South Asia to serve on the Parkchester South board, has recalled that he personally spoke to a top official of the parent corporation about infrastructure and security concerns and was told: "We know the problems, but we are thinking of getting out." No redress was in the offing; when push came to shove on many contentious issues, the sponsor had the majority of the votes.[72]

In May 1995, three hundred renters and condo owners, having had enough of management claims that it didn't "have the money to make all necessary improvements," initiated a rent strike that lasted into the winter of 1996. The latest in a long line of advocacy groups, the Parkchester Alliance, hired an attorney and demanded "the renovation of at least 50 buildings." The protesters called for "more resident representation." Alliance president Kay Washington told reporters that withheld rent was going into escrow for use "as a bargaining tool with the management." But the sponsor was not easily moved. Some renters availed themselves of the option of "voting with their feet." Fifty-five years after Parkchester opened, the "city within a city" was seemingly on the verge of self-destruction.[73]

FIGURE 8.1. Photo of restored, graffiti-freed Parkchester buildings and Metropolitan Avenue, 2005. Courtesy of Ronald L. Glassman.

8

RENEWAL EFFORTS

ALTHOUGH HARRY HELMSLEY ASSERTED IN 1968 that it was glamorous to own Parkchester, a decade later he was already exceedingly frustrated with the state of his Bronx acquisition and, in fact, with the whole business of residential real estate. In 1980, he told a reporter that if he could divest himself of "residential properties" he would be pleased to do so. In 1984, Helmsley started quitting the rental market in a significant way, selling "some of his buildings in the 2,700 apartment Tudor City complex" on Manhattan's East Side, contending that such housing was "an impossible business to be in." By that time, rent-control and rent-stabilization laws had thoroughly undermined his condominium conversion plans in many parts of the city. Parkchester, his long-time headache, was the foremost case. Almost from the outset, in his view, delaying tactics "gave rise to state legislation, since amended, that impeded conversions in the city for several years." By the early 1990s, with all the turmoil around the neighborhood about the company's ownership practices and the welter of legal problems faced by his family on a variety of fronts, it was time for the aging real estate mogul and his associates to move on.[1]

In the winter of 1994, a highly placed representative of the Helmsley group in charge of Parkchester approached the not-for-profit Community Preservation Corporation (CPC) with a proposal to sell the now unwanted and physically distressed property. For CPC president Michael Lappin, this augured to be the most ambitious project for his organization, which for more than twenty years had been working with bankers and government to prevent housing abandonment and rehabilitate blighted neighborhoods in various parts of the metropolis and upstate New York.

The CPC was an initiative of the New York Clearing House Association, a highly influential combine of major commercial banks, whose legacy in the city dated back a century. Under the leadership of David Rockefeller, who chaired the group's urban affairs committee, a valiant effort was made "to demonstrate that the city could marshal its resources to combat the wave of abandonments that plagued the metropolis." At the very time when Gotham was in steep decline, top officials of financial outfits like Chase Manhattan Bank and the New York Bank for Savings were working to rebuild the city, in which they were heavily invested.

This mission intersected both with Lappin's professional experience and his personal agenda. As a self-described "social justice activist," while a college student in the mid-1960s, and later while in graduate school, he had worked down south in Mississippi and Kentucky, helping build schools in which he taught poor black youngsters, and participating in other endeavors under Lyndon Johnson's poverty programs and subsequent federal initiatives that aided the families of sharecroppers and tenant farmers. Returning to New York in the early 1970s, he secured a position in the Office of Programs and Planning within the city's Housing Administration. Having previously attempted "to make a difference in people's lives," he chafed at his desk job, which consisted mainly of surveying housing conditions and "surveying the surveys," with no discernible impact. He soon left to join the newly created CPC, first as its point person for development. Lappin believed, much like the old money capitalists who hired him, that they could help revive New York City.

The corporation's game plan, launched in 1974 in Crown Heights, Brooklyn, and in the Washington Heights–Inwood section of Manhattan, was to use their expertise and connections to assist building owners in securing public and private financing to fix up their declining properties with the ultimate goal of making their buildings "financially and physically sound and affordable for residents" both presently and for "another generation to come." The CPC was also on the scene to guide their clients when it came to practical matters such as meeting construction and other capital costs for upgrading their real estate holdings. As Lappin put it, what the organization called "one stop shopping" involved "developing construction scopes and specifications and coordinating construction and permanent financing with a variety of public subsidies and mortgage insurance."

However, for work to go forward, not only did landlords have to agree to the CPC coming in, but tenants' approval was required as well. Though they would ultimately benefit from better plumbing, improved electrical wiring, new roofing, and so forth, the renovation efforts would not only disrupt their lives, but a portion of the costs would be passed on to them. The CPC turned to religious leaders and local politicians to help make the case within the two neighborhoods it initially targeted. With the help of these well-positioned civic spokespeople, particularly in Washington Heights–Inwood where over a five-to-six-year period some ten thousand units were improved, the CPC acquired a sterling reputation for concern and efficiency.

During the 1980s and early 1990s, with Lappin now as its president, the corporation expanded its purview and began the even more arduous job of rehabilitating abandoned buildings in other, more depressed parts of the city. During this period, with the co-op and condominium markets in steep decline—a situation that obviously had a major impact on Parkchester—the CPC facilitated the restructuring of co-ops in Queens, even as it also involved itself in housing problems in upstate New York. In sum, the

Helmsley group's offer was made to a widely tried and well proven organization.

In contrast to its prior efforts, CPC was now being courted to become the actual owner of a property that was far larger than any of the buildings it had helped preserve and rehabilitate. Lappin criticized the Helmsleys for their mismanagement of the Parkchester property and allowing its infrastructure to deteriorate while running an annual $4 million deficit, with many vacant apartments. Accordingly, the CPC "didn't believe that there was a suitable owner to meet . . . [the] triple goals of physical integrity, financial soundness and affordability." Yet the CPC "took the leap of ownership for the first time."[2]

In the negotiations, which extended from 1995 to 1997, the CPC adopted a two-pronged approach to both making a success of the sale and ultimately changing Parkchester for the better. Even as Lappin "began negotiating the purchase" and looking for ways to finance the endeavor, he sought out a partner or partners to oversee the actual restoration work. Getting funds and securing tax abatements was the CPC's strength, not the hands-on work of rebuilding and long-term management. After talks with, among others, the Lefrak family, who owned and operated their own massive "city" in Queens, proved unproductive, the CPC turned to real estate principal Morton L. Olshan, who in turn brought in Jeremiah W. O'Connor Jr. Together they set up a for-profit subsidiary, the CPC Resources Company.

Olshan came to the effort with substantial experience in real estate ownership and management, although his career had started out on a different path. As a student at CCNY and NYU, he had studied accounting. As a CPA at the firm of Duff and Brown, Olshan was mentored by real estate entrepreneur Joseph Janoff while he handled some of his client's books. Having learned the ins and out of owning and operating buildings and properties from Janoff,

Olshan would go on to partner with his mentor's family, including Joseph's sons, Ronald and Milton, in his first real estate investment. The property was a high-rise, rent-controlled apartment building at 60 West 76th Street, a few steps west of Columbus Avenue. Olshan family tradition has it that Morton "cobbled together" the finances necessary to make the deal, "seeded by the money he had made waitering in the Catskills." Today, the part of town where that prescient investment was made is a toney spot, but in the 1950s, it was a neighborhood long in decline. Subsequently, the Janoffs and Olshan bought and managed buildings in Flushing, Queens, and in Brooklyn Heights, even as Olshan's real estate company diversified, becoming a significant player in the development of regional malls and suburban retail centers. Back in Manhattan, Olshan worked on several residential upgrade efforts with the CPC in Washington Heights. But for all his experience, for Olshan just as for Lappin, the Parkchester project was a massive undertaking. Looking back on the endeavor, Olshan, who sounded in this regard much like Parkchester's original owners, would assert that he "believed in town centers where people live, work and enjoy entertainment and outdoor recreation in one facility." To compliment his efforts and those of the CPC, Olshan brought into the partnership Jeremiah O'Connor, who was making his mark in suburban real estate. Parkchester would be his first urban residential endeavor.[3]

Together, they tendered a $5 million offer to the Helmsley group, which initially countered with a price of $10 million, However, time was clearly not on the prior owners' side, as they "struggled with more than 700 vacant apartments that they had kept off the market," an onerous monthly burden. The CPC and its CPC Resources partnership had the upper hand. Through a newly established entity called the Parkchester Preservation Corporation (PPC), Lappin's organization, Olshan, and O'Connor ultimately succeeded in buying not only the "6,362 money-losing" apartments that Helmsley still owned but also all of the neighborhood's commercial interests for $4 million after the cost of the necessary removal of harmful asbestos was factored in. The financial challenge ahead of the group was to find funding in the amount of "$178 million to replace plumbing, wiring and more than 65,000 windows throughout the complex which sprawls across 129 acres." It was initially estimated that "once approved the project is expected to take three to four years."[4]

But consent from within the Parkchester community was not readily forthcoming. The PPC partnership had to use all the powers of persuasion that the CPC had honed over the years in smaller endeavors elsewhere to gain the assent not only of the South and North boards but also of the rank and file of condominium owners. For Parkchester alumnus Fernando Ferrer, who had been serving as Bronx borough president since 1987, the initiative constituted the neighborhood's only reasonable chance of ending decades of neglect. He had previously been on the record as lamenting that Parkchester's problems were his "biggest worry for the Bronx." Stewart Epstein, president of the Parkchester Merchants Association, could not have agreed more. "You have to be foolish," he said, "not to support CPC. . . . This is the one chance that Parkchester has to improve." Still, these vocal backers and those who shared their view, including local politicians and religious leaders, also heard from dissenting voices within the community. Ferrer has recalled that "decades of broken promises" had left many residents highly suspicious of another group of outsiders' grandiose plans. Even more pointedly, there was fear, particularly among those with fixed incomes, that "increases in . . . monthly carrying charges'" and a new requirement that residents pay their own electric bills galvanized opposition. As at earlier moments in Parkchester's history when residents had rejected infrastructure improvements, clearly once again there were tenants and owners in the complex who did not want to pay more even in return for far better living conditions.[5]

Gary Hall, a North Quadrant condominium board member and a spokesman for PORA, an organization of CPC opponents (its acronym, he said, stood for the fact that "we have become *poorer* [emphasis mine] ever since we moved to Parkchester"), alleged that the proposed renovations did "not go far enough to fix the problems that have plagued Parkchester for years." Most critically, "what the owners will be paying for [is] an incomplete job that will not solve the owners' problems," such as decaying electrical supply lines, which "will cause many owners to go into debt for the rest of their lives to pay for it." He also asserted that a pivotal election of board members, who would determine the future course of the neighborhood, had been "illegally influenced by the Community Preservation Corporation." In Hall's view, what was going on was all too reminiscent of what he saw as the Helmsley group's shenanigans.[6]

His PORA associate Gladys Williams even threatened street protests to dramatize residents' plight. "We're going to lay down in the streets," she said. "We're going to stop traffic. We're going to jump up and down and scream, this is not a good deal for Parkchester." PORA initiated a court action challenging the board election procedures, but it was rebuffed by the New York State Supreme Court.[7]

In response to these ardent critics, and also to answer more moderate skeptics concerned that "this is the biggest rehabilitation CPC has undertaken and it's the most complicated both in terms of the scope of the work and the financing," Lappin replied that "it is a difficult process, much like going to the dentist. But if the work is not done now, then there will be a much bigger need in the future, It will be a disaster." Moreover, he insisted that his group's "investment is long-term," and promised that they would engage "a highly-qualified management firm to make sure that the development is maintained after the work is completed." He admitted that to make the plan work financially "each owner will have to pay about $95 a month towards the debt." However, because of real estate tax abatement legislation that was moving smoothly between Albany and City Hall, residents "could save $53 a month in charges." Additionally, "a $25 monthly electricity charge will be eliminated, replaced by individual electrical bills, estimated at $44 a month." Putting these numbers all together, "the net increase should not exceed $74 a month." As far as senior citizens with fixed incomes were concerned, the corporation agreed, due to Msgr. Derivan's wise intercession, to spend $7.5 million to subsidize the cost increases for elderly residents. To sweeten the deal further for residents of every age, the new investors committed "to turn over a parking garage for a community center and to provide for an annual contribution of $100,000 a year for 10 years." Finally, in addressing Hill's claim that the plan did not go far enough and that residents would ultimately have to bear additional unmanageable costs, Lappin declared: "We're trying to keep the project as affordable as possible and we are replacing what needs to be changed. But there are many lines in good shape and it would be foolish to change them if we don't have to." On the political front, Assemblyman Peter Rivera declared, "We're anxious to go forward. . . . Right now, CPC seems to be the only option for Parkchester."[8]

In November 1998, the partnership's search for approval took a large leap forward when it passed muster with the Parkchester South board, but only after the new owners answered some trenchant questions from the community's leaders. For the move to succeed, the PPC needed a combination of the board seats it inherited from the Helmsley deal along with the votes of resident directors. These men and women, who still carried battle scars from their dealings with the Helmsley group, were concerned about "surrendering their independence" and wanted substantial input on the reconstruction process, including the details and costs of remodeling. While appreciative of the newcomers' approach and keenly aware of the money being expended on their behalf, board president Edward Watkins and his colleagues wanted a strong say when it came to "contracts, construction and accounting." Watkins had told the *New York Times*: "I'm for it as long as it doesn't interfere with the independence of the board to function." When they were sufficiently reassured that they would have a presence in future decision-making and accountability, the board voted up the proposal unanimously. Several weeks after this decision, Watkins told the *Times*: "It means a rebirth for Parkchester. It will bring us into the 21st century." Ruminating on what he and his fellow residents endured, Watkins remarked: "Imagine where you live, blowing 15-amp fuses every day." After twenty-seven years in the complex, he was ready for the change. Michael Lappin's take on what transpired during these critical deliberations was that "while there was some dissension among board members, they pulled together and recognized that this was a very good deal for the residents." What remained to be concretized down south was a go-ahead on the proposal from the community rank and file.[9]

As a January 1999 vote among the owners in that part of the development approached, the partners placed numerous full-page ads in the *Bronx Press Review* to encourage the residents whom Lappin called "the silent majority" to turn out for the meeting at which time the proposal's fate would be decided. The Parkchester Preservation Corporation pledged complete transparency as to "why we want to restore and preserve Parkchester," emphasizing, above all, affordability. The gathering, held at the Parkchester Baptist Church, site of contentious resident-management exchanges in the past, ended favorably for the plan. The rallying of religious leaders and politicians had paid off. Ferrer, for one, told the assemblage: "the place is falling apart.... [W]e have to fix the place ... no one has a better idea." Resident Howard Hall echoed these sentiments. Rising from his seat in the audience, he vehemently asserted that when he "bought an apartment last November, [he] was deeply dissatisfied with the conditions he found when he moved in. 'If I have to pay a few more dollars to fix the place up, I'm in.'" Kumar Kancherla strongly seconded Hall's opinion, declaring that "we can trust the new sponsors." Although angry dissenting voices were heard—Lappin has recalled that the "battle [was] punctuated by physical threats, smears and efforts to pit the various ethnic groups against one another"—the rehabilitation plan passed by more than the necessary two-thirds majority. Both long-term and newly arriving residents, owners and renters alike could look forward to improvements—not least, the prospect of air-conditioning was finally in the offing.[10]

However, by the end of summer 1999, questions were already being raised on neighborhood streets about whether the new management was really intent on following through on its grand promises. That September, "a protest over the garbage piling up in front of the complex's buildings brought out scores of residents to Metropolitan Avenue." They alleged that in one building, where workmen did appear, they proved to be less than proficient. It was said that "dozens of mice became stuck in the fresh paint, died and began rotting." One complainant compiled a three-page inventory of "problems with electricity, leaking pipes and moldy walls." Making matters worse, in the view of those who spoke up, "the landlord began distributing flyers offering rent breaks in return for luring tenants to the complex, which has 700 to 800 empty apartments." Pamela Sanchez, a resident of twenty years, told a reporter: "they can't even take care of the place and they are using us to get more people here. . . . If I was younger, I would move. I just want to warn people not to live here."

Michael Lappin's reaction to this palpable impatience was that "we know that the place is in bad shape. This is a big ship and it will take a long time to turn around. There are more than 60 plumbing breakages a day, so simple maintenance will not resolve the situation." Among the residents, a new president of the Parkchester South board struck a more positive note about the future, asserting that "the rental markets have already improved, because people know that renovations will take place."[11]

The perception that improvements were proceeding too slowly did not help the partners in their difficult task of convincing the Parkchester North board and that area's condominium owners to vote them in to their part of the complex. Part of the reticence has been attributed to a wait and see attitude as the northerners watched the course of change transpiring down south. On the board level, as well, there was the familiar issue of the relative power of the sponsor versus that of the resident directors. Here the difference of perspective became contentious and enduring. Indeed, when Lappin and his associates moved to effectively increase the number of board members who would support their positions—a tactic that they believed was permitted under New York State real estate law—lawyers for the Parkchester North board went to court to stop the sponsors. The legal fight would last more than two years, holding up renovations. As the battle was joined, board president Harry Brown, a strong advocate for the partners' plan, argued that there was no alternative. "Parkchester," he contended, "cannot survive without it being renovated at this time." Those standing in the way, in his view, were doing more than just voicing dissent, which he allowed takes place "every time you make progress." He alleged that fellow board members, some of whom were closely connected to the existing management, were benefitting financially from past deals that had been struck with various contractors and vendors.[12]

While Parkchester North's board balked over signing up with the CPC and its associates, down south, residents began to benefit from their affirmative vote as the proposed improvements started to come through. By the spring of 2002, when that key creature

FIGURE 8.2. Michael Lappin (center) and CPC allies Harry Brown (left) and Rev. Hilary Gaston (right). Courtesy of Ronald L. Glassman.

comfort of air-conditioning was becoming a reality on southern streets like McGraw Avenue, it could be said that "the twin developments [were now] as different as Hot and Cold." Twenty-five-year-old school teacher Eddie Del Vallo cheered the fact that the era of his taking "three showers a day" while his "ceiling fans were on 24/7" during "sweltering summer days and nights" was coming to an end. With the plumbing and electrical systems upgraded, Del Vallo now had his "first air conditioner, a $345 Friedrich model that the windows were designed to hold ready to be installed." A CPC motto declared, "Parkchester—a cool place to live." Meanwhile there was no such relief in store for seventy-two-year-old Robert Parr, a Parkchester North resident since the early 1970s. He lamented: "You go over there [to Parkchester South], you think you're in a different world." Still, some of Del Vallo's neighbors were not as "thrilled" as he, since "maintenance fees have risen and some residents complain that the new windows [that were part of the deal] do not open all the way, reducing the breeze for those without air conditioners."[13]

Meanwhile, the upgrades of residential life, along with the inflow of the partners' funds, had a positive effect on the neighborhood's Metropolitan Avenue shopping strip. By the end of 2002, it was reported that "85 percent of the commercial tenants had renewed their leases and that 30 of the forty stores had complete renovation." Neighborhood staple Zaro's added Italian marble to its frontage and improved its fixtures. The American movie theater became a multiplex. Chain stores such as Bolton's, Payless Shoes, and Dunkin' Donuts improved their looks. In a sure sign that the neighborhood was on an upswing, a Starbucks arrived in 2001. Most notably, Macy's, a community partner with Parkchester from the very outset, installed "new mannequins and bold displays, higher quality music systems, new fixtures . . . and new carpeting and tile throughout." The famous department store made clear that it intended to stay for the long haul when it signed a fifteen-year lease extension, with an option to remain for another forty-five years. All of these improvements, of course, benefitted residents in both the north and south communities.[14]

In August 2002, following a court decision that affirmed the CPC's right to vote in board members favorable to their plans, the rank and file of Parkchester North owners approved the renovation plan. In garnering approval, it helped that the sponsor agreed to subsidize the forthcoming rent increase, which would be higher than the one obtained down south.[15]

By April 2004, with the renovations in the south almost done and a scheduled completion date for repairs of July 2005, residents began to see that the value of their apartments was significantly on the rise. This was due in part to "first-time buyers, who were enticed by low interest rates but priced out of homes in New Jersey

and then in other sections of the Bronx," who "found they could afford to buy condominiums in Parkchester." The *Village Voice* spoke,
in 2006, of "a stampede of young professionals" as "condo values
breached the six-figure mark." In 2003, a three-bedroom apartment
went for under $100,000; three years later, it could fetch as much
as $215,000. As so often in the past, it was noted that commuters
who lived in the "city within a city" could get to work quickly via the
subway or express buses. Six and a half decades after Parkchester
had come into existence, the lifestyle advantages it had always possessed over suburbia— and for less money—could once again be
emphasized. Long-term residents could also see that the people
coming in were quality individuals. Toward the dismal end of the
Helmsley era, there was at best inadequate screening of potential
occupants of the many empty apartments. The neighborhood was
afflicted, as well, by illegal squatters, who cared little for the upkeep
of places where they should have not been. These problems were
exacerbated by the difficulties faced by departing residents in selling their apartments due to a depressed market. "If they needed to
move for personal reasons, they either rented out their units or sold
to investors, often with little screening" of those who would live
there. Now, both the north and the south communities, harkening
back ironically to Parkchester's earliest days, were committed to
"tougher screening criteria . . . which include criminal background
checks, credit cards and a requirement that renters show evidence
they have the income to pay their rent." Once again, Harry Brown
was in the lead, asserting: "You've got to have a job or you've got
to have the income. It is important because it gives you a stable
community."[16]

Amid this period of revival, in 2007, the *New York Times* real estate
section took another look at Parkchester's worthiness as a residential destination. The findings unquestionably pleased the sponsors
and managers, not to mention the tenants and owners. Some twenty-

one years earlier and then again, in 1992, the area had received mixed reviews in two "If You Are Thinking of Living in Parkchester" surveys, which had highlighted the problems of encroaching crime and the deterioration of once-pristine buildings and grounds. Now, the *Times* printed hardly a single discouraging word about life in the neighborhood. No security concerns were mentioned while, of course, there was praise for the "flowers, benches, and a fountain where bronze-cast statues spout water" at the Oval.[17]

The protagonist of the piece was Evelyn Liston, president of Parkchester North Condominium, whose search for "quiet surroundings" that brought her to the neighborhood in 2004 was characterized as a "heroic quest . . . marked by high ideals, momentary defeats and, in the end, redemption." The now fifty-year-old "consultant to music composers and organizations," previously of Washington Heights, had started out looking in Brooklyn and Queens for an affordable dwelling, unsuccessfully. After riding the subway to the Bronx, she found her "green oasis" with people who "were so nice. They're not yuppies or whatever. They're just really good people with solid income who want to invest and have a nice place to live." Impressed, Liston bought her "airy one-bedroom for $74,000" and was pleased to report that "the 55 buildings in her quadrant were all to have new roofs'" by the following year. The article also emphasized that the value of her and, indeed, all the complex's apartments was on the rise and "show[s] no signs of faltering."

Affirming that much-improved economic situation, Zakir Kahn, owner of Parkchester Real Estate, said that while the "real estate market has become unstable in some places, Parkchester has still been strong. It's not a high-profile neighborhood, but it's a good neighborhood." Pat Shapiro, operations director for the management company, chimed in: "Since the renovation and revitalization, there has been a tremendous change. As Manhattan's gotten more expensive, more and more people are attracted."

The lone, muted critical voice in the upbeat article came from octogenarian Margaret Walsh, president of Parkchester South Condominium, who, it will be recalled, had lived in the neighborhood since 1943. For her, "the biggest problem and the biggest complaint" was "the unavailability of sufficient parking." Walsh, who had been through all of the Helmsley wars, noted that decades earlier few tenants had vehicles. Now, "there just isn't room in the garages or on the city streets."[18]

Life in a renewed Parkchester garnered additional public praise some four years later when, in conjunction with the community's seventieth-anniversary commemoration, self-described "first-generation" resident Hank de Cillia and John Dalpe produced a video testimony to the neighborhood's past and present. The documentary premiered at the American as a centerpiece of the celebration, which saluted both continuity and change. The twenty-five-minute film played over and over again to a packed audience of both current residents and some fifteen hundred alumni who returned to the neighborhood on May 15, 2010. The voiceover narration of the largely black-and-white film made sure to observe that while De Cillia was growing up contentedly in "a place where families of hard working people of modest means could be part of the American dream," no "people of color" were allowed in Parkchester. The closing section, shot in Technicolor, showed people of all races and ethnicities taking part happily in street activities. The film conveyed the message that "the new millennium breathed new life into the old grand neighborhood [as] a consortium of socially concerned and fiscally competent corporations gained ownership of Parkchester and began a program of comprehensive renewal and improvement to the apartments and condominiums." Though no mention was made of the Helmsley years in what was an admittedly rosy account, Michael Lappin appeared on screen, describing many of the improvements that the CPC and its associates had brought in, including the sixty-five thousand new windows in the complex. He asserted that Parkchester was becoming "one of the most livable and affordable communities in New York City." Fernando Ferrer characterized the neighborhood as a "building block foundation of the new New York." The film's closing line was that, at seventy years of age, Parkchester was "a shining example of how good housing and fairs prices can improve the lives of those who live there."[19]

FIGURE 9.1. Celebrating diversity at St. Helena's Church. Msgr. Thomas Derivan with Ernestina Mensah and Kwasi Mensah, St. Helena's first Ghanaian parishioners, circa 1985. Courtesy of Msgr. Thomas Derivan.

IMMIGRANT ARRIVALS AND OLD-TIMER DEPARTURES

T HE FIRST PUBLIC RECOGNITION THAT THE ETHNIC, national, and racial balances of Parkchester residents were once again undergoing a major shift had occurred in the late 1980s, when the *New York Times* noted that the families of some of the high-achieving students in the local public school were recently arrived from countries such as Bangladesh, Puerto Rico, Ghana, Ecuador, the Dominican Republic, Cambodia, Vietnam, Yemen, Cuba, and the Soviet Union. Subsequently, in 1990, commemorating the development's fiftieth anniversary, Amit Sikdar, a Helmsley management vice president, proudly declared that "the latest wave of newcomers are Indians, Asians, Pakistanis and other Orientals . . . a mosaic" of different peoples living together. Left out of these enumerations, but surely a presence in the neighborhood's mix since the 1970s, were Afro-Caribbeans from places like Antigua and Guyana and Africans from countries like Nigeria and Ghana.

These newcomers, except for the Puerto Ricans who, of course, were United States citizens, were Parkchester's first substantial immigrant cohorts. The majority of the neighborhood's earlier residents, whether they were Jews, Irish, Italians, or members of other white ethnicities, had been the children and grandchildren of those who came to America and to Gotham in the late 19th and early 20th centuries. The community's African Americans were, likewise, New Yorkers of long-standing. In many cases, they were descendants of those who moved up north during periods of major black migration. Puerto Ricans came to the American mainland and to the metropolis en masse after World War II. Although each of these groups of new-comers to the country from the Third World had their own unique stories to tell of how they made it to the East Bronx neighborhood, they had benefitted in common from the United States Congress's passage in the mid-1960s of new immigration legislation. These statutes rescinded the prejudicial national-origins quota acts of the 1920s that had favored Northern and Western Europeans. Breaking through the gates to America, the new visa system placed all nations on an equal footing while emphasizing an "opened door to those with occupational skills required in the United States." Under this mandate, immigrants from "Asia, the Caribbean basin and South America . . . accounted for about three-quarters of the four million immigrants of the 1970s, and the pattern continued into the 1980s."[1]

Upon admission to America, most of those immigrants who set-tled in New York City found their initial places of residence "near their compatriots for convenience [and] mutual support, organi-cally forming communities within the ethnic mosaic of the city." For example, Dominicans tended to congregate in Washington Heights in Upper Manhattan and various neighborhoods in Queens. This cohort, three hundred thousand strong, became as, of 1990, "first in population among the city's foreign-born." Brooklyn neighbor-hoods such as Bedford-Stuyvesant, Flatbush, and Crown Heights were home to a growing number of Afro-Caribbeans, while "the more prosperous settled in Queens." The latter, especially its Flush-ing and Jackson Heights neighborhoods, was a first stop for many new Asian Americans, including Koreans, Indians, and Bangla-deshis. Chinatown in Manhattan continued its decades-long ten-ure as home to that national group, even as significant numbers of Southeast Asian refugees joined the mix. Well into the first decade of the new millennium, New Yorkers could still speak of "a welter of immigrant neighborhoods." Bangladeshis, by then, were ensconced in Kensington, Brooklyn; Ghanaians in the Concourse Village, Highbridge, and Morris Heights sections of the Bronx; Guyanese in Richmond Hill, Queens; Sri Lankans in Staten Island. For one observer, these were the "Kleindeustchlands of the 21st century"— cultural enclaves reminiscent in many ways of the distinctive and insular German-immigrant neighborhood on the Lower East Side in the mid-19th century.[2]

From the mid-1980s through the first decade of the new millennium, Parkchester was the first home in America for members of each of these and other national and racial groups of immigrants. But the relative size of the cohorts from every South American, Asian, and African country in the neighborhood, and in the Bronx generally, lagged well behind other communities and boroughs in the city. As earlier in its history, an ethnically diverse Parkchester was not overwhelmingly the province of one specific group of newcomers. From 1983 to 1989, of the approximately 610,000 people who found their first American homes in the city, only some 80,000 (13 percent) settled in the Bronx as compared with the over 200,000 (33 percent) who landed in Brooklyn. During those same years, Parkchester, along with the streets immediately north and northeast of the complex, was "the initial place of settlement" for just 3,200 immigrants. Similarly, in 1990–1994, when 200,000 foreign-born people came into Brooklyn, only 76,000 went to the Bronx. Within Parkchester's environs, only 4,000 people (some 5 percent of the borough's total newcomers) joined the neighborhood immediately upon arrival in the United States. It is very likely that those who came directly to the East Bronx neighborhood had relatives already in the area. If so, Parkchester witnessed a classic example of immigrant family chain migration. In all events, this reportedly "extremely diverse immigrant stream" included those from countries like the former Soviet Union, the Dominican Republic, Bangladesh, the Philippines, Guyana, China, Vietnam, and India. But no one group predominated. Besides which, they were now sharing Parkchester both with African Americans and Puerto Ricans, now of long standing, and the minority of aging white folks who remained in their apartments of old.[3]

In many cases, Parkchester was not the first but a second or even third place of settlement for those who initially may have settled in their own larger and more homogenous immigrant enclaves. These "outliers" were now willing and able to pay more to own a condominium, or to take over a rental, in a more salubrious setting and were comfortable residing in a mixed middle-class neighborhood. One cultural issue for many was the degree to which they wished to maintain the customs and traditions of their past in this new heterogeneous environment. Some were very keen to do so, others not so much. In either event, their experiences resembled those of Parkchester's first residents, for whom the neighborhood was a family's second or, perhaps, third step up and away from the ethnic streets of the downtown tenement district or the black ghetto in Harlem where their ancestors first struggled to find jobs that would lift them out of poverty.

One such family, Ghanaian natives William and Vera Acquah, rented a one-bedroom apartment at 28 Metropolitan Oval in 1992. It was their third place of residence since their marriage in 1988. William had emigrated in 1974; Vera came over a decade later. Previously, Vera, a home health aide, and William, a hotel worker, had lived in Flatbush, Brooklyn, among Africans and people of other ethnicities and then in the Mosholu section of the Bronx, which, as of 1990, had a minuscule African population. Feeling that their second neighborhood was "in decline," they jumped at the opportunity to secure a space in Parkchester where they could raise their two sons. The foursome dealt with their cramped quarters much as some Parkchester residents of prior decades had done. The boys were given the bedroom, the parents slept in the living room. But then again, when they were children back in Africa, Vera's family had lived in even more cramped quarters. When the Acquahs moved in to their tenth-floor digs, there were some "old whites, three African Americans, and three Pakistanis" on their floor. A quarter century later, their neighbors were African Americans, Bangladeshis, Dominicans, and Puerto Ricans. As avowed "assimilationists," the Acquahs did not seek out fellow Ghanaians as neighbors. Rather, they saw themselves as a "St. Helena's family." Their youngsters were educated in the school affiliated with the church, where they worshipped among an increasingly racially diverse religious community.[4]

Meanwhile, though those from South Asia, mostly natives of India and Bangladesh, were a minority among Parkchester's multicultural immigrant groups, they were the most noticed newcomers to the neighborhood. The Dominicans, Parkchester's largest Spanish-speaking group of newcomers, surely differed culturally from Puerto Ricans who had preceded them to the area and from the English-speaking Jamaicans who had also started moving in. But at least these Latinos all spoke the same languages. And those so disposed largely attended the area's churches of long-standing. Similarly, churchgoing Africans and Afro-Caribbeans found their way into existing Christian houses of worship. These congregations faced the challenge of integrating folks who, to the outside world, simply looked black or spoke Spanish or their own accented English, but differed widely in many cultural ways.[5]

The presence of South Asians—mostly Muslim, some Hindus, often with distinctive dress and mores—was, on the other hand, readily visible to all Parkchesterites as they walked down Metropolitan Avenue en route to the subway to their city jobs or their mosques and temples. In keeping with Parkchester tradition, religious institutions continued to be situated outside the neighborhood. Interfaith rows were still part of the scene on Virginia and Benedict Avenues and around neighboring Olmstead Street and Newbold Avenue. But now churches would share street space with mosques and Hindu temples rather than synagogues.

Muslim institutional life began very modestly in 1987 in a private house on Taylor Avenue, located a few blocks south and east of the 177th Street/Parkchester subway stop, where ten worshippers gathered to pray according to their Sunni tradition. Two years later, with more than a hundred affiliates, mostly hailing from Bangladesh, Parkchester Jame Masjid was built on Virginia Avenue south of the neighborhood. In time, the multistory mosque would attract over five hundred devotees to Friday prayers. Among the early worshippers were a few newcomers from West Africa—Senegal, Gambia, and the Ivory Coast—who looked forward to the day when they would have a house of worship that celebrated their own national and regional Islamic customs. In 2001, with assistance from a "self-help organization" founded in 1991 by "West African livery drivers," enough money was cobbled together to purchase a St. Helena's parish building that the Dominican Sisters of Sparkhill had previously occupied. When the Jamhiyatut Tahaawun Islamic Center moved into its own ramshackle three-story brick building, the decades-old interfaith row now had friendly Muslim neighbors. In the following decade and a half, five additional mosques opened in close proximity to Parkchester and attracted ever-increasing numbers of worshippers to their five-time-daily and extended Friday prayer services. All of these mosques are Sunni and multinational, but with Bangladeshi pluralities, and each started out in rented or purchased private houses or even their basements.[6]

While as of the late 2010s, Parkchester Jame Masjid, the first Muslim house of worship on the scene, remains the largest mosque servicing the neighborhood, the Baitul Aman Islamic Center on

Newbold Avenue—situated a few blocks southeast of Parkchester—was well on the way in constructing a four-story, ten-thousand-square-foot edifice, with plans to build four more stories if need be, that could potentially hold three thousand worshippers every Friday. Typically, this institution started out in 1994 in a private house and moved to the other side of Newbold Avenue fifteen years later with a congregation made up of Bangladeshis, Indians, Pakistanis, Guyanese, and a large cohort of Yemenis, growing from its initial 150 Friday worshippers to 500 as of 2017, who avail themselves of both religious services and educational activities for adults and children. Its worship leader, Imam Mohammed Uddin, is well positioned to minister to his diverse group of followers, speaking no less than six languages, including Farsi, for the small number of Iranian worshippers.[7]

The Hindu presence began in 1993 when Guyanese immigrant and pundit (religious leader) Vishnu Sukul, with the help of a local realtor and fellow Hindu, Joe Ramharack, opened a temple in the basement of a private house for twenty worshippers. Two years later, with his followers growing significantly, the Vishnu Mandir house of worship moved to more permanent quarters on Fteley Avenue, on the outskirts of Parkchester. Five years later, in 2000, a disagreement within the ranks over Sukul's leadership prompted some dissidents to break with the pundit and begin worshipping again in a basement temple on Nereid Avenue in the northeast of the Bronx. Many in the breakaway group returned to Parkchester in 2003 and established the sizable Shri Vishnu Mandir temple on Newbold Avenue, several hundred feet from the well-established Fourth Presbyterian Church and around the corner from a mosque, joining yet another interfaith row.[8]

In 2015, a group of Bangladeshi Hindus, a minority among their nationality in Parkchester where most from their country are Muslim, began the process of establishing their own distinctive

FIGURE 9.2. Shri Vishnu Mandir temple, summer 2018. Courtesy of the Yeshiva University Office of Communications and Public Affairs.

religious and cultural institution on Olmstead Avenue, around the corner from Shri Vishnu Mandir. Previously, organizational leaders like Dev Podder, an accountant by profession, who moved into the Bronx neighborhood in 2005 after living for a while in a Bangladeshi enclave in Jackson Heights, Queens, would pray with his family either in Parkchester's Guyanese Hindu temple or travel back to Queens for services among his own ethnic-national group. But in early 2017, with the financial assistance of the Bronx Puja Committee, Podder and his associates on the executive committee purchased a small two-story, pink-shuttered private house for the congregation's forty-some members. Their plan was to use the first floor for services and the upstairs for an apartment for a full-time pundit whom they hoped to engage. Although the executive committee had yet to grant an official name to their religious services, in October 2017, again with the help of the Bronx Puja Committee, a Sree Sree Shyama Puja and Diwali festival was held within the unfinished premises.[9]

Beyond their carved-out places on renewed interfaith rows, South Asian newcomers also became active participants in the Parkchester area's real estate activities as they contributed a very apparent entrepreneurial spirit to the neighborhood. Among the world's worth of post-1970s immigrants to the United States, South Asians have been credited with bringing to their new homes an impressive level of "Westernized education" that had not led to highly gainful employment in their home countries but which provided them with a high degree of business acumen that assisted them in quickly rising economically in America. Indians and Bangladeshis in particular brought their abilities to Parkchester, taking advantages of opportunities to own and manage units for themselves, their fellow South Asians, and others, even as they grappled with the difficulties of the late Helmsley and early CPC years.[10]

One such entrepreneurial Indian American, Kumar Kancherla, known in the community as "K.K.," had become a recognized neighborhood presence by 1987, though he and his family had lived in Parkchester for only a short time. Kancherla arrived in the United States in 1985 after earning a degree in electrical engineering. After an initial stay in New Jersey with his brother, a physician, who had come to America a decade earlier, he secured a job in his field in Texas. A year later, when that position did not work out, he took an apartment on Gleason Avenue, east of Parkchester, with plans to return to his home country. As he found what he described as "odd jobs" in his profession and his financial position rapidly improved, he and his wife decided to stay in the country and neighborhood, renting and then buying an apartment in Parkchester. Not fully cognizant of all that was wrong with the area during the Helmsley era, his family soon concluded that they "had made the worst mistake possible." After reprimanding Amit Sikdar, Helmsley's man on the scene, and hearing that improvements were not in the offing, the Kancherlas moved out in 1987 but retained ownership of their leaking apartment. Keen to protect their investment, K.K. became a board member, and, as previously noted, was there during the battles over the arrival of the CPC, allied with Michael Lappin. Indeed, he weathered complaints from resident owners who resented someone who was now not an apartment dweller having such a major say in the community's future. In the years that followed, which saw successful rehabilitation efforts all over Parkchester, K.K. acquired additional units while working in his chosen profession as an electrical engineer until his retirement in 2008. As late as 2017, K-Pro Realty and Management Inc. was still very active in the sales, rentals, and management of its close to sixty units all across the neighborhood.[11]

Profiled in a Bronx weekly as "immigrants living [the] American dream," Bangladeshis Saleh (Sal) Uddin and Shariful (Sharif) Islam entered the Parkchester real estate business in 2002, almost a generation after K.K, and other South Asians, started buying and renting. It was a propitious time, with the rehabilitation of the neighborhood well underway. Uddin had come to the United States in 1991 with a degree in public administration and settled initially in Woodside, Queens. During his first decade in America, he worked as a salesman-consultant and eventually as a district manager for Vitamin Shoppe, a pharmaceutical chain. Though advancing in the company and saving his money, he chafed at his inability to make a really substantial living as an employee. He was meanwhile aware of the possibilities in local real estate and the recent history of Parkchester, having rented an upstairs apartment from a fellow Bangladeshi on Virginia Avenue not far from the complex. He joined Shariful Islam in a start-up firm and began buying and renting to fellow Bangladeshis and members of other nationalities who were seeking residency in the affordable neighborhood.

Islam had come to the U.S. in 1990 and earned a business degree from Baruch College. While he pursued higher education, Islam worked as a waiter in Manhattan restaurants. Together, Uddin and Islam demonstrated their commitment to the ethnically diversified neighborhood when they bought condominiums in Parkchester—Islam in 2004, Uddin a year later. In 2012, Islam purchased a home on Gleason Avenue; as of 2017, Uddin and his family still resided in Parkchester and their operation, Parkchester Bronx Reality, Inc., was flourishing.[12]

While the substantial improvements in the quality of life and availability of services benefited the diverse new immigrant and now more senior African American and Latino minority groups who, at the start of the new millennium, together predominated in Parkchester, the changes for the better came at least a generation after almost its entire Jewish population had aged out of the community. At the Young Israel of Parkchester, the decline already evident in the early 1970s accelerated in the two decades that followed. The calls for minyan maintenance became plaintive cries as early as the spring of 1983, when, for example, the synagogue president sent "An Emergency Open Letter" to the congregation warning that if volunteers did not step up, "we will have to abandon the daily minyan and have services just for Shabbos." For Fred Kutner, it was a source of great humiliation that "the rabbi makes the same plea for you men to help. Every night he makes personal phone calls asking for volunteers for the following morning. He could write a book about the excuses and insults."[13]

Just a few years earlier, from 1979 to 1981, there was some hope that membership numbers might revive due to the influx of Jewish immigrants from the Soviet Union. As a charter constituent organization of the Parkchester-Unionport Jewish Community Council, founded in 1978 with "the ultimate goal of stabilization of the Jewish community," the YIP added to its mission the intention "to greet and serve as hosts to Russian-Jewish immigrants," with the aspiration of "their becoming our neighbors in Parkchester and become part of our Jewish community." Toward the dual ends of fulfilling the Jewish commandment to help newcomers, while surely seeking to replenish their own congregation, synagogue leaders also reached out to the New York Association for New Americans, promoting their neighborhood as a welcoming destination. In 1980, the YIP organized a monthly social club with the Friends of Refugees of Eastern Europe at which "lectures [were] given in Russian with Torah content." Observant congregants were invited to "adopt" Russian families and to "become their spiritual mentors." That same year, the congregation sponsored Passover seders for this new potential Jewish community cohort. In the end, while the YIP would be proud that due to its influence a few children of immigrants ended up being enrolled in yeshivas, religious participation was not high on most of these immigrant families' agendas. While Parkchester in the 1980s was an acceptable place to settle, and for a brief period a decade later newcomers to Parkchester from the Soviet Union—including both Russian Jews and non-Jews—even outnumbered the Dominicans, Bangladeshis, and Filipinos, synagogue life was neither a need nor an attraction for Russian Jews. Besides which, by that time, the YIP did not have sufficient resources to help them out.[14]

Indeed, throughout the 1970s and 1980s, presidents of the shul publicly bemoaned the decline of the synagogue's membership and revenue sources. Among the concerned lay leaders was Bernard Horowitz, who served as president from 1976 to 1979. Julius and Irene's second son stayed in the neighborhood with his growing family—his wife, Roberta, was the daughter of another prominent YIP family—largely out of allegiance to his widowed mother at a time when his siblings, cousins, and other so-called YIP "whiz kids" of the 1950s–1960s were moving out. During his administration, he was proud that the congregation had joined with the Jewish Association for Services for the Aging in providing Jewish education for "our Senior Citizens" and that they had established a "mailgram bank" which enlisted "100 members and friends to make our views [in support of Israel] known in Washington." Along these same lines, his still-spry mother continued to deliver informative talks about the Jewish state to the members of the Hadassah (the women's Zionist organization) that met regularly at the synagogue. But Bernard Horowitz admitted that "my administration has been unable to halt the erosion of our financial picture. Our loss in membership through death and to retirement villages has not been offset by any influx of new members. Skyrocketing costs have not been matched by new revenues. The situation is serious." While he trusted that the "new administration will continue to seek solutions to this problem," there was no ready remedy at hand.[15]

In the years to come, Bernard Horowitz would continue to assist the congregation of his youth and early adulthood. But beginning in 1981, he would do so primarily from his new home in Riverdale. He and Roberta moved because "there were simply few other Jewish children around with whom their kids could play and few Jewish adults with whom to socialize." For many years thereafter, Horowitz would return on the High Holidays to be the chief cantor. In 1985, Kalman Winkler, a congregational founder and long-time lay officiant, and his wife retired to West Orange, New Jersey. Horowitz understood that the YIP could not hire a salaried cantor, and he would not leave his mother and her contemporaries bereft. In addition to Horowitz's profound commitment to the old shul, there was some financial support from former members, young and old, who lived in the city or in Florida. Indeed, the synagogue often sent out its bulletin and letters with requests for donations to which alumni, who harbored fond memories of what the YIP had meant to them, responded affirmatively.[16]

Congregational continuity suffered another blow in April 1984 when, after more than a quarter century of service, Rabbi Maurice L. Schwartz left his Parkchester pulpit. In tendering his resignation to assume a post in Pelham Parkway, he explained that "the recent changes in the community have put undue pressure upon me" and with "a vibrant synagogue in a Jewish community seeking spiritual leadership offering me a challenge," he could not refuse. According to his son Hayim, himself a rabbi who by then lived in Queens, Rabbi Maurice L. Schwartz left because "he believed that the basis of the shul is the daily minyan. Once the shul can no longer maintain the daily minyan, then the shul is not as viable as before."[17]

Six months after Schwartz's departure, the fading congregation obtained some temporary relief on the minyan issue when the YIP and the neighboring Beth Jacob Congregation, faced with the same dilemma of declining membership, decided to join together for weekday services, with worshippers attending their "respective synagogues for Friday night, Saturday and Sunday morning services" where a prayer quorum was still assured. This "merger," as it was then called, foreshowed the "unification" of the two shuls when Beth Jacob, whose physical plant was in total disarray and with almost no money in its account, sold its building to the Iglesia Bautista Cristiana de Soundview and joined up with the YIP.[18]

The shut-down shul's Rabbi Seymour Schwartz, Maurice's younger brother, known in Parkchester circles for his work as an organizer of the Thursday Community Walk of the 1970s, assumed the pulpit of the conjoined synagogues. With YIP coffers ever dwindling, he maintained a second job as a public school administrator in the Bronx. But he could do little to stem the tide of the actuarial decline of his Jewish community. In 2001, the YIP sold its building to the Neighborhood Enhancement and Training Center for $43,000 with the provision that the congregation would be allowed to use its half-century-old sanctuary for another two years. In 2015, the

Virginia Avenue building became the Parkchester Islamic Center—the mosque had been established two years earlier just around the corner in a private home owned by a Bangladeshi worshipper.[19]

To help keep the synagogue afloat, a YIP alumnus and his wife had bought one of the Parkchester shul's Torah scrolls, which they rededicated at the Hebrew Institute of Riverdale. With the proceeds from the sale and other contributions, a storefront operation was opened on White Plains Road, almost equidistant from where Beth Jacob and the YIP were previously located. For a number of years, with the help of several Yeshiva University students who walked a few miles every Saturday from their Washington Heights dormitories, a minyan was maintained for the elderly YIP remnant and others who once prayed in now-defunct congregations situated outside of the neighborhood.

The last years of the congregation were not without some legal controversy. When the YIP sold its Virginia Avenue home, the National Council of Young Israel claimed that since the shul was a constituent member, it was subject to its protocols: "if a branch is dissolved or expelled, all its assets, both personal and real shall become property of the Organization." However, with Bernard Horowitz returning as president to lead the shul's defense and protect the interests of his mother and her friends, the Bronx County Supreme Court found in the local congregation's favor. In dismissing the suit, Judge Betty Owen effectively held that the ongoing presence of the storefront on White Plains Road meant that the YIP was still alive and thus entitled to the sale proceeds.[20]

In 2007, time and funds seemingly had run out for the bare-bones congregation. The congregational treasurer, seventy-eight-year-old Leon Bleckman, wrote a plaintive letter, addressed simply to "Chabad 770 Eastern Parkway," asking for last-ditch assistance. The Hasidic group had earned a worldwide reputation for its outreach efforts, most notably in establishing religious community life in areas where previously co-religionists had no synagogues or other basic forms of Jewish life. Now they were asked to save a dying community that once had stood tall. Chabad responded positively to the request. Four emissaries appeared at what was to be the farewell service at the storefront to declare that their movement was ready to adopt the elderly congregants. Bleckman declared their arrival to be nothing less than a "miracle; like the messiah coming down from heaven." By that time, a Jewish communal organization had estimated that the average age of Jews in the entire Unionport-Soundview and Parkchester area was 78.1—almost exactly Bleckman's age. In any event, the YIP was renamed Bais Menachem of Parkchester, in honor of the Lubavitcher Rebbe Menachem Mendel Schneerson, Chabad's late spiritual leader.

Also extending a helping hand, Sheik Moussa Drammeh, leader of Masjid Al-Iman Mosque, situated a block south of Parkchester, stepped up with an offer of assistance late in 2011 that drew significant media attention. During an era when Muslims were routinely characterized as hostile to American values, let alone to Judaism, the imam was widely applauded for offering room in his house of worship to Bais Menachem. To some extent, Drammeh's largesse was friendly payback for the help Bleckmen and the YIP seniors had given the Islamic community in the neighborhood when, several years earlier, the Jews had organized a clothing drive for indigent Muslim families. Drammeh was also mindful that on September 11, 2001, St. Helena's Church first provided space for a school under the auspices of the Islamic Cultural Center of North America. For Patricia Tomasulo, a Catholic and a Democratic precinct captain in Parkchester, this coming together of faith communities was "so unique ... nowhere in the world would Jews and Muslims be meeting under the same roof." Hyperbole aside, her estimation of this relationship suggested that the neighborhood tradition of the interfaith street had survived the aging of one religious group and the emergence of others.

Chabad's young rabbis also earned substantial street credibility for trekking by foot some fifteen miles from their homes in Crown Heights every Saturday to keep the minyan going. As highly observant Orthodox Jews, they were prohibited from driving or riding the subway to the Bronx on the Sabbath. In 2012, Drammeh made their efforts appreciably easier when he provided two of the travelers with sleeping quarters in his center. Meanwhile, a married Chabad couple, Rabbi Meir and Hana Kabakow, rented a room in a motel only a mile from the mosque-qua-synagogue. Eventually, this family on a mission drew even closer when they rented an apartment a block from the sanctuary. Chabad was also on the scene for Purim and Hanukkah parties and commemorations of other special days in the Jewish calendar. These minor religious festivals drew larger crowds than Sabbath and High Holiday services since the emissaries were permitted under Jewish law to drive around the neighborhood to pick up the very elderly Jews who were unable to walk even the few blocks to the house of worship.

In 2013, the Chabad-Muslim efforts gained a degree of wider Jewish communal recognition, when the Jewish Community Relations Council negotiated a "refurbishment . . . Unity Grant from the city." Subsequently, Drammeh's center began partnering with Congregation Tehilla of Riverdale, the Riverdale YMHA, and that West Bronx neighborhood's Kinneret Day School in an interfaith "Synagogue in the Mosque Project," an initiative still active as of 2017. Some of the Riverdale youngsters who helped clean up the East Bronx locale, among other educational activities, were the children of former Parkchester residents. These efforts caused Bleckmen to assert "there are still Jews in Parkchester, but they don't know we have a synagogue. We need to get the word out." He also dreamed that, with funding, there could be a revival of Jewish life in Parkchester. He said, "Hopefully, someday we could have a building with a dormitory that could fit about forty students who'd want to sit and learn. They could have a study hall here. We could have a mikveh."

In the summer of 2017, Chabad was still a minimal presence in Parkchester, ministering to barely a handful of Sabbath worshippers complemented with Chabad people. The outreach organization was working without the encouragement, hopes, and prayers of Leon Bleckman, who had died that February. In the fall, due to the burden of "finances and expenses to maintain the size of their building," the mosque and its school closed their doors, at least temporarily. A "delinquent tax debt" led to the sale of the property at a public auction. The Drammehs' prayer that a "benefactor" would step up did not materialize. As of fall 2018, while maintaining an office near Parkchester and publishing a newsletter called *Parkchester Times*, Drammeh and his wife, Sharina, were in the process of establishing a "temporary" mosque in Co-op City, hopeful still of remaining a force for good within the East Bronx neighborhood. In Sheik's words, they were "not finished in the neighborhood" and were still determined through their efforts to offer "a counternarrative" to the negative depictions of Muslims in America and indeed worldwide.[21]

Temple Emanuel stalwarts Herbert and Miriam Korman were Bernard Horowitz's and, later on, Leon Bleckman's counterparts in the efforts to stave off the demise of Parkchester's other signature synagogue. Bronx-raised Herbert, a corporate controller, and Miriam, who had focused on raising their two children and then become a school aide, moved to the neighborhood in 1948, four years after Miriam's parents had relocated there from Elder Avenue, a few miles away. In 1955, with Jay and Iris approaching bar and bat mitzvah ages, the couple affiliated with the Conservative synagogue and enrolled their youngsters in its then large Hebrew school. In due course, they both assumed lay leadership positions. He was a member of the board of trustees and also participated with the congregation's brotherhood. She was deeply involved with the sisterhood and the Women's League for Conservative Judaism. They were thus on the scene when "it was busy and crowded . . . a large middle-class synagogue with lots of school teachers . . . open to everyone." It boasted of "clubs for the women and men" and dealt with the joyous dilemma of the massive number of twelve- and thirteen-years-olds in the Hebrew school by scheduling multiple bar mitzvahs on the same Sabbath. And sadly, for the Kormans, they watched the decline of membership beginning in the 1970s. For Herbert, "the Cross Bronx Expressway and Co-op City killed the neighborhood. People left Parkchester because Co-op City was new. It had new furniture and air conditioning."[22]

Signifying the lack of future viability of Jewish life in Parkchester, in 1976 Temple Emanuel's last full-time rabbi, J. Leonard Romm, left the community for a position at the Baldwin Jewish Center on Long Island. By the time he left after a four-year stint right out of rabbinical school, there were only "100 individuals, mostly elderly, in the congregation." Rabbi Romm felt that he was ministering to his "grandparents" even as he was grateful that they "doted on his two children," born on West Avenue in Parkchester.

A few of the younger members who lived in Co-op City retained an allegiance to the synagogue. They sent their children to the Hebrew school, where Romm was one of the two instructors. Others returned from their new neighborhood to Parkchester on the High Holidays. One North Bronx resident, who enjoyed serving as a cantor, frequented the shul on many Sabbaths and was offered the opportunity to lead the prayers. By the 1970s, Temple Emanuel could not afford a full-time professional cantor and its lay choir was no more.[23]

In the decades after Romm moved on, some twenty rabbinical students from the Jewish Theological Seminary of America ministered to the remaining synagogue members before they were ordained and called to pulpits on Long Island, other U.S. locales, Canada, and Israel. Romm's younger brother, Edward, was the first to assume the temporary post before his career took him to Canada and ultimately to Israel. In 2009, Jesse Olitzky, the penultimate rabbi-in-training in Parkchester, took over the congregation for one and a half years, where on the best of Saturdays some "thirty to thirty-five people" might attend services. There was no chance of conducting Friday night services since the elderly members were not venturing out after dark. On the High Holidays, approximately sixty "extended families" drove in to accompany their parents and grandparents. The holiday return to the old synagogue was by then an established tradition among these Jewish former Parkchesterites. They sat in a sanctuary that once held hundreds of worshippers. Much like the Chabad contingent, Olitzky and his wife lived a Spartan existence during their Sabbath labors. The erstwhile full-time rabbi's study became their bedroom and the former secretary's office was their dining area. For a while, during the week, Olitzky conducted a Bible study class for a few members who also turned out for a hot lunch in the synagogue that a Jewish "meals on wheels" operation provided. Upon ordination, Olitzky became the spiritual leader of the Jacksonville (Florida) Jewish Center and as of 2017 was the rabbi of Congregation Beth El in South Orange, New Jersey.

During this long good-bye of three decades for Temple Emanuel, the Kormans remained committed to the place that they called "their second home." Over the years, additional responsibilities devolved upon the couple as those who shared the pews with them passed on. In the 21st century, Miriam became president of a congregation that no longer held formal synagogue meetings. Herbert was its one-man ritual committee. They sank some of their own money into the failing operation and leased space to a senior center for needed income. In 2008, the Bronx Jewish Community Council assumed ownership of the synagogue, providing financial help for a while prior to the eventual sale in 2011 of the Benedict Street building to the Bronx Charter School of Excellence. The final Temple Emanuel service took place on Yom Kippur 2011.

In the very last days of the Conservative synagogue, the emissaries of Bais Menachem reached out in an "informal recruiting effort." They were hopeful, at least, to add some men to their minyan since their own prayer quorum was also often in doubt. But the remnant of Temple Emanuel did not take up the offer, despite the emolument of a hot Sabbath lunch. The extra blocks to be walked from their Parkchester homes were too arduous for the elderly. And, at least for the Kormans, there was a residual loyalty to the synagogue of their youth and now of their old age. About a week after Temple Emanuel closed, a reader of an online article about the denouement, who apparently grew up in the congregation and had long since moved away, saw things in an even darker light, writing in a comment that "it is sad that the remaining members . . . are boycotting the new Bais Menachem synagogue." In his view, undeniably referring to the Kormans, "Solidarity was never their outstanding quality. Now that Mr. Korman has passed away at the age of 90, let us pray that the Jewish community, which has so dwindled, will unite." But by that time, there were hardly any Jews around to come together.[24]

During this period, Parkchester's churches continued to service the parishioners of their several denominations. But the men and women in the pews and choruses were racially and ethnically different from the original worshippers, reflecting the demographic shifts in the neighborhood that had begun in the 1970s. By the early decades of the 21st century, African Americans, Africans, Latinos, Afro-Caribbeans, and a few Asians predominated in Christian faith communities, where they shared neighborhood religious life with the multiplying Muslim mosques and Hindu temples. Like the Jews who aged out or left their synagogues behind, white Protestants and Catholics were rarely to be seen in Parkchester's houses of worship. Nonetheless, one of the issues that sometimes disquieted congregations was that, ironically, of integration. While the outside world might observe that the worshippers were clearly all people of color, culturally they were quite diverse. Bringing them together in communities of faith was a sensitive task, a fact not lost on the area's religious leaders.

The Fourth Presbyterian Church actively embraced diversity in pursuit of what its pastors and laity called its "poly-racial mission." Though never one of the largest denominations in a neighborhood that was overwhelmingly Catholic and had more Jews than Protestants when it was all white, it had still claimed, for instance, some eleven hundred members in 1958. Some fifteen years later, when the first black members joined—a family from Antigua—the white constituency was in steep decline. In the decade that followed, as most of the remaining Italian Americans, German Americans, Hungarians, Scots, English, Canadians, and white Puerto Ricans passed away or moved out of the area, not only did Afro-Caribbeans and African Americans replace them, but the church also attracted worshippers who had emigrated from Nigeria, Hong Kong, and the Philippines.

In 1982, armed with a redevelopment grant from the national Presbyterian Church that funded the hiring of its new minister, Rev. Robert Foltz-Morrison, the congregation redoubled efforts already underway to build on its new multi-racial identity. Foltz-Morrison, a recent graduate of Princeton Theological Seminary, arrived with a proud calling card of three years of "field work in urban settings" and the desire to be engaged in "urban ministry." Settling with his family at 1460 Unionport Road, he was reminded daily of how diversified Parkchester was. Next door was an "old Irish women."

Across the hall was a Portuguese family. Near the elevator lived Sri Lankans. Puerto Ricans were also there along with an "Indian couple," and at the end of the floor was an "older German woman." Foltz-Morrison invited his neighbors to his church, but none took up the offer. If they were Christians, they were likely members of Catholic, Pentecostal, or Assembly of God churches in the vicinity of Parkchester. Still, members of all these ethnicities and more would appear for services, and Foltz-Morrison was sure to "follow up with home visitations" to grow his flock.[25]

Anxious that Fourth Presbyterian respect the spiritual needs of his new majority of non-whites while keeping his older Parkchesterites comfortable, on alternate weeks he would either tweak the Sunday liturgy and practices, making them "less formal and more casual" to be "representative of the culture of the new group," or conduct services in the classic style to head off "grumbling" from oldsters in the pews.

Foltz-Morrison also oversaw significant shifts in the lay leadership hierarchy, integrating those who controlled the church's purse strings. One of the new board members, a native of Antigua, who became an important figure as congregational treasurer, assumed his post with a most impressive resume. In his day job, he was a vice president at Manufacturers Hanover Trust. Though the church's diverse members seemed comfortable with each other, the congregation did not grow exponentially. Still, by the time Foltz-Morrison left for a pulpit in the Midwest, the number of regular attendees at Sunday devotions had risen from between twenty and thirty-five in 1982 to some seventy.[26]

Recent decades have witnessed a decline in worshippers at the church due both to the passing of its oldest white members and a second-generation brain drain from among its families of color. As of September 2017, Rev. Clark Bradley, who had served since 1995, counted approximately forty-five regular Sunday communicants, remaining members of what he has characterized as his "transitional neighborhood." Much like Parkchester's Jewish story, many of the high-achieving children and grandchildren of Christian immigrants, and of the Latinos and African Americans who moved from Harlem and the South Bronx in the 1970s–1980s, are pursuing their professional careers in suburbia or more gentrified parts of Gotham. Those Presbyterians who remain continue to be a minority faith community. When Rev. Clark Bradley attends a community clergy meeting, he sometimes sits with more imams than priests and ministers.[27]

By the time Rev. Hilary Gaston assumed the pulpit of the Parkchester Baptist Church in 1990, the congregation had already been, for a decade or more, overwhelmingly African American, Afro-Caribbean, and Latino. Like the Presbyterians and the Jews, most of the white worshippers either had died or left the neighborhood in the 1970s. As the first minister of color to serve the church, Gaston set out to "establish a special immigration ministry for Caribbean and West Indian members." Outside of the sanctuary, he showed a particular concern in helping newcomers to America with their immigration issues. Some of the remaining white worshippers were less than comfortable with a black man at the congregation's helm. A few of these elderly folks gravitated to the Presbyterian Church only to have Rev. Foltz-Morrison question their devotion to his particular denominational doctrine even as he was willing to have them worship in his sanctuary. Trying to stay clear of "racial antipathies," and after talking with Rev. Gaston, Foltz-Morrison suggested to those who approached him that they look for an alternate Baptist church.

Gaston's leadership initially also seemed strange to some of his Caribbean parishioners who back home had never been in a church with a black minister. Ultimately, however, the integration issue that most challenged Gaston was bringing his African American and black immigrant newcomers together in "developing a sense of real community within a highly diverse flock." To that end, he, for example, transformed African American history month into a multicultural celebration not only of the story of blacks in America but also the island heritages of those who had recently arrived. In the eleven years of Gaston's Bronx ministry, due also in part to his personal visits to new Parkchester families who were used to traveling back to churches in places like Harlem, a congregation that numbered some 75 families when he arrived, with about 40 regular attendees at Sunday service, grew to a congregation of 350 families, with close to 275 in the pews on Sunday.[28]

In 2005, Rev. Dr. Laura B. Sinclair assumed the Parkchester Baptist pulpit. By that point, Gaston had risen to become president of the New York Theological Seminary. During her ten-year tenure, Sinclair continued her predecessor's efforts to bring together African American, Latino, and Afro-Caribbean members with their many differing backgrounds. There were no longer any white members of her flock. The service was sure to use Caribbean music, while some Latino worshippers recited scriptural readings in Spanish. The sermon was in English. Church suppers and other repasts included the foods of several cultures. In Sinclair's early years, there was nonetheless a slight decline in church membership and attendance. Fewer than two hundred worshippers showed up regularly and often the balcony was half-filled. To counteract dissociation, the clergy and lay leadership kept after those who were frequently absent from devotions, sending them postcards imploring their attendance. If no favorable response was forthcoming, the uninterested were removed from church rolls. As of 2017, under the leadership of Rev. Dr. Felicia Smith, the church remained vibrant. Some 150 men and women were attending on a week-in and week-out basis with both long-time, older members and younger folks in the pews. Parkchester Baptists thus continued to be a significant religious presence in Parkchester and its environs.[29]

Much like their sister Baptist Protestant congregation, during the last decades of the 20th century Parkchester's St. Paul's Lutheran Church witnessed profound ethnic and racial transitions, endured some static over changes in ministerial leadership, and saw those in charge make efforts to meld the cultures of their new majorities into its worship services. When African American Evelyn McCatty moved to the Bronx community in 1979 from Staten Island, she became one of the few blacks to attend the church. An informal 1974 survey of the congregation had revealed that fewer than ten out of three hundred member families were black. McCatty has recalled that when she affiliated some five years later, she was met "with caution" by older white members who "had to adjust" to the racial changes that soon came to the Lutheran church. By 1984, the faces in the pews had changed significantly as close to 30 percent of the member families were now people of color. As demographic shifts continued, a 2011 church census of "active participants in the life of the congregation" showed that of the 160 adults and children who took part in religious activities, 74 were African American, 36 were either African or African Caribbean, 34 were Asian, 9 were Latino, and only 7 were white.[30]

As St. Paul's increasingly ministered to non-white families, there was a call from the pews and several members of the lay congregational council for a black pastor. In 1995, African American Rev. James Thomas assumed the post, but not without some controversy, reminiscent of what had transpired at Parkchester Baptist when Hilary Gaston ascended to the pulpit. Approximately 40 percent of St. Paul's members were still white as of 1995. Most were elderly. A significant percentage of the church lay council was also white and many of those members were not comfortable with a black minister. Joining them were Afro-Caribbean congregants who had been part of a religious culture back home where the man at the altar had always been white. When African American worshippers questioned their attitude, the response was "We are not yet ready." Some of the more outspoken American blacks in the council deliberations retorted: "When will you be ready?" Within this religious community, congregants had to learn to get along despite clashing visions of what their leadership should look like. Ultimately Rev. Thomas was elected and served in Parkchester until 2009, when he assumed an academic post at the Lutheran Theological Southern University in South Carolina.[31]

Thomas's successor, Rev. Fernando Otero, the church's first Latino minister, has redoubled efforts to mesh his "multicultural" group of African, African American, Guyanese, and a few Latino congregants "into a cohesive faith community." Like other churches, St. Paul's has relied upon music, sensitive to different tempos for prayers and often including "calypso beats" to bridge cultural differences for the approximately hundred and ten regular worshippers who attended services and bible classes on Virginia Avenue.[32]

Among Parkchester's Catholics, St. Helena's, a predominantly Irish American and all-white church in its 1950s and early 1960s heyday, could boast back then of some four thousand "parishioners at a typical Sunday mass." As late as the 1970s, when the first persons of color affiliated with the congregation, some twenty-five hundred worshippers were still showing up regularly. At Christmas and Easter, several masses had to be celebrated to accommodate the thirty-five hundred communicants who wanted to pray and hear the homilies. Back then, Father Joseph J. O'Shea recalled in 2002: "To get a seat at midnight Mass, you had to show up at 11 p.m." However, in the decades to come, according to the priest, who had been serving at St. Helena's since 1942, "most of the young [white] folks" left. They went to the country"— meaning Long Island and New Jersey.[33]

Thomas Derivan, who followed O'Shea as lead priest, fostered his ministry's dual mission as continuing to service what he called his "pioneer souls" while swinging the church's doors wide open to the Latinos, Africans, African Americans, and "some Asians" who by the 1990s constituted 75 percent of his flock. To that end, in the early 1980s, he had instituted a "multicultural mass" with children from various nationalities and traditions, "including some Hindu kids and other non-Catholics, dressed in the clothes of their places of origin," taking part in the devotions. To head off any naysaying among the primarily elderly white faithful about this shift, Derivan constantly preached that instigation of "racial discord was a cardinal sin." In 1985, St. Helena's instituted its first Spanish-language Mass for a community that now included worshippers from "14 national groups." By the beginning of the 21st century, a 4 a.m. celebration of the Feast of Our Lady of Guadalupe, an observance particularly venerated by Latinos in the pews, had become an important date on the church calendar. In recent years, enrollment figures at its parochial school evidence the reality that St. Helena's future resides in the souls of non-whites. A "student racial/ethnic origin" census conducted for the 2015-2016 academic year revealed that 93 percent of pupils were categorized as "black or African American, Hispanic or Latino," 5 percent were Asian, and only 2.6 percent were white—seven Caucasian students in total.[34]

When Msgr. John Graham assumed the pulpit at St. Raymond's in 2004, the issue of white resistance to people of color had long since passed. At that juncture, the majority of worshippers were Latino, and a Spanish-language Mass had already been instituted. Many of the congregants were second-generation Parkchesterites, while the church serviced immigrant worshippers from some forty different countries. As with the other houses of worship in the area, the remaining whites, who constituted approximately 15 percent of communicants, were elderly men and women, described by Msgr. Graham as "long-time residents with no interest in leaving . . . happy with what the community had to offer." Much like what Derivan had done at St. Helena's, to bring the disparate Third World groups in his congregation together, Graham endeavored to "celebrate ethnicity" by defining Black History Month as more than just an American historical commemoration. He added West African dance to the Mass—hardly a style of worship that would be seen in an "Irish church"—and countenanced religious societies attuned to the South American and Mexican traditions that his congregants had brought to the neighborhood. During Graham's tenure, St. Raymond's also connected with Bangladeshi and Pakistani immigrants who were majority non-Catholic but who turned to the church's school for the quality education that it provided their youngsters. St. Raymond's new profile was complete in 2016, when Father James Cruz, who as a boy had attended St. Raymond's High School, became the church's first Latino pastor.[35]

FIGURE 10.1. Zaro's Family Bakery, back in the neighborhood, summer 2018. Courtesy of the Yeshiva Office of Communications and Public Affairs.

10

AS A BRONX NEIGHBORHOOD
APPROACHES EIGHTY

I N OCTOBER 2016, A DECADE SINCE ITS LAST LOOK-SEE, a real estate correspondent for the *New York Times* revisited life in Parkchester.[1] Vera Haller determined that the "vibe" on the neighborhood's streets was decidedly upbeat, with much of what had always made the area attractive still very much in play. For her, "the heart of Parkchester lies in . . . Metropolitan Oval, where residents relax on benches as they gaze at the water-spouting nymphs in the plaza's central fountain." There, she continued, "children ride scooters and parents push babies in strollers. A bulletin board in the Oval displays flyers for adult exercise classes and an international potluck Thanksgiving dinner at the Boys and Girls Club. There are also art classes, salsa dancing and knitting, among other activities." For the athletically inclined, "the recreational facilities include playgrounds, a baseball field and basketball and handball courts." Commuting to and from work in midtown Manhattan, she reported, took, as in the past, but thirty-five minutes via subway. The express buses went into and out of the "city" in about an hour. And there was serious talk that Metro-North was planning a Parkchester stop. Interviewee Lara Miranda, an administrator at Hunter College, said, "Coming home around 5, I like seeing all these people, working people, leaving the train and going home to care for their kids." Turning attention to the commercial side of the street, Haller observed that Macy's still anchored Metropolitan Avenue, with a Starbucks situated a few steps south of that famous emporium and an Applebee's one block to the north.[2]

Had Haller returned to Metropolitan Avenue just four months later, in January 2017, she would have learned that local shoppers were enormously pleased that their Macy's branch was not slated to be shut down, even as the famous chain was cutting back all over the country. At that point, some sixty-eight stores, mostly in suburban malls, were scheduled to close due to "a disappointing holiday shopping season." Several months later, the number of operations on the termination list rose to 100. Although Parkchesterites, like other Americans, were increasingly shopping online, the neighborhood retail anchor was still holding strong.[3]

There was similar good news in August 2017, when Bronx borough president Ruben Diaz Jr. happily announced that Zaro's, the "iconic Bronx bakery," would reopen only two storefronts down from its original spot across from Hugh J. Grant Circle. Two years earlier, after close to fifty years of service in the neighborhood, due to a dispute over the lease, its space had been rented to a Boston Market. Residents enthused about the return of Zaro's hoped the move would be a harbinger of the return of another Parkchester institution of long-standing that recently had shut its doors. In 2014, their Loew's American movie theater had been replaced by a Marshalls low-cost department store. Sara Serrano Harris emoted: "First Zaro, hopefully the movie theater next." Ria Cee agreed: "The Parkchester Movie Theatre was a community stable [*sic*: i.e., staple]. . . . [It] needs a chance to comeback as well!" However, the prospects for its return were questionable. Back in the mid-1990s, local businessman Stewart Epstein, an early and vocal supporter of the CPC, had attempted a revival of the entertainment venue, which like so much of Parkchester had fallen into disrepair. But ultimately the renovated multiplex did not generate enough box-office receipts. Meanwhile, satellite disks could be seen on the roofs of Parkchester's apartments, making it possible for residents

FIGURE 10.2. Marshalls, on the former site of the Loew's American, summer 2018. Note the preservation of one of Parkchester's emblematic art deco façades. Courtesy of the Yeshiva University Office of Communications and Public Affairs.

to watch many of their favorite films in the comfort of their homes. Still, for Robert Rodriguez, who was on the scene on East Avenue as the American was gutted to make way for Marshalls, with its passing came a palpable sense of lost community. "Losing this is a hardship," he opined. "Everyone from the Bronx used to come over here. There are a lot of memories here. A lot of relationships started here." Morton Olshan, on the other hand, believed that if so many of the people who mourned the movie theater's end had only continued to be regular patrons, it would have remained viable. But such was not the case.[4]

Meanwhile, in the demographic realm, the *Times* reporter, attuned to both continuity and change among the residents of the nearly eighty-year-old neighborhood, observed that "middle-class New Yorkers have looked to Parkchester for reasonably priced housing ever since the Metropolitan Life Insurance Company completed the complex in the early 1940s." Haller quoted a local real estate agent who remarked that, as always, "nurses, police officers, firefighters live here. They come here because they have friends or friends who already live here." A 2010 statistical study evidenced how true that statement was, revealing that contemporary Parkchesterites worked at many of the same occupations as did their Irish, Italian, and Jewish predecessors. A full one-quarter of the men and more than one-third of the women were engaged in "sales and office occupations." (Unlike studies in the 1940s, questions were asked of both genders.) Meanwhile, more than one in four men worked in "service occupations," a share slightly below that of their female counterparts. Parkchesterites were employed in both categories at significantly higher rates than their fellow New Yorkers, living as they did in what was still a solid working- and lower-middle-class community.[5]

Haller did emphasize that "what has changed over the years is the makeup of the population. Until 1968, only whites received leases." Quoting the chief executive of Parkchester's management, Haller reported that, as of 2016, "the approximately 41,000 residents include Hispanics, African Americans and South Asians." The decennial federal census of 2010 substantiates that description: As of the start of the second decade of the 21st century, more than eight out of ten residents were either black or Latino and a solid 12 percent were Asian. The specific countries of origin of the one out of eight who were immigrants from Asia cannot be ascertained. However, the numbers show that the Asian population had been on the rise since 2000, when only 6 percent of the neighborhood's residents hailed from that part of the world. As before, it is evident that the immigrants in the community, no matter what their continental or national origins, had chosen to settle in an ethnically diverse neighborhood and not in one of the enclaves elsewhere in the city where their own kind predominated. Michael de los Santos, thirty-two, a porter for a residential building in Tribeca and his wife, Andelkyz, thirty-three, a teacher, who moved into a one-bedroom condo in August 2016, reflected a typical Parkchester attitude when they told Haller: "[We] want our daughter to be raised in a place where there are different colors and cultures. A lot of people say we can't get along, but that's not the case."

Beyond these statistics, a five-minute, one-block walk from Starling Avenue to Odell Street, east of Unionport Road, long known as an ethnic food street and now bearing an official "Bangla Bazaar" signpost, also evidences the growing presence of Bangladeshis, Indians, and Pakistanis as well as Muslim West Indians and West Africans. Amid the sit-down and fast-food restaurants with various ethnic menus, halal meat stores, groceries with Arabic frontages, and a cut-rate communications operation offering cheap phone calls to relatives back home stands Jerry's Pizza, under its present ownership since 1993. This small corner store is a reminder of the time when local streets were home to Italian and Jewish delis and other ethnic European food places. The neighborhood mosques are busy with the daily prayers of the devoted and even more men and women in attendance for Friday services. By contrast to the ongoing growth of Parkchester's Third World constituency, when the government last looked in 2010, it determined that only 3 percent of the neighborhood's population was white, half what it had been ten years earlier. Although the 2010 census report did not break down the age of those surveyed, it is plausible that the community's approximately eleven hundred whites were nearly all elderly.[6]

Parkchester management offered its own take on how the neighborhood was doing in two videos that it produced around Parkchester's seventy-fifth anniversary. The first, dated December 2014 and called "Parkchester: A Great Way to Live," used words and phrases reminiscent of ones employed by Frederick Ecker back in 1939. Parkchester residents gushed about where they lived as "the jewel of the Bronx" and as "a village in the heart of the city" with "all the conveniences of the city" and readily accessible to downtown through public transportation. It was depicted as a "community where everyone knows one another . . . feels safe, a place where life is good." And, of course, "every one-, two-, and three-bedroom Parkchester home . . . has a spacious foyer, ample closets and a spacious sunny living room."[7]

Several months later, a second video appeared, co-produced by an Olshan Properties executive. The leitmotif of "Parkchester's 75th Anniversary: Thriving @75" was how the multicultural community exemplified the virtues of diversity and was a model for others to emulate. Much like De Cillia and Dalpe's seventieth-anniversary presentation, the scenes of the early years were in black and white. No mention was made of the segregated past. The glorious human mosaic of contemporary times was offered in Technicolor. The video also provided leaders of the neighborhood—each of whom have also appeared in this book—with "curtain calls" in which they extol the atmosphere of acceptance that pervades Parkchester. For example, Parkchester North's president, Lady Anne Dunbar, depicted where she lived, for four decades by then as a "microcosm of New York City" with its "mixed cultures." Former North president Harry Brown, who a decade earlier had fought long and hard for the CPC and its reha-bilitation plan, chimed in with praise for the neighborhood's diversity. Parkchester NAACP president Beverly Roberts, who as a high school student wanted very much to live in the then segregated Parkchester, spoke movingly about a place that was "an oasis in the Bronx where families of all cultures" resided, all "looking for the American dream."

Morton and Andrea Olshan also had their say about how they had been attracted to help restore Parkchester, which they attrib-uted to "the fact that it was occupied by middle-class, hard work-ing people." Reflecting on their efforts, they were well satisfied with what they had done to ensure the future of a "beautiful, safe, well-maintained community . . . for young families." Looking ahead, they suggested that Parkchester's long-existing commutation advantage over the suburbs would only grow if that talk of the creation of a Metro-North station linking the neighborhood with a line that ran from New Rochelle to Manhattan's Penn Station became a reality.[8]

It is not known how many people received copies of the "Thriving @75" video as part of the anniversary commemoration. But as of late 2017, some twenty-eight thousand had viewed the 2014 "A Great Way to Live" video via YouTube. The few who took the time to comment on what they saw tendered mixed reviews about the neighborhood scene. While some offered praise punctuated with exclamation points, others wrote that all was not totally well. One writer complained about a problem that had persisted throughout the neighborhood's eight-decade history: "I want to move there. Once you have kids, it [has] additional cost. Extra bedrooms. That sucks!" Another, more expansive critic offered what he or she characterized as a balanced view. This respondent, identified only as "joyous pro," submitted on the "pro" side: "for what it's worth, a decently pleasant community with security and the NYPD responds quickly and many of the security personnel are helpful. A community with year round activities and adolescents." On the other hand, "Parkchester management," the writer contended, had not done enough about some complaints like "brown water coming out of faucets, about staff not providing proper shoveling of walk ways during winter months . . . and in them really making a full effort to educate residents on how to recycle garbage and proper disposal of garbage. . . . About security, crime does happen here more than the management wants residents to know about."[9]

Underscoring much that was good as well as some enduring problems, the Spring/Summer 2017 edition of Parkchester South's official newsletter reminded residents that Metropolitan Oval was still very much in bloom. It was described, as always, as a perfect place "to experience a cool spring day . . . just soaking up the views and the beautiful flowers." This central spot, it was announced, would be the place to be for an Annual Health Fair in June, a Night at the Movies in July, a Summer Concert Series in July and August, and an all-day Annual Summer Fest "with food and music" on August 5. Significantly, the organ also noted that on August 1, the Oval would be the location

of the NYPD National Night Out for Crime. Some of Parkchester's oldest tenants who were on the scene in the late 1970s may well have
remembered how Rabbi Seymour Schwartz, with John Dearie's assistance, organized an after-dark street patrol when crime was the
prime topic of discussion among residents who may have sat in the
Oval by day and early evening but rarely at night. As YouTube commentator "joyous pro" suggested, crime has remained an issue in the
neighborhood. In this regard, an appended annual report from the
Parkchester Department of Public Safety reported that "property
wide for 2016 a total of 364 arrests were made. DPS issued 867 Criminal Court Summonses, 35 Environmental Control Summons, 38 Moving Violations and 2106 Parking Summonses addressing Quality of
Life issues on property." Given this unavoidable reality of city life, the
newsletter chimed in with reminders to residents to take care in not
letting in through the locked front doors or up the elevators people
who "make you feel uncomfortable." All were admonished to adhere
to the "rules and regulations of Parkchester South Condominiums."

These strictures—which read much like the MLIC's ordinances
of the past, but without the hard edge of the old "Parkchester cop"
surveillance of the area's largely law-abiding tenants—focused on
three "frequent quality of life complaints." First, "noise should be kept
at an acceptable level that does not disturb . . . neighbors." Apartment floors, the newsletter advised, "should be covered by carpets to
muffle sound." Back in the 1940s, such carpeting had been mandated.
Second, proper garbage disposal was deemed imperative as it "affects
all of the residents in the building [and] . . . allows everyone to live in
a clean pest-free environment." Finally, everyone was reminded that
"littering is illegal." Moreover, it draws "mice and bugs. . . . The condition of your home and neighborhood depends on you."

The most pressing concern that the board leadership identified
was the need to keep the aging infrastructure of the complex in
prime working order, and to do so without overly burdening resi-

dents with heavy increases in common charges. At that moment, as Parkchester passed its seventy-seventh birthday, in addition to operating the heating plant "as efficiently as possible," a major worry in Parkchester South was roof and façade leakages. Water seepages and damages were daily issues for "top floor neighbors across all 116 buildings that reside in our condominium association."[10]

As of 2018, the Olshan group was already instituting plans to transform the demographics of Parkchester once again as it moved close to its eightieth anniversary. In an era of gentrification throughout Gotham, efforts were being made to attract residents willing and able to pay for "Contemporary Collection" one- to three-bedroom apartments or "Premier Collection" one- and two-bedroom residences. In keeping with its commitment to diversity, certainly no restrictions of any sort would be placed on the racial, national, or ethnic backgrounds of people ready to invest in the community. But for the first time in its history, Parkchester's quintessential new occupants presumably would not be civil servants or working-class people, but the better-heeled who would have access to "over 100 retail stores," starting with Macy's and Starbucks, "medical facilities, restaurants, public, private, and parochial school[s]," and the ever-important counter to the burdens of suburban migration, the "30 minutes to Midtown by No. 6 subway line (Express and Local)/Express bus." The pitch for the "Prestige Collection" digs addressed the decades-long family-space problem in an upbeat manner, asserting that its "two-bedroom residences are ideal for couples, for roommates who are sharing, for a single seeking a home office or media room, or for growing families." Its three-bedroom option was presented as a "very affordable housing choice for extended families." Meanwhile, the "Premier Collection" could boast of "beautifully appointed kitchens with granite countertops, shaker-style cabinets, dishwashers, microwaves, maple cabinetry and stylish ceramic tile floors." More changes are in play within a neighborhood that has served its borough and city for almost eight full decades.[11]

CONCLUSION

An Enduring Get-Along Spirit

N EW YORK NEIGHBORHOOD HISTORIES ARE REPLETE
with the stories of residents who have felt that where
they lived was a special place and were committed to its
maintenance and preservation. Armed with proprietary perspectives, even if they usually did not own their apartments,
they often have been on the guard against forces and circumstances that have been seen as threatening their turfs. In
many regards, for eight decades, Parkchesterites have been
no different. For example, though activists among them never
explicitly connected their actions to what their predecessors
had done, generations of spokespeople have protested landlord, and later sponsor, policies deemed unfair or inimical to
the future of the development. Early on, tenants rallied when
"Mother Metropolitan," in their view, failed to act maternally.
Subsequently, the deeply concerned gave the Helmsleys no
quarter when their real estate priorities and neglect of properties threatened to undermine the complex. There even were
suspicions of and objections raised to the plans of the CPC and
its associates when they stepped up to rebuild Parkchester.

Where the history of this community has differed from that
of most other enclaves in Gotham is in its inhabitants' mutually held conviction, notwithstanding their varying colorations,
nationalities, or religions, that they all were living together in
a special place. Most critically, they generally behaved in a way

that suggests that they believed that no "other" ethnic, religious, racial, or immigrant group's presence threatened to destroy their community. If anything, during Parkchester's most difficult times, angry words were directed far more at management, and at outside troublemakers, than at those who lived on the same floor. This feeling was not born out of any rarified egalitarian belief that the world all around them had to be changed. Rather, it grew from a sense among the majority of men and women on Parkchester's streets that they shared common values and outlooks that endured.

In this regard, two aforementioned intergroup relationships in two different eras stand out and are worthy of revisiting. From the 1940s through the 1960s, the Jews and Irish of Parkchester saw themselves as part of the same community, a marked turn in the groups' history of disputes. The way the MLIC constructed and filled up their coveted properties set the stage for family-by-family coexistence. An early news report that "the Akuskas, the Abbotts, the Breslaus, the Devores," and I shall emphasize "the Gershowitzes and the McCahans" lived together in their randomly populated buildings helped to create that get-along spirit even if some Jews believed that the management gave Catholic applicants preferential treatment. But Jews also had to know that in some other places in the city they were not wanted. The family of future Msgr. John Graham would not have agreed with the allegation that members of his faith came first when their quest for an apartment was turned down. In all events, as a result, due to Ecker, the Lowe brothers, and their associates' policies—and unlike older neighborhoods and many postwar enclaves in the city—there was no "Jewish street" and "no Christian street." Moreover, the decades-long lack of air-conditioning was a reality that has to be remembered, afflicting everyone and perforce bringing people together. In summertime when neighbors kept their doors and windows open to deal with their overheated apartments, pleasant nodding relationships and in some cases, friendships developed among Jewish, Irish, and, to be sure, other Christian neighbors.

For religious leaders of the Jewish minority, the MLIC's rental system created an issue to be addressed when they contemplated the dilemma of how to maintain their younger generations' interest in their distinctive identity. But assimilation was a minor concern for most Jewish lay people in Parkchester. Many of them were uninterested in living in a predominantly Jewish neighborhood as they had in the past. As a collateral plus, the absence of their own definitive area within the large complex may have served as a deterrent to potential troublemakers who could not readily find those whom they might hassle.

The turnout of all Parkchesterites as patriotic supporters of the war effort that started just a year after the development opened also contributed to good feelings. It is noteworthy that when, in 1943, a Mrs. Minnie Levine, clearly possessed of a Jewish surname, was arrested for price gouging, no mention was made in the newspapers of people pointing to her apparent religious background. If there were any former Coughlin followers still around, they were silent. That Lorraine Helfond—very possibly a Jew—was instrumental in hauling Levine into court may have helped thwart any anti-Semitic insinuations. But even more significant, Helfond was also a leader of the United Victory Committee, whose stalwarts had surnames like Johannes, Ferraro, Sosis, and Elkin, not to mention Lehman and Kozerwitz. Similarly, neighborhood people of all backgrounds showed signs of this get-along spirit when they came together in work and prayer within the AWVS and the Bronx Unit of W.I.V.E.S., "an organization of the wives of men in the armed forces."[1]

But perhaps Parkchesterites got along from the very start because Jews, the Irish, and other Christians were all coming into a fresh, new neighborhood. There was no sense of one group invading the others' turf, a feeling that had fueled earlier interethnic conflicts. If anything, given the MLIC's complex, invasive vetting procedures, members of every group surely felt fortunate to be chosen to live in the area. Concomitantly and powerfully, in the postwar era of prosperity the neighborhood's Jews and the Irish both did well economically. The unemployment pressures of the Depression era were past and there was a consequent decline in competition and jealousies among a new generation of New Yorkers. Indeed, Parkchester's men, especially its army of police, firefighters, and other civil servants, worked at many of the same jobs and marched to the subways together.

Finally, a number of Catholic religious leaders, most notably Msgr. Scanlan and, during a later period, Msgr. Derivan, were committed to brotherhood. That the story of Msgr. Scanlan playing a role in the rise of Temple Emanuel became part of St. Helena's historical lore says much about the possibilities for religious tolerance in what was identified as the "Interfaith Rows" almost from the beginning of Parkchester.

However, while organized anti-Semitism was never part of Parkchester's scene and Jews could speak affirmatively of their "Christian neighbors," nonetheless there was an edge to the friendliness that limited the closest of relationships. Such were the realities of that time in America. At the end of the day, as one veteran Irish American writer who grew up in the neighborhood put it so well: "we lived separately together." Deeper and enduring interfaith relationships would await subsequent generations.

The second and more complex intergroup relationship that also demands further analysis involved whites and blacks and the integration of Parkchester. Here, to begin with, the main opponents of African Americans moving in were not the tenants of Parkchester but the owners. To be certain, during its first decades of control, MLIC behavior was fully in line with how most Americans and most realtors then acted. Institutional racism ruled in housing as in so many other aspects of the country's life. It cannot be asserted with complete certainty what that reporter for the *New York Times* meant in his 1939 description of how Ecker was bringing to the East Bronx an "integrated colony." Most likely, Lee Cooper was impressed that Parkchester would have "thirty-nine blocks" that were not "cluttered up" and that the "vast plot has been divided into four big quadrants, each of which will have stores, playgrounds, parking fields and garages." Conceivably, this observer may also have been taken with the vision of how people from different white ethnic and religious backgrounds would be living together. In 1941, Edgar Beigel, writing in the *New Republic*, offered an even more explicit depiction of different nationalities and religions behaving as an "integrated group." But unquestionably, neither Cooper nor Beigel meant the different races would be residing in the same places. Parkchester's early history underscores how powerful the tradition of segregation was in New York City as both the law and custom of the land.

Thus, within this discriminatory spirit, when in 1953, an attempt was made to integrate the complex, the MLIC found easy relief from the state court and the interlopers were evicted. Not only that, a year later the MLIC's general counsel, Churchill Rodgers, published an article in the *American Bar Association Journal*, based on a University of Chicago Law School Conference, where he matter-of-factly described the sit-in at the MLIC's downtown offices and the attendant "public furor" and calmly defended his company's "freedom of choice in the selection of tenants." The law, he was satisfied to note, was on his clients' side. His learned piece also defended the MLIC's stance against the Jehovah's Witnesses a few years earlier while asserting that MLIC's investments were "a prime example of private enterprise productively devoted to public service." It constituted a position that in his view was challenged by "those who have sought to make this realm of endeavor an area of social and political conflict."[2]

Eventually, in the 1960s, law and public opinion moved toward creating open housing statutes. Yet until 1968, the MLIC kept

Parkchester almost all white. Tried and untrue methods to maintain the racial status quo were kept in play. The most common refrain was that the company was agreeable to desegregation, but that blacks, whom it was said for the longest time did not really want to live in the neighborhood, would have to wait their turn. They almost never got off that voluminous waiting list. Meanwhile, whites with the right family or religious connections and clearly the right complexions often jumped the line. It was only in 1968, when the City Commission on Human Rights threatened recalcitrant MLIC officials with jail time, that more than just a minuscule number of minority applicants entered the community. Even then it took a while for the word to come down from the home office to the operatives on the ground in the East Bronx. The studied methodologies of exclusion in Parkchester, which also underscore the long legacy of functional segregation in Gotham, serve as a primer on how those who wanted to drag their feet found ways to avoid complying with legal mandates.

Where the Parkchester race story departs most strongly from the experiences of other communities both in New York and nationally is how the indigenous white majority reacted to the newcomers when they finally were allowed in. While some of the first blacks in Parkchester had to deal with instances of nastiness from other tenants, like having elevator doors slammed in their faces, there was no organized opposition to their presence in the area. The tactics that the Urban League and the NAACP used to force the hand of the MLIC, which focused on using legislation and court decisions to open doors, a studied conservative approach to civil rights advocacy, played a substantial role in the uncommonly calm transition. No street demonstrations or other public protests took place in the neighborhood that might have raised white resident consciousness either about the importance of change or trepidations that their comfortably segregated community was under attack. Given this environment, with the exception of a small, resolute cohort of white activists who spoke out in the early 1950s in an unsuccessful attempt to end the MLIC's racist policies, during the development's first three decades there was little public discussion of the race question. Young white boys and girls grew up perhaps aware of the battles over race taking place elsewhere, but without much thought about why there were no racial minorities in their concrete backyards.

Moreover, the African Americans and Latinos who moved into Parkchester were on the whole solid working- and lower-middle-class folks. Occupationally, they were much like the original tenants in the neighborhood and were perceived as such. They shared many family values with Parkchester's white people. Thus old-time residents were able to set aside whatever feelings they may have had about the integration of the area. Indeed, in some cases, upstanding African Americans who fled deteriorating areas were concerned that the neighborhood they moved into not become overwhelmingly black, in which case they would consider moving out too. They also wanted a racially mixed neighborhood. Put differently, in Parkchester, commonalities in economic and social class among groups and a mutual feeling that they were all living in a special place worth preserving trumped racial animosities. The white-black relationship echoed the prior Irish-Jewish spirit of amiability. This atmosphere created its own get-along attitude that was missing from other areas during an era when fears of underclass black "invasion" led to massive white flight from integrating neighborhoods. In Parkchester, first-generation residents and their upwardly mobile children may have moved out or aged out en masse but they did not flee.[3]

And then in the 1970s–1990s, during the Helmsley era, whites and blacks had a common enemy, the real estate mogul who brought them closer together. They rallied and worked in tandem for years on the issue of condominiums as well as in denouncing how Helmsley-Spear was letting the infrastructure of Parkchester deteriorate. At contentious meetings, the owners faced off against a racially mixed cohort of protesters that by the 1990s would include the neighborhood's first outspoken immigrants.

This racial conviviality was noticed in 1991 at the very time when racial confrontations were roiling neighborhoods elsewhere in the city, such as Canarsie and Crown Heights in Brooklyn. Although Parkchester was not the only place in Gotham or nationally where "peaceful change was achieved and neighborhoods did not deteriorate," the persistence of calm on its streets had much to do with the ability of groups in this "relatively middle class area . . . to meet on neutral territory . . . to address concrete problems."[4]

In the first decades of the new millennium, although tolerance of diversity is not a by-word nationally, notwithstanding intermittent and troubling tensions among groups that on occasion have caused racial problems, New York is among America's most paradigmatic multicultural urban areas. Much of the best of this sensibility is reflected in racial, religious, and national relationships today in Parkchester. However, though the community is open to all who can afford the apartment charges, a different, if more subtle form of integration has been required to maintain that get-along spirit. What has transpired in the religious realm offers a useful teaching moment for both residents and outside observers—scholars and the general public alike—about race and culture.

At first glance, non-white, and in many instances, foreign groups of worshippers, indistinguishable to the uninitiated, predominate in the neighborhood's churches, mosques, and Hindu temples. But upon closer examination it is evident that African Americans, Afro-Caribbeans, and Africans, possessed of similar pigmentation, and who may share the same pews, have different cultural values and even attitudes toward leadership. By a similar token, Parkchester's half-dozen mosques serve people from a multitude of Middle Eastern and Asian origins, while Hindu congregants hail from both the

Indian subcontinent and Guyana. Priests, ministers, imams, and pundits have been challenged to create religious experiences that bring groups together and seemingly have found ways to meld their adherents into communities.

Yet in my frequent returns to my old neighborhood—full disclosure, I grew up in Parkchester from 1949 to 1974—I have picked up some floating discomfort among some of the older African American and Latino residents toward the most recent newcomers. Bangla Bazaar on Starling Avenue has been referred to negatively as "Banglaville." Complaints have been articulated about the "strange smells" emanating from Indian apartments as "their large families" consume their pungent ethnic foods.

One personal experience in the summer of 2017 encapsulated for me that there are lessons some still need to learn in Parkchester about intergroup conviviality, never a simple matter. One evening, my wife and I took two of our grandchildren to Metropolitan Oval for a children's concert. The four of us were among the few white folks at this pleasant event. While waiting for the music to start, I conversed with a thirty-eight-year-old Latina woman whose kids, like my grandchildren, were patiently waiting to have their faces painted. I told her about my book in progress and she, like so many of the people I had interviewed the past year, was intrigued that I had been a Parkchester boy. When I asked her: "How do you like living in Parkchester today?" she replied: "It used to be great. But now there are so many people in the neighborhood from Bangladesh. It just is not the same." I did not challenge her statement. She already knew that her grandmother long had difficulties getting an apartment in the all-white community of the 1960s. But it did seem to me that if her views were at all representative, people of all backgrounds who have been attracted to this "city within a city" have been challenged, as they have been for eight decades, to get along, to live well together, certainly as neighbors but hopefully also as friends.

A few months later, returning once again to my old neighborhood on a research trip, I met a young man whose friendly demeanor and behavior has reassured me that Parkchester continues to house the "right type of people," as the MLIC characterized the first well-behaved working- and middle-class white tenants whom they admitted to its then restricted residences. I first encountered Tamzidul Islam, a second-generation Bangladeshi American and a devout Muslim, in fall 2017, when I appeared at his mosque on the site of my erstwhile synagogue, the YIP. My quest was to interview the religious and lay leaders of that house of worship and perhaps learn more about the other five mosques that now serve the growing Islamic community in the area. I arrived just as early afternoon prayers were concluding. Imam Obaidul Hoque greeted me warmly and attempted to respond to my several questions about the history of his group's religious institutional life and the background of his worshippers. However, it quickly became clear that I was having trouble understanding his heavily accented English. A native of Bangladesh, his native tongue was Bangla. Sensing my difficulties, Tamzid—as he likes to be called—stepped up and helped me to communicate more effectively with the imam. After we were finished, he inquired if I was interested in speaking with leaders of Parkchester's other mosques. I happily agreed and a week later, with Tamzid as my guide, I met five additional imams and members of some of their families. In each instance, my additional entrée to conversation was my ready statement that I had grown up in the area, which led everyone to inquire about what life had been like in Parkchester generations earlier. I had many stories to tell, starting with how I frequently evaded the "Parkchester cops" when I had committed the misdemeanor of climbing over the fence of a closed playground.

In the course of our two hours together, I also found out that Tamzid, this bright nineteen-year-old, had graduated from the

Bronx High School of Science, one of New York City's best public high schools, and was now a scholarship student at New York University, an elite private college, where he was studying civil engineering with a minor in business. It immediately occurred to me that his educational progress to date was reminiscent of the path that many of the young men and women who grew up in my synagogue had successfully taken. I started to think: "He was one of us." Then I made a remark that drew me even closer to him. "You know," I said, "we lived very close to the synagogue and on a snowy morning the phone would ring at 6:30 a.m. with my rabbi on the line requesting that the Gurock man and boys rush down to 'make a minyan.' As a reward for my participation, while my father hurried to the subway and the old-timers imbibed a shot of whiskey to warm themselves before venturing out into the cold, I was handed a shovel to clean the sidewalk." Tamzid laughed and said, "I attend services on similar wintery days, and afterwards they also hand me a shovel." Perhaps it is the same shovel; if so, it is the only artifact that remains on-site from the building's Jewish days. In subsequent conversations, I found out that Tamzid held a weekend post in his mosque as a youth leader and teacher. I had a comparable job some fifty years ago in precisely the same religious space. Time will tell how long Tamzid will remain in Parkchester after he starts his own professional career and, perhaps, marries. Right now, he already has his own apartment across the hall from his parents and siblings as this second-generation Parkchesterite copes, much like we did, with the limited space available for families. But then again, his digs are air-conditioned. We did not have that crucial creature comfort available to us.

For me, writing about my newfound friend in the old neighborhood is a good place to end this history of the people who have resided in a "city within a city" that has changed much over time. But in some crucial respects it has remained the same special place.

FIGURE C.1. Photo of Jeffrey S. Gurock and Tamzidul Islam outside the Parkchester Islamic Center, summer 2018. Courtesy of the Yeshiva University Office of Communications and Public Affairs.

Acknowledgments

IT IS A DISTINCT PLEASURE TO THANK THE MANY PEOPLE
and institutions that assisted me in the writing of this book. Residents of Parkchester past and present have an uncommon affection
for their neighborhood and so many of them were willing to open
their homes and hearts to tell me their poignant stories. Their
recollections have richly complemented the literary sources of
several genres that undergird my research. In connecting me with
Parkchesterites who now live in the area, several individuals were
extremely helpful in linking me up with the neighborhood's many
contemporary groups as well as with tenants of the longest standing. I am especially grateful to genealogist extraordinaire Karen
Franklin, Assemblyman John Dearie, Msgr. Thomas Derivan, Bernard and Rivka Horowitz, Phil Schneider, Dorothy and Harold
Jackman, Abu Shakoor, Nicole Tambini, Kumar Kancherla, and
perhaps most notably to Tamzidul Islam, who took me on a memorable and extraordinarily useful tour of Parkchester mosques and
introduced me to his religious group. All interviewees are identified
in the notes and have my thanks for their openness to an inquisi-
tive questioner. I am likewise very thankful for the willingness of
Michael Lappin, former president of the Community Preservation Corporation and Andrea Olshan, CEO of Olshan Properties,
to discuss their organizations' pivotal roles in the renovation of
Parkchester from the 1990s through the early 21st century. For the
early years of the neighborhood, the archives of the Metropolitan
Life Insurance Corporation, carefully managed by Daniel May, but-
tressed strongly the oral histories that the first tenants and their

children provided me. Prof. Emita Hill and the library staff at Lehman College alerted me to important newspaper sources in their collection.

In working on this topic, I was blessed with the tireless efforts of my prized student and research assistant, Mindy Schwartz of Yeshiva University's Stern College for Women. As always, my university's outstanding library staff, especially the indefatigable Mary Ann Linahan, were of inestimable help. I am also very happy to acknowledge the financial and intellectual support our provost, Dr. Selma Botman, provided my efforts. Her ongoing interest in, and encouragement of, my work motivates me to continue my scholarship.

I am so pleased that this book is my fourth work appearing under the auspices of NYU Press. My editor and friend Jennifer Hammer and her associates have been uncommonly helpful in each of these endeavors. Their wise efforts included Jennifer's reaching out on my behalf to anonymous scholars whose reviews of a penultimate draft of this work improved my study. As always, Professor Benjamin R. Gampel of the Jewish Theological Seminary of America and Professor Marc Lee Raphael of the College of William and Mary were wise readers and critics of sections of the book. Any misconstructions of the advice that they and other colleagues rendered are mine alone.

Among friends, near and far, who had shown interest in my work, two individuals stand out because of their deep commitment to seeing this project move forward. Joshua Landes has shown an unflagging willingness to hear me out about Parkchester, and so many other scholarly pursuits, as we exercise together at record speed at adjoining stationery bikes in our gym. As a long-time member of the board of trustees of the American Jewish Historical Society, he has shown great devotion to the advancement of scholarship in the field that we both cherish. In that same positive spirit, Leonard Grunstein, an active and dedicated member of the board of the Bernard Revel Graduate School, where I have been privileged to

teach for four decades, has supported Jewish scholarship of varying genres in so many ways and in my case has actually helped with
a critical part of my research on this very special community. I am
enormously grateful for Josh's and Len's friendship.

Finally, my family, beginning and ending with Pamela, make my
efforts worthwhile. I hope that my children and grandchildren will
dip into this book for what it tells them about their father's and
grandfather's early life as a son of Parkchester. Perhaps the high
school students, Audrey and Mira, will read large portions of my
work. Maybe Eli and Sheri, Rosie and Dan, and Michael and Elise
will find time from their busy professional activities, which make
me very proud, to move this volume from their coffee tables to their
night stands. And hopefully, Zev, Margot, Hannah, Dahlia, and Sophie will show the pictures that accompany the text to Adison Rae,
our latest, wonderful addition to our clan to whom this book is
dedicated with abundant love. It is her turn.

Riverdale, NY, February 2019

Notes

INTRODUCTION

1 On the size of Parkchester, its number of apartments, and estimates of its number of residents when it opened, see "Metropolitan's Parkchester," *Architectural Forum* (December 1939): 412–26; Henry Robinson Luce, "Metropolitan Life Makes Housing Pay," *Fortune* (April 1946): 133–34. The 171 buildings were in 51 "interconnected" areas or clusters, themselves sometimes referred to as "buildings." For examples of Parkchester being referred to as "a city within a city," see Lee E. Cooper, "'City within a City' Fast Taking Form," *NYT* (November 12, 1939): 133; "City within a City," *NYT* (January 13, 1941): 14. See also Ed García Conde, "Parkchester 75 Years Later: A Brief History of a City within a City," *Welcome2TheBronx* (August 5, 2015), www.welcome2thebronx.com. The neighborhood also was occasionally referred to as a "town within a city." See, for example, John Stanton, "Town within a City," *NYT* (May 11, 1941): SM 12.

2 On the MLIC's openness to differing nationalities and religions, see Edgar Beigel, "Parkchester Middle Class Houses," *New Republic* (September 29, 1941): 401. No mention is made of its racial segregation.

3 On Ecker's pet dreams, see "Metropolitan's Parkchester," 413.

4 On the distinction between Parkchester and "projects," see Paul Goldberger, "Tradition in Housing," *NYT* (August 21, 1981): B3. For a fuller discussion of the difference between Parkchester and "projects," see chapter 1, note 16.

5 Ronald H. Bayor, *Neighbors in Conflict: The Irish, Germans, Jews and Italians of New York City, 1929–1941* (Baltimore: Johns Hopkins University Press, 1978), 3–5, 25–26, 150–57.

CHAPTER 1. THE BUILDING OF PARKCHESTER

1 "Ecker Fifty Years in Metropolitan," *NYT* (May 6, 1933): 19; "Metropolitan Life Honors F.H. Ecker," *NYT* (May 7, 1943): 27; Churchill Rodgers, "Life Insurance Investments: Some Legal Phases," *American Bar Association Journal* 40 (August 1954): 676–77; Luce, "Metropolitan Life," 133; Robert E. Schultz, *Life Insurance Housing Projects* (Homewood, IL: S.S. Huebner Foundation, 1956), 26n6.

2 On the housing crisis in New York and comparisons with other cities, see Gurock, *Jews in Gotham: New York Jews in a Changing City, 1920–2010* (New York: NYU Press, 2012), 9–10. On the Metropolitan Bill, see Marquis James, *The Metropolitan Life: A Study in Business Growth* (New York: Viking Press, 1947), 253.

3 Roberta M. Moudry, "Prudential Insurance and Housing Development," in *Encyclopedia of American Urban History*, ed. David Goldfield (Thousand Oaks, CA: Sage, 2007), 613–14; Walter Stabler, *Comfortable Homes in New York City at $9.00 a Room a Month* (New York: Metropolitan Life Insurance Company, n.d.), 4, 10, 11; James, *Metropolitan Life*, 254; Schultz, *Housing Projects*, 26.

4 Stanton, "Town within a City," 27. On the economic profile of early Parkchester residents, see "3,000 Get Suites at Parkchester," *NYT* (July 8, 1940): 31.

5 The text of the April 15, 1938, radio interview "Pall Mall Broadcast—Dorothy Thompson, People in the News" is in the MLICA.

6 "Metropolitan's Parkchester," 414; "U. S. Housing Projects," *Architectural Forum* (May 1938): 356–58. On the rationale for passage of the bill, see Roberta M. Moudry, "Architecture as Cultural Design: The Architecture and Urbanism of the Metropolitan Life Insurance Company" (Ph.D. diss., Cornell University, 1995): 346–47; Luce, "Metropolitan Life," 136. See also Beigel, "Parkchester," 400.

7 On the costs of purchase of the property, see Beigel, "Parkchester," 400. On the team that Ecker assembled, see Eric Mumford, "The 'Tower in a Park' in America: Theory and Practice, 1920–1960," *Planning Perspectives* 10, no. 1 (1995): 26; Sara Stevens, *Developing Expertise: Architecture and Real Estate in Metropolitan America* (New Haven, CT, and London: Yale University Press, 2016), 108–14; "Man over Manhattan," *Architectural Forum* (January 1946): 96–99.

8 Richard Plunz, *A History of Housing in New York: Dwelling Type and Social Change in the American Metropolis* (New York: Columbia University Press, 1990), 184–90, 253; Mumford, "Tower in a Park," 18–19; Stevens, *Developing Expertise*, 104–7.

9 "Model of Housing Displayed at Fair," *NYT* (May 5, 1939): 47; James, *Metropolitan Life*, 255.

10 "Metropolitan's Parkchester," 413.

11 Cooper, "City within a City," 153; James J. Nagle, "Housing Interest Rising in Bronx," *NYT* (January 28, 1940): RE 13; "Parkchester Area Being Landscaped," *NYT* (April 27, 1941): RE 2; Stanton, "Town within a City," SM12. On the assessed value of Parkchester as of 1941, see Beigel, "Parkchester," 401.

12 The MLICA maintained these out-of-town articles. See RC/12 Printed Materials-Housing Parkchester-Book 1-1938–1942 [MLICA]. See also "City Within a City"; Lee E. Cooper, "Insurance Funds May Aid Housing in Post-War Era," *NYT* (February 22, 1942): RE 2.

13 "Parkchester Information Sought by Many Sources," *BHN* (March 4, 1940): 5; "Parkchester Manager Will Conduct Course in Housing for Graduate Students at N.Y.U.," *BHN* (March 20, 1940): 10.

14 Charles Grutzner, "Housing Is Sought for Middle Group" *NYT* (May 12, 1952): 31. See also "Realty Investor and Planning Expert Debate Future of the 'Vertical City,'" *NYT* (April 1, 1951): 22.

15 "Pelham Bay Subway Gets Express Trains," *NYT* (October 15, 1946): 26.

16 Luce, "Metropolitan Life," 136; Beigel, "Parkchester," 401. On subway improvements, see "6 Parkchester Trains Added," *NYHT* (September 17, 1940): 21. Approximately two decades later, the "tower in the park" concept would absorb withering criticism; in some cases, Parkchester was used as an example of its deficiencies. See Plunz, *History of Housing*, 253, which states that "Parkchester was an omen of the mass isolation that would be heightened for all form of middle class housing after the war." And "the towers of Parkchester were prophetic of the 'tower in the park' form of public housing that evolved after the war." Although Jane Jacobs did not focus extensively on Parkchester in her upbraiding of planned communities, her 1961 manifesto that attacks Le Corbusier's ideas as applied to American cities was striking and impactful. See Jane Jacobs, *The Death and Life of Great American Cities* (New York: Random House, 1941), 17, 21–24, 195. On criticism, see also Mumford, "Tower in a Park," 29, 30, 38, 39. On the other hand, a distinction has been made between this building concept, said to have worked successfully despite "a certain monotony" in Parkchester and also in the MLIC's other major development, Stuyvesant Town, as opposed to its "less successful attempts," such as public housing projects that "yielded cold and austere buildings that, according to many critics, have been a contributing factor in the social problems that public housing was intended to solve." See Goldberger, "Tradition in Housing," B3.

CHAPTER 2. FORTUNATE APARTMENT DWELLERS AND THE BEGINNINGS OF COMMUNITY LIFE

1 "3,000 Get Suites at Parkchester," *NYT* (July 8, 1940): 31. Descriptions of the tour offered to prospective tenants appear in John Carlfield Smith, "Homes-American," *Mclean's Magazine* (December 1, 1945): 43–44, and Gretta Palmer, "Middletown-on-the-Subway," *Reader's Digest* (December 1941): 132–34. See also a retrospective report on the visits, "Parkchester Five Years Old Today Is City in Itself," *Parkchester Press Review* (March 1, 1945). See also "A Visit to Parkchester," undated flyer circa 1940, in the MLICA. For the Frigidaire ad, see *NYT* (July 16, 1939): 24.

2 Hyman Sandow, "Parkchester: Design for Community Safety," *Safety* (October 1941): 274–76; Bill Twomey, *The Bronx in Bits and Pieces* (Bloomington, IN: Rooftop Publishing, 2007), 173.

3 Morris Markey, "40,000 Neighbors," *Saturday Evening Post* (May 18, 1940): 42.

4 Schultz, *Housing Projects*, 32–33.

5 James, *Metropolitan Life*, 317–18; "3,000 Get Suites"; "Parkchester to Open Three Model Suites near Pelham Bay Subway Line This Week," *BHN* (April 28, 1940): 10; "Couple on Honeymoon to Live in Parkchester," *BHN* (March 27, 1940): 9.

6 Maretta Krista and Joe Krista, "Reminiscences of Old Parkchester" (unpublished memoir dated April 19, 2005, made available courtesy of the Church of St. Helena), 1.

7 Smith, "Homes-American," 43–44.

8 On the Horowitz family's entrance into Parkchester, see "Once upon a Time in the Bronx," NY1 television interview with Irene Horowitz (August 22, 2010). Video in the possession of Rivka Horowitz. On the interview process, see also Markey, "40,000 Neighbors," 42.

9 "Another Step Is Taken towards the Completion of Parkchester," *HO* (August 1940): 10–12. The MLIC also used its house organ, *Home Office*, to shoot down rumors that the company inspected the apartments of renters monthly, that there were restrictions on the use of electric lights—utilities were included in the rents—and that visitors had to leave at a certain hour. All of these allegations were deemed "absurdities." See also "Parkchester: A Case Study in Management," *Real Estate Record and Builders Guide* (December 6, 1941).

10 For basic demographics of the building on McGraw Avenue discussed here, see "Population Schedule: Sixteenth Census of the United States, Enumeration Date April 3, 1940." See also NY1 interview with Irene Horowitz. On the MLIC's selectivity, see "Parkchester: A Self-Contained City," *Bronx Times Reporter* (February 10, 2000): 41.

11 Interview with Msgr. John Graham (October 30, 2017).

12 "Real Estate Transactions in the City and Suburban Fields," *NYHT* (February 23, 1940): 32.

13 "Tenant Keeps a 2-Year-Old Date," *New York Post* (February 22, 1940).

14 "Second Parkchester Baby Born at Mt. Eden Hospital," *BHN* (April 21, 1940): 1.

15 "Parkchester Five Years Old Today."

16 On the social control agenda of the MLIC that excluded houses of worship and schools from the neighborhood, see Moudry, "Architecture as Cultural Design," 368n114.

17 On the history of St. Raymond's, see "St. Raymond's Church in Bronx Celebrates 125th Anniversary," *NYT* (October 30, 1967): 40; *135th Anniversary 1842–1977 Parish of Saint Raymond Bronx New York* (New York: n.p., 1977.). On the founding of St. Helena's and its school, see "New Parish Gets Site," *NYT* (September 6, 1940): 39; "St. Helena History and 75th Anniversary Celebration," *Church of St. Helena's*, https://churchofsthelena.com. On the competition between the parishes, see Jean Meyer Campbell, *A Priest and his Parish: Monsignor Arthur J. Scanlan, St. Helena's Bronx, NY* (New York: R.C. Church of St. Helena, 2003), 98–99. See also untitled document dated July 11, 1940, signed by Scanlan and Tierney; "The Boundary Lines of the Parish of St. Helena's, The Bronx, September 12, 1940," in the St. Helena's file (Archive of the Archdiocese of New York).

18 On youthful perceptions of which parish was superior, see interview with Peter Quinn, November 6, 2017. See also Quinn, "Recollections of a B.I.C.," in *The Writing Irish of New York*, ed. Colin Broderick (New York: Fordham University Press, 2018), 18–30; Graham, interview.

19 Interview with Peter Carolan, February 17, 2017; interview with Msgr. Thomas Derivan, January 24, 2017. For information on the demographics of Mott Haven as of 1943, see "Bronx Profiles: St. Mary's Park," *New York City Market Analysis* (1943; accessed January 17, 2019), www.1940snewyork.com.

20 Interview with John B. McInerney, interview #123, conducted by the Bronx Institute Oral History Project, Lehman College, November 1, 1982.

21 On the history of the two synagogues that predate the 1940s, see Ellen Levitt, *The Lost Synagogues of the Bronx and Queens* (Bergenfield, NJ: Avotaynu, 2002), 57, 83. On the founding of the Young Israel of Parkchester, see Sydney Schwartz, "Maintaining the Minyan: The Struggle of a Storefront Synagogue" (unpublished essay, Columbia University School of Journalism, 2005), 13. On the size of the Jewish Center of Unionport and the career of Rabbi Silver, see interview with Sheri Silver, February 9, 2017.

22 On the history of the Young Israel movement, see Gurock, *Orthodox Jews in America* (Bloomington: Indiana University Press, 2009), 126–27, 154–55, 163, 193, 306; interview with Rabbi Solomon I. Berl, February 22, 2017.

23 Schwartz, "Maintaining the Minyan," 3–15. See also Robyn Winkler Shoulson email to Gurock, January 6, 2017. On the growth of the congregation, see "Young Israel of Parkchester: The First Ten Years, 1940–1950" (YIP).

24 Bernard Horowitz email to Gurock, February 8, 2017; Berl, interview.

25 There is a possibility that the need for a Conservative congregation was tied to a change in rabbinical leadership at the Jewish Center of Unionport. *The Parkchester News, Souvenir Opening Issue 1941* contains an invitation to newly arrived Jews in the area from the Jewish Center and its rabbi, Isadore Budik, to join the institution. Budik was a recent graduate of the Jewish Institute of Religion, a Reform Jewish seminary, and the invitation notes that services were held Friday night, not daily as in an Orthodox synagogue. There are no sources on why and how Budik left and the strictly Orthodox Rabbi Silver came to that pulpit. But it is conceivable that those at the Jewish Center who supported Budik's religious orientation might have gravitated to Temple Emanuel, only a few blocks away from the Ellis Avenue shul. On Budik's ordination, see *Graduates*

of the Hebrew-Union College-Jewish Institute of Religion: A Centennial Register of Graduates (Cincinnati: Hebrew Union College–Jewish Institute of Religion, 1975), 6.

26 On the founding of Temple Emanuel, see "Residences Figure in Bronx Trading," *NYT* (July 24, 1941): 32; Daniel Beekman, "Temple Emanuel, Parkchester's Last Synagogue, Closes after Years of Serving Dwindling Congregation," *NYDN* (October 31, 2011), www.nydailynews.com. On the lore that Msgr. Scalan interceded to make the synagogue building possible, see Derivan, interview.

27 On the acoustic problem at Emanuel, see interview with Rabbi J. Leonard Romm, September 11, 2017.

28 The year of the Parkchester Baptist Church's founding was ascertained by a look at its cornerstone. See also on the founding of that church, "New Parkchester Church Is Begun," an undated article that appears to be from 1949, in the MLICA. See also on the groundbreaking, *BPR* (September 22, 1949): 2. On the founding of St. Paul's Lutheran Church, see "St. Paul Lutheran Church," *New York City Chapter of the American Guild of Organists* (accessed January 17, 2019), www.nycago.org. On the movement of members into the "Olmstead church," see "1785 Church Moving Out to the Bronx: Population Change Spurs Merger," *NYT* (November 12, 1954): 29. For the term "Interfaith Row," see "Churches Give Day to Race Relations," *NYT* (February 14, 1949): 17.

29 On exchange of pulpits and candle lighting, see, for example, "Church Will Be Host in Temple," *BPR* (January 10, 1963): 9; "Growing Ecumenism in the Bronx," *BPR* (December 1, 1966): 2; "Presbyterians Will Attend Temple Thanksgiving," *BPR* (November 22, 1967): 7; "Parkchester's Christmas Display Lighted Up," *BPR* (December 12, 1966): 4.

30 On a "happy town," see Louis I. Dublin, *A Family of Thirty Million: The Story of Metropolitan Life Insurance Company* (New York: Metropolitan Life Insurance Company, 1943), 353. For Ecker's recruitment efforts, see "Our Veterans Are Told about Parkchester," *HO* (May–June 1940): 12–14; *The Home Office: Convention Supplement 1941*, 15. On the chauffeur driving youngsters home, see interview with Michael Horowitz, April 2, 2017.

31 "'Ask Meyer,' Is Byword at Parkchester: Tenants Find His Legal Judgment a Boon," *BHN* (March 14, 1940): 6.

32 For profiles of in-house employees who lived in Parkchester, see, for example, *HO* (March 15, 1945; July 7, 1945; August 2, 1945; August 9, 1945; September 6, 1945; September 13, 1945; September 20, 1945). See also "500 Parkchester 'Cousins' of the Home Office Family Keep This Company Running Smoothly," *HO* (January–February 1940): 8–10.

33 "More for Parkchester," *NYT* (February 28, 1940): 23; "3,000 Get Suites at Parkchester," *NYT* (July 8, 1940): 31; "Fall Rush Is On for Apartments," *NYT* (September 1, 1940): E1; "Parkchester Draws 2,400 More Families," *NYT* (September 5, 1941): 36.

34 On the draft issue, see "Parkchester Marks 25 Years," *BPR* (February 25, 1965).

35 On moving in to Parkchester, see "More for Parkchester"; "Parkchester Comes Alive as the First 550 Families Move In," *HO* (February–March 1940): 5–9; "Parkchester Five Years Old" (Metropolitan News Service press release, March 14, 1941); Linda Greenhouse, "Parkchester: Trouble in Paradise," *New York Magazine* (February 17, 1969): 38. See also "Frank Lowe Just Retired Placed 25 Year Impress on Parkchester," *BPR* (November 5, 1964), and "What It Was Like When the First Tenants, the First Vans Came" *BPR* (August 29, 1965). Other early arriving tenants have been presumed to be the first to arrive on McGraw Avenue, the first major street through the complex with completed buildings. Among those who entered at the outset were Oswald and Ruth Kramer, who resided near the Crandall family at 2049 McGraw Avenue. See Jack Hirschfield email to Gurock, July 25, 2018.

36 "Van Arsdale Agrees to Confer with U.T.O. on Parkchester Differences," *BHN* (April 16, 1940): 3.

37 For the statistical breakdown, see "One-Quarter of Suites Already Leased," *NYHT* (July 18, 1940). Several other sources provided by the MLIC identify proudly the same type of occupational distribution without assigning numbers to the categories. See, for example, "Parkchester Comes Alive"; "500 Parkchester 'Cousins'"; *Metropolitan Life*, 318. See also Stanton, "Town within a City," SM 27, for the statement concerning neither rich nor poor in Parkchester.

38 Markey, "40,000 Neighbors," 44.

39 Memorandum "Reds Try to Hang Plutocrat Tag on Parkchester People" information derived from *National Underwriter* (March 11, 1949) in the MLICA.

40 Beigel, "Parkchester," 401; Stanton, "Town within a City," SM12. On the economic profile of early Parkchester residents, see "3,000 Get Suites at Parkchester," *NYT* (July 8, 1940): 31.

41 In 1941, the MLIC also invested in Parkfairfax in Alexandria, Virginia, but this development was a group of smaller townhouses constructed near the Pentagon at FDR's behest. See Rodgers, "Life Insurance Investments," 676.

42 Hilary Ballon, "Robert Moses and Urban Removal," in *Robert Moses and the Modern City: The Transformation of New York*, ed. Hilary Ballon and Kenneth T. Jackson (New York and London: W.W. Norton, 2007), 242.

43 On the problem of the size of apartments, see Plunz, *History of Housing*, 258.

44 "Parkchester Marks 25 Years." See also Joseph Alsop, "The Pallid Issue," *NYT* (August 3, 1962), 14.

45 "A Silver Anniversary for Parkchester," *HO* (April 1965): 13; "Parkchester—City within a City," *HO* (October 1950): 4–7.

46 Cooper, "City within a City," 153. See also Dominic J. Capeci Jr., "Fiorello H. La Guardia and the Stuyvesant Town Controversy of 1943," *New York Historical Society Quarterly* 62 (October 1978): 289–310.

CHAPTER 3. FAMILY LIFE IN "STORKCHESTER"

1 Untitled press release from the Metropolitan Information Service, November 6. 1942 (MLICA); "Parkchester Comes Alive," 9. See also "East Bronx Area Has New Shopping Center," *NYT* (August 10, 1941): RE3.

2 "Macy Branch to Open," *NYT* (October 12, 1941): 54.

3 Brochure entitled "Macy's Accepts the Invitation" circa 1941 (MLICA). See also "Macy's to Close Syracuse Store After Year of Experimentation," *NYHT* (December 27, 1941): 19.

4 On the opening of Macy's and its appeal to young families, see "Macy Branch to Open: 5,000 Attend Preview of New Store in Parkchester," *NYT* (October 12, 1941): 54, and "Model Suite on Exhibit in City's Largest Housing Project," *NYT* (November 11, 1942): RE1. On the MLIC's sense of the community, see untitled Metropolitan Information Service press release dated December 8, 1942 (MLICA). See also "East Bronx Area Has New Shopping Center."

5 "Women Rush Store for Paper Draperies," *NYT* (March 5, 1946): 22.

6 "Beck to Open in Parkchester," *NYT* (January 5, 1941): F7; "Restaurant Leases Parkchester Space" *NYT* (September 22, 1945): 28; "Parkchester to Get H&H Retail Store," *NYT* (November 9, 1945): 34; "East Bronx Area Has New Shopping Center," *NYT* (August 10, 1941): RE 3; "Story of Retail Enterprise—Downs and Ups over 25 Years," *BPR* (April 29, 1965); Stanton, "Town within a City," SM13.

7 "Wandering Children and Mislaid Articles Keep Parkchester 'Lost-Found' Busy," *NYT* (February 21, 1943): RE1.

8 For an account of the activities in the playgrounds, see the documentary film "Parkchester—The Grand Old Neighborhood," *Vimeo* (Hank [Harry] de Cillia, exec. prod. and co-writer; John S. Dalpe, prod., dir., and co-writer, 2010), 28 min., https://vimeo.com/28477257. On the polio scare of the 1950s, see "Living in Fear: America in the Polio Years," *Lauren's Space*, http://teachspace.org. Hank de Cillia has also recalled that the recreational directors maintained 3-by-5 index cards with the names of the youngsters who regularly played in the East Quadrant playground, noting their good and bad behavior. He presumes that parents were notified if their children were a "problem." See De Cillia email to Gurock, September 14, 2018. On the management's wartime beautification efforts, see untitled Metropolitan Information Service press release dated April 2, 1942 (MLICA).

9 "News of Food," *NYT* (December 3, 1946): 40; "6,500 Pound Wash Handled Daily in Launderettes at Parkchester," *NYT* (August 10, 1948): 19.

10 On the frequent struggles among ethnic groups in New York neighborhoods before World War II, see Bayor, *Neighbors in Conflict*, 161.

11 On the different ethnic names of people drawn to Parkchester, see Stanton, "Town within a City," 27. The names of the Jewish and Christian residents of 2055 McGraw Avenue were derived from the previously noted 1940 U.S. census records. The religious backgrounds of the residents are approximations based on the last names. The census did not inquire about religion. See "Population Schedule." On older ethnic segregation in New York housing, and how Parkchester was different, see William H. Farrell, "Projects Become Home, Sweet Home," *NYT* (June 21, 1949): 27.

12 Rivka Horowitz email to Gurock, July 23, 2017. On Jewish businesses denoting postwar Jewish presence on the Grand Concourse, see Gurock, *Jews in Gotham*. On the popularity of delis in other Jewish neighborhoods, see Ted Merwin, *Pastrami on Rye: An Overstuffed History of the Jewish Deli* (New York: NYU Press, 2015), 110–11. See also Krista and Krista, ""Reminiscences," 3–4.

13 "Jack Slove to Member," June 24, 1942 (YIP).

14 On the persistence of defined ethnic neighborhoods in postwar New York—but not Parkchester—see Joshua M. Zeitz, *White Ethnic New York* (Chapel Hill: University of Noirth Carolina Press, 2007), 15–17. On suburban neighborhoods clustering with sensitivity toward whom different groups would live with, see Herbert J. Gans, *The Levittowners: Ways of Life and Politics in a New Suburban Community* (New York: Random House, 1967), 49. See also Albert I. Gordon, *Jews in Suburbia* (Boston: Beacon Press, 1959), 16, 171–72. On references to Parkchester life evoking a suburban social-neighborly lifestyle, see Markey, "40,000 Neighbors," 44.

15 On neighbors opening doors during summertime, see I. Horowitz, interview; Derivan, interview; Carolan, interview; Krista and Krista, "Reminiscences," 3. On the Castle Hill Beach Club, see Anna Quinlan, "About New York," *NYT* (September 8, 1962),

www.nytimes.com. For these additional demographics of the building on McGraw Avenue, see "Population Schedule." It may be noted that in describing the mothers' theater excursions, Irene Horowitz did not indicate whether the invitees were a mixed ethnic group. If so, that would indicate an additional level of budding friendship in the building among women of different religious and ethnic backgrounds.

16 McInerney, interview. It might also be suggested that the different ethnic and religious groups came together because they shared comparable political allegiances. On this observation and the difficulties of determining voting patterns, see chapter 4, note 16.

17 On the attempt to form an America First branch in the neighborhood prior to December 7, 1941, see Lloyd Ultan, "Life in Parkchester, 1941," *BPR* (September 25, 2008): 8. For a postwar accounting of the numbers of veterans and those killed in action from the neighborhood, see an untitled Metropolitan Information Service report, circa 1948 (MLICA).

18 On the activities of the United Victory Committee and the involvement of the YIP, see United Victory Committee of Parkchester to Young Israel of Parkchester (April 16, 1942) and Jack Slove to Members (June 24, 1942). See also flyer dated March 28, 1942, calling on YIP members to attend a Victory Committee dance (YIP).

19 See "Blackout Instructions Given to Development," BHN (April 9 1942): 6. On the secret labyrinth of tunnels, see interview with Mark Winnegrad, April 30, 2017. Interestingly, a major architectural examination of the infrastructure of Parkchester in 1939 that ran fourteen pages and included schematic diagrams of the area did not mention the tunnel labyrinth. See "Metropolitan's Parkchester," *Architectural Digest* (December 1939): 412–26.

20 On the activities of the Reliance Civic Association, see "Officers Elected by Reliance Assn.," *BHN* (March 25, 1994): 4.

21 "Pickets Yield to Holiday," *NYT* (July 5, 1942): 18.

22 "La Guardia Will Ration Hot Water," *NYT* (August 17, 1942): 1; "City Acts to Set Priorities on Oil," *NYT* (December 28, 1942): 21; "Parkchester to Convert 171 Buildings for Coal," *NYT* (April 18, 1943): 44.

23 "Waste-Paper Pile Rises," *NYT* (December 22, 1943): 12; "100 Trucks Aid Paper Salvaging," *NYT* (January 2, 1944): 12; "Half-Hour Red Cross Canvass Brings $63," *BHN* (March 12, 1943): 13.

24 "Wives of Service Men Unite," *NYT* (March 8, 1944): 22; "Service Wives Will Hear Address on Rehabilitation," *BH* (March 25, 1944): 4.

25 "Parkchester Women Down Price Violator," *NYT* (March 22, 1944): 22. On Helfond's involvement with both groups, see "Victory Group's New Officers Are Honored," *BHN* (March 25, 1944): 4.

26 On the range of activities conducted just in March 1944, see "AWVS Brotherhood Lunch," *BHN* (March 5, 1944): 5; "AWVS Makes Survey of Child Care Needs," *BHN* (March 12, 1944): 8; "St. Patrick's Day Marked by AWVS Business Girls," *BHN* (March 19, 1944): 5; "More than 500 at AWVS Dance: Part of Proceeds Will Go to Mobile Kitchen," *BHN* (May 10, 1942): 9; "Advanced First Aid Training Is Planned by Local AWVS," *BHN* (May 17, 1942): 9; "Services for Roosevelt to be Held in Parkchester," *BHN* (May 4, 1945): 9. See also, from May 1945, "Parkchester Women See Movie of Aid to Veterans," *BHN* (May 23, 1945): 3.

27 On the fire engine incident, see "Reminiscences of Old Parkchester," 1; on the YIP report of Jews in the military and its inaccurate numbers of murdered Jews, see *YI* (December 1945): 6.

28 Jane Nickerson, "News of Food," *NYT* (January 31, 1946): 18.

29 "Crowded School Arouse 800 Parkchester Mothers," *NYHT* (January 27, 1947). See also "Editorial," *BHN* (January 22, 1947). When it came to school problems—unlike rent issues and heavy-handed MLIC controls over children's behavior—seemingly more Jewish than Catholic mothers were involved, since only a minority of Catholic families sent their children to public schools.

30 "1,000 Children, Parents Parade in Bronx to Remind City That Area Needs a School," *NYT* (June 10, 1949): 24.

31 Murray Illson, "Priority Changed in Schools Scored," *NYT* (July 26, 1949): 29. See also Gene Currivan, "Education in Review," *NYT* (September 8, 1957): E11.

32 "City Plans School-Home Teamwork," *NYT* (March 19, 1950): E9; "Civic Groups Here Aid in School Plan," *NYT* (June 12, 1950): 16. See also "Misleading Ads of Films Deplored," *NYT* (March 20, 1949): 68.

CHAPTER 4. "DON'T PICK THE FLOWERS"

1 Markey, "40,000 Neighbors," 42. Signs forbidding canines were clearly posted. There is, however, some evidence that less-problematic cats were brought in quietly by tenants.

2 "Parkchester: The First Five Years," *Parkchester Press Review* (July 7, 1945). On defense of management, see "Frank Lowe Just Retired," and "What It Was Like in Parkchester." See also Twomey, *Bronx in Bits*, 174.

3 Untitled and undated memoir of the early years of Parkchester written by Jay Becker and contained in the Parkchester files of the Bronx Historical Society.

4 On the history of controlled play in New York, see Cary Goodman, *Choosing Sides: Playground and Street Life on the Lower East Side* (New York: Schocken, 1979).

5 "Tenants Fight Ouster," *NYT* (October 17, 1944): 25. See also Patricia Napolitano, "Recollections of My Life in Parkchester," *Bronx Historical Society Journal* (Spring 1985) 27–28; "Changes in Parkchester Bring a Fear Oasis in City May Go," *NYT* (December 29, 1968): 56.

6 "Parkchester Boys Not as Docile as Statistics Actually Find," *NYHT* (October 14, 1944): 13.

7 Carolan, interview.

8 Matthew L. Wald, "Parkchester Rally Asks Preservation of Bronx Project," *NYT* (November 21, 1977): 43.

9 Interview with Ruby Lukin Langer, August 8, 2017.

10 The several rules that are identified in this chapter were selected from among some eighteen rules enumerated in a 1959 Parkchester lease document at the Bronx Historical Society. See also, in that collection, an undated "Letter to Parkchester Residents," which notes the prohibition of children playing in the snow except in the playgrounds. On the 1940 boast about elevators, see "206 Elevators That Even a Child Can Run Will Serve Parkchester Apartment Tenants," *BHN* (April 3, 1940): 6. On using a false or incomplete name to avoid a Parkchester police citation, see interview with Roberta Stern Horowitz, April 1, 2017; Krista and Krista, "Reminiscences," 2.

11 For the positions of the Jehovah's Witnesses, see Hayden C. Covington, *Brief for Plaintiff-Appellants, Watchtower Bible and Tract Society, Inc. against Metropolitan Life Insurance Company* (Court of Appeals, State of New York, 1948). For the positions of the

MLIC, see Rodgers, "Life Insurance Investments," 677. See also "'Witnesses' Fail in Appeal," *NYT* (December 7, 1948): 33.

12 "Tenants Fight Ouster," *NYT* (October 17, 1944): 25.

13 "72 Parkchester Families Face Eviction as Nuisances," *BHN* (August 19, 1947); "Manager Explains a Tempest in a Tea Pot," undated *BHN* undated article in MLICA.

14 "Quill Asks City to Probe Met Life Eviction Attempt," *Daily Worker* (September 6, 1947).

15 "Hint Parkchester Will Drop Nuisance Eviction Case," *BHN* (October 16, 1947). On Isaacson's political career, see Rafael Medoff, *Jewish Americans and Political Participation: A Reference Handbook* (Santa Barbara, CA: ABC-Clio, 2002), 295.

16 For a report on November 1948 election returns, see "Yesterday's Vote for the President in City, State and Nation; Composition of New Congress," *NYT* (November 4, 1948): 5. It cannot be determined exactly how Parkchesterites voted since the 11th Assembly District included not only Parkchester but a large section of the Bronx north of the area. However, clearly the vote in that entire district for Wallace was minuscule. On the dimensions of the 11th Assembly District, see the map entitled "Bronx County Districts" (Municipal Archives). Parkchesterites who liked Isaacson could not vote for him since they were in the 25th Congressional District, while he was in the 24th, centered in the South Bronx. In future elections, the 25th Congressional District went either Democratic or Republican. Finally, although it is impossible to determine how Jews and the other white ethnic groups in Parkchester and its environs voted in 1948, the voting patterns suggest that in politics, as in so many aspects of their lives together, the varying groups shared mainstream political identities. As a contrast, at that very moment, in November 1948, in predominantly Jewish neighborhoods in the Bronx, like the Grand Concourse and Mosholu Parkway, Jews, many of whom had strong left-wing proclivities, supported Wallace. See Rafael Medoff, "When Jews Backed a Third Party: Henry Wallace and the 1948 Race," *Connecticut Jewish Ledger* (June 1, 2016), www.jewishledger.com. I am grateful to Dr. Medoff for his assistance with this election data.

17 "Urges Tenants Council," *BHN* (October 1947).

18 "Rents to Go Up 12% at Parkchester," *NYT* (July 22, 1948): 40.

19 "Fight Parkchester Rent Hike," *BHN* (July 18, 1948); "Tenants Association," *Parkchester Press Review* (November 18, 1948). For the rentals on various-size apartments, see, "A Description of Parkchester" (1948), typescript of the New York Housing Authority (Municipal Archives).

20 "Over 8,000 Parkchester Leases at Higher Rents Signed to Date," *Parkchester Press Review* (November 23, 1948); "Tenants Association: Reply," *Parkchester Press Review* (December 7, 1948).

21 "Parkchester Unit Fights Rent Rise," *NYT* (May 27, 1952): 56.

22 "Court Bars Move to Oust Army Wife from Home," *NYHT* (October 27, 1944): 21.

23 "Veterans and Housing," *BHN* (August 1946). On displacements due to construction of the Cross Bronx Expressway, see Robert A. Caro, *The Power Broker: Robert Moses and the Fall of New York* (New York: Knopf, 1974), 850–93.

24 "Changes in Parkchester," 56. On very negative attitudes toward the Parkchester police, see "Parkchester Boys Not as Docile."

25 For a retrospective listing of Bronx gangs and for maps plotting where they were located, see New York City Fighting Gangs (http://newyorkcitygangs.com). For the identification of the Golden Guineas, see interview with Fred Dicker, March 21, 2017.

26 "Hold-Up in Housing Unit," *NYT* (November 25, 1940): 16.

27 "Crime Kept Down by Housing Police," *NYT* (December 11, 1949): 120.

28 On the reasons for the rise of gangs after World War II in New York, see Eric C. Schneider, *Vampires, Dragons and Egyptian Kings: Youth Gangs in Postwar New York* (Princeton, NJ, and Oxford: Princeton University Press, 1999), 27–28.

CHAPTER 5. "NEGROES AND WHITES DON'T MIX"

1 On Lowe's attitudes about race, see "Frank Lowe, Just Retired, Placed 25 Year Impress on Parkchester," *BPR* (November 5, 1964): 4.

2 For a discussion of this statement quoted in the May 20, 1943, edition of the *New York Post*, see Capeci, "Fiorello H. La Guardia," 292.

3 James Egert Allen, *Black History: Past and Present* (New York: Exposition Press, 1971), 83–84.

4 For a comprehensive study of governmental involvement in housing discrimination, see Richard Rothstein, *The Color of Law: A Forgotten History of How Our Government Segregated America* (New York and London: Liveright, 2017). For his basic thesis statement about the denial of African Americans' rights to settle in middle-class neighborhoods, see p. xiv.

5 Seth M. Scheiner, *Negro Mecca: A History of the Negro in New York City, 1865–1920* (New York: NYU Press, 1965), 30; Gilbert Osofsky, *Harlem: The Making of a Ghetto: Negro New York, 1890–1930* (New York: Harper & Row, 1964), 130, 248.

6 C. Morris Horowitz and Lawrence J. Kaplan, *The Jewish Population of the New York City Area, 1900–1975* (New York: Federation of Jewish Philanthropies of New York, 1959), 163, 187, 265. See also Osofsky, *Harlem*, 248.

7 John L. Fox, *Housing for the Working Classes: Henry Phipps, from the Carnegie Steel Company to Phipps Houses* (Larchmont, NY: Memorystone, 2007), 81–83. See also "Henry Phipps and Phipps Houses: Millionaire's Effort to Improve Housing for the Poor," *NYT* (November 22, 2003), www.nytimes.com.

8 Osofsky, *Harlem*, 151–58.

9 On "Striver's Row" and other black neighborhoods, see Gurock, *The Jews of Harlem: The Birth, Decline and Revival of a Jewish Community* (New York: NYU Press, 2016), 209, 227.

10 Mark Naison and Bob Gumbs, *Before the Fires: An Oral History of African American Life in the Bronx from the 1930s to the 1960s* (New York: Empire State Editions/Fordham University Press, 2016), xi–xiii, 173.

11 Kenneth B. Clark, *Dark Ghetto: Dilemmas of Social Power* (New York, Evanston, IL, and London: Harper & Row, 1965), 57; James Baldwin, "Fifth Avenue, Uptown: A Letter from Harlem," in *Collected Essays* (New York: New American Library, 1998), 175.

12 For important, overlapping sources of information on the battles for integration in Stuyvesant Town, see Arthur Simon, *Stuyvesant Town, U.S.A: Pattern for Two Americas* (New York: NYU Press, 1970), 43–106; Martha Biondi, *To Stand and Fight: The Struggle for Civil Rights in Postwar New York City* (Cambridge, MA, and London: Harvard University Press, 2003), 121–36; Capeci, "Fiorello H. La Guardia," 289–310. On the proportion of minorities evicted from the area to make way for Stuyvesant Town, see Rothstein, *Color of Law*, 107.

13 For a comprehensive discussion of the twist and turns in the tenant-MLIC battle in Stuyvesant Town, including the census statistics, see Simon, *Stuyvesant Town*, 79–102. The census statistics are quoted on p. 106.

14 Derivan, interview.

15 On the YIP apartment efforts, see Douglas Lowe to Charles Rubinstein, November 18, 1958, published in *Kovetz Moreshet Avinu* (New York: n.p., 2005), 86; Zvi Gitelman email to Gurock, August 17, 2017; Hayim Schwartz email to Gurock, August 17, 2017. For an example of a Rubinstein letter to the editor, see "Stay in Bronx Month Urged by Rubinstein," *BPR* (February 7, 1963): 31.

16 Hayim Schwartz suggests in a privately published memorial volume for Rabbi Maurice L. Schwartz the possibility that there were "quotas" limiting the numbers of Jews in Parkchester. He asserts that the "limitations" mentioned in Lowe's letter to Rubinstein reflected "a quota in place limiting the number of Jews." See *Kovetz*, 86. There is no hard evidence of such discrimination, although other Jews also believed it was taking place and Catholic clergy may have been given preferential treatment in dealing with a waiting list that was often estimated as in the thousands of families. Moreover, newspaper and magazine reports of the time emphasize the planned diversity of the white ethnic religious mix of the community. See the discussion in chapter 2 about the diversity of the community as reported when Parkchester opened. On religious integration, see also Markey, "40,000 Neighbors," 42. And through the struggles over racial segregation in which Jews took an active role in the fight on behalf of blacks, no mention was made of them having comparable problems during an era when Jewish defense organizations also rallied against the remnants of the housing discrimination that they had faced for many decades.

17 "Parkchester Tenants Rap Housing Bias," *NYAN* (May 14, 1949): 21.

18 "Survey Reveals 'Negroes' Welcome," *NYAN* (June 24, 1950): 9.

19 On the Committee's mission and other early activities, see "Call to a Conference on Ending Discrimination in Parkchester" (Papers of the NAACP, New York Public Library Part 5 Campaign against Residential Discrimination, 1914–58).

20 "Pickets Stage Demonstration at Parkchester," *NYAN* (May 9, 1953): 5. Mrs. Simon is identified as the white occupant of the contested apartment. See "Delany Lashes Met's Parkchester Jimcrow," *NYAN* (October 25, 1952): 7. However, the lawsuit identifies an "Orlansky" as the defendant in the eviction case. See *Met. Life Ins. Co. v. Orlansky et al* (L.&T. 5301–1952).

21 Biondi, *To Stand and Fight*, 228; "Housing Bias Alleged," *NYT* (January 11, 1953): 76; "Chain Selves as Protest," *NYHT* (May 20, 1953).

22 The information on the activities of the two related protest groups is derived from dated and undated flyers, press releases, and open letters that are part of the Papers of the NAACP Papers, New York Public Library Part 5 Campaign against Residential Discrimination, 1914–58. See "Call to a Conference"; "Dear Friend" (January 14, 1953; March 10, 1953); "End Jim-Crow in Parkchester"; "Flash, Flash, Flash, Flash: Our Publicity Staff Announces a Television Program"; "For the Press, Draft Letter to Frederick Ecker." See also "Denies Remark on Parkchester Bias Policy," *NYAN* (February 28, 1953): 16.

23 "Women in Chains Protest Eviction," *NYT* (May 20, 1953): 31; "Batter Down Door to Evict Negro Family," *New York Post* (May 20, 1953): 52.

24 On the eviction, see "100 Cops Used to Evict Parkchester's First Negro Family," *Daily Worker* (May 21, 1953): 1; "Bail 2 in Resisting of Bronx Eviction," *NYDN* (May 22, 1953).

25 "Call for Showdown on Parkchester Bias," *NYAN* (May 30, 1953): 5.

26 Although the Bronx branch of the NAACP was listed as a supporter on the activism and its president issued a statement threatening a boycott, there is some evidence that suggests that the national office was concerned that a so-called "Communist organization" was leading the protests. In October 1952, the NAACP told its 'branches to refrain from association" with the Parkchester group since "it is a typical; Communist maneuver tying together isolated incidents . . . to develop the thesis that there is a national conspiracy inspired by the federal government against Negro citizens." Such activities, in its view, "undermine legitimate protests." See "Delany Lashes Met's Parkchester Jimcrow." *NYAN* (October 25, 1952): 7.

27 Biondi, *To Stand and Fight*, 229.

28 Robert Stone and J. Philip Waring to Frank Lowe (March 11, 1954) (RFW).

29 "Parkchester Protest," *NYT* (March 13, 1954): 17; "Metropolitan Disgrace," *New York Post* (March 16, 1954). See also *NYAN* (March 20, 1954), noted in Biondi, *To Stand and Fight*, 326n15, 229.

30 This information on MLIC directives on how agents were to handle requests from blacks and others not wanted in Parkchester was derived from "office notations" that Arthur Simon saw before 1970. The MLIC would not let him "publish these office notations verbatim." See Simon, *Stuyvesant Town*, 105–6, 120n2.

31 "Parkchester: Barrier to Democracy," printed meeting program, September 23, 1954 (RFW).

32 Waring to Anne Hedgeman (September 28, 1954); Warren Moscow to Hedgeman (September 27, 1954); Stanley Lowell to Stone (October 25, 1954); Robert F. Wagner to Lowe (October 25, 1954) (all RFW). See also Abel Silver, "Mayor Urged to Act on Parkchester Bias." This clipped article, which appears in the Wagner Papers, does not indicate a date or publisher, but it clearly is from September 1954.

33 For examples of the similarly written letters to City Hall, see Ruth Kurtz to Lowell (October 23, 1954); Lillian Kittner to Lowell (September 23, 1954); Frances C. Rawlins to Lowell (September 28, 1954); Sylvia Perlman to Lowell (n.d., 1954) (all RFW).

34 For an example of the identically worded letter, see Lowell to Ruth Kurtz (October 27, 1954). For a memo that suggests that a "policy decision" was necessary, see Moscow to Hedgeman (October[?] 1954). See also Mayor to Lowell (November 15, 1954) (all RFW).

35 For Dowling's activities and attitudes, see "Man over Manhattan," *Architectural Forum* (January 1946): 96–99; "R.W. Dowling Heads Citizens Budget Group," *NYT* (November 29, 1944): 7; "Age of Cities Only Starting Dowling Says," *NYT* (April 16, 1944): B4; "Energy Personified: Robert W. Dowling," *NYT* (June 1, 1956): 12; "Robert Dowling of City Investing Dead; Spearheaded Civic and Planning Drives," *NYT* (August 29, 1972): 40; "Speeches and Articles, Robert Dowling, 1954–56," National Urban League Box I:E 29, Library of Congress. Dowling was also involved with other affluent city leaders, like David Rockefeller in the mid-1960s, in hatching plans to upgrade the public school educational system that affected blacks. See Clark, *Dark Ghetto*, 153.

36 Clark, *Dark Ghetto*, 221. On the MLIC's pride in company training and hiring practices, see "Education at the Metropolitan," *HO* (September 1959): 1, which also includes a cover photograph of a black and a white trainee at an educational program. See also "The College Recruiter," *HO* (September 8, 1966): 105, which indicates that the MLIC by this later date actively recruited in historically black colleges. I am grateful for the insights of Professor Matine Spence, who has done important work on the mission and focus of the National Urban League during this time. The conclusions about the reasons for Dowling's behavior are mine alone. See Spence email to Gurock, March 30, 2017.

37 On the efforts of the civil rights group to use the new law to its advantage, see NAACP Bronx Branch, Executive Board Meeting, April 14, 1958; Bronx Branch NAACP General Membership Meeting, October 27, 1958; Minutes of the Executive Committee, Bronx Branch, March 14, 1960 (Papers of the NAACP, New York Public Library). See also Marta B. Varek, "The First Forty Years of the Commission on Human Rights," *Fordham Urban Law Journal* XXIII (1996): 982. On the issue of enforcement, see also Simon, *Stuyvesant Town*, 199–201. On Lowe's evasiveness, see also "Builders, Realty Men Back an Anti-Bias Housing Bill," *NYHT* (January 28, 1960): 15.

38 Interview with John Dearie, January 18, 2017; Sara Wyner Gootblatt, "Prejudice Spelled Backwards Is Ecidujerp—Either Way It Doesn't Make Sense" (unpublished diary memoir made available courtesy of the author).

39 Carolan, interview; Winnegrad, interview. On the question of anti-Semitic epithets, Peter Quinn has contended that he "never heard anti-Semitic professions by teachers or clergy." See Quinn, "Recollections," 22. However, some Jews have recalled religious name-calling.

40 Interview with Robert Krain, October 9, 2017; interview with Robert Lewis, October 10, 2017. For a mini-history of the Vikings, see "The Gift of Friendship," *Amit Magazine* (Fall 2017), https://amitchildren.org.

41 On his lack of friendships with Jewish boys and girls outside of street interactions, see Quinn, "Recollections," 22. See also Sara Wyner Gootblatt, "Irish Eyes" (unpublished diary memoir made available courtesy of the author).

42 Interview with Roberta Stern Horowitz, April 13, 2017; McInerary, interview.

43 On the possibility of avoiding stations in the South Bronx, see Gurock, *Jews in Gotham*, 133–34. On the implications of the subway system as a geographical barrier, see also Greenhouse, "Parkchester," 42.

44 For a comprehensive examination of the Castle Hill Beach Club case, see Brian Purnell, "Desegregating the Jim Crow North: Racial Discrimination in the Postwar Bronx and the Fight to Integrate the Castle Hill Beach Club (1953–1973)," *Afro-Americans in New York Life and History* (July 2009): 47–74.

45 Simon, *Stuyvesant Town*, 108, quotes the *New York Telegram and Sun* statement. On the threat of public protests, see "NAACP Demands Response," *BPR* (July 25, 1963): 1, 22. See also "Metropolitan and NAACP Join in Housing Statement," *BPR* (August 1, 1963): 1, 8.

46 Simon, *Stuyvesant Town*, 110.

47 On the tactic of checking, see Brian Purnell, *Fighting Jim Crow in the County of Kings: The Congress of Racial Equality in Brooklyn* (Lexington: University Press of Kentucky, 2013), 75–88, noted in Christopher Hayes, "Thoughts on Operation Open City and the First, Second and Third Reconstruction," paper delivered at The Urban History Biennial Conference, October 2016. I am grateful to Professor Hayes for sharing his important research with me. For the instructions on checking, see "Instructions for Homeseekers and Checkers," circa 1966 (Papers of Operation Open City, Urban League of Greater New York on file at the Schomburg Library).

48 Joseph P. Fried, "City Charges Bias at Three Projects," *NYT* (May 28, 1968): 27.

49 For a biographical sketch of Mildred Hall, see "Board Presidents Bring Experience to Their Positions," *Parkchester's Fiftieth Anniversary, 1940–1990* (New York: n.p, 1990): 4. See also interview with Dr. Valerie Hall Daly, April 10, 2017.

50 On the back-and-forth negotiations between civil rights groups and the MLIC during 1963–68, with references to newspaper coverage, see Simon, *Stuyvesant Town*, 107–10. See also Fried, "City Charges Bias," 27; "Metropolitan Life Denies Racial Bias." *NYT* (May 29, 1968): 18; "Met Eyes Booth Charges of Bias." *BPR* (May 30, 1968): 1; Steven V. Roberts, "High Court Ruling against Discrimination in Housing Is Hailed," *NYT* (June 19, 1968): 28.

51 "Parkchester Staff Waits New Rules," *BPR* (July 25, 1968): 1, 21.

52 David K. Shipler, "Negroes Say Pact on Housing Lags," *NYT* (July 28, 1968): 27.

53 "Changes at Parkchester Bring a Fear Oasis in City May Go," *NYT* (December 29, 1968): 56. See also "Company States Policy in Leasing Apartments," *HO* (August 2, 1968).

CHAPTER 6. A MIXED RECEPTION

1 Michael Horowitz email to Gurock, January 5, 2017; interview with Michael Horowitz, April 2, 2017. See also Irene Horowitz's recollections of that event in her NYl interview. It should be noted that in 1976, more than seven years after Parkchester was desegregated, the synagogue invited Rabbi Meir Kahane, founder and president of the Jewish Defense League. His presence may indicate some congregational affinity for his controversial stance on race relations in America. However, the topic was "There Is No Palestine, There Is No Arab Problem," which suggests that his focus that night was not on local Jewish concerns but on international issues. See *YI* (November 1976): 1.

2 Langer, interview; Gerard J. Pellison and James A. Garvey III, *The Castle on the Parkway: The Story of Dewitt Clinton High School and its Extraordinary Influence on American Life* (Scarsdale, NY: Hutch Press, 2009), 98–99.

3 On the YIPs forums, see "Oneg Shabbat Forums [1961–1967]" (YIP, Box 25). See also, "Documents of Our Time," *YI* (March 1967): 4, which discusses interfaith dialogue and reprints a statement by the eminent Orthodox rabbi Joseph B. Soloveitchik defining the levels of interaction appropriate for Orthodox Jews. For other examples of topics discussed at the forums, see *YI* (November 1965): 1; *YI* (November 1966): 1; *YI* (November 1967): 1; interview with Hayim Schwartz, July 25, 2017.

4 Peter Quinn, *Looking for Jimmy: A Search for Irish America* (New York: Overlook Press, 2008), 191.

5 David Gonzalez, "Fr. John Flynn: People's Priest of the Bronx," *America Magazine* (October 1, 2002), www.americamagazine.org; "Father John C. Flynn," *Catholic New York* (October 4, 2012), www.cny.org; Patrice O'Shaughnessy, "Father John Flynn Walked His Way into the Hearts and Minds of the Bronx Community He Served and Loved," *NYDN* (September 27, 2012), www.nydailynews.com; Winnie Hu, "As the People's Priest, He Fought for the Forgotten of the Bronx," *NYT* (September 21, 2012): A21; Quinn, interview.

6 See Hayes, "Thoughts on Operation Open City," 3, for a comparison of the National Urban League's tactics with those of the Congress of Racial Equality.

7 "New Neighbors in Parkchester," *BPR* (August 10, 1963): 10.

8 On the changes in Brownsville, see Wendell Pritchard, "From One Ghetto to Another: Blacks, Jews and Public Housing in Brownsville, 1945–1970" (Ph.D. diss., University of Pennsylvania), 175–77, discussed in Gurock, *Jews in Gotham*, 131–32. For Tripodo's statement to the *Times*, see "Changes at Parkchester," 56.

9 Simon, *Stuyvesant Town*, 112–13, 116–17.

10 Reynolds Farley and William H. Frey, "Changes in the Segregation of Whites from Blacks during the 1980s," *American Sociological Review* 59 (1994): 27–28; Stephan and Abigail Thernstrom, *America in Black and White: One Nation, Indivisible* (New York: Simon & Schuster, 1997), 221–22.

11 Greenhouse, "Parkchester," 43.

12 The untitled memo date September 24, 1968, seemingly written by "CLF, Jr." is in the MLICA.

13 Greenhouse, "Parkchester," 41.

14 Interview with James Kibler, June 27, 2017.

15 Interview with Beverly Roberts, May 2, 2017. There is also the possibility that the Helmsley group was sued for its unwillingness to rent to a black applicant even after the forced desegregation. Eae James Mitchell has contended that his lawsuit in 1969 that garnered for him a $10,000 judgment led to the desegregation of Parkchester. However, his memoir does not indicate against whom he brought the case and from all reports the decision on integration clearly was rendered before 1969. Additionally, this possible suit was not mentioned in any of the city or local newspapers. Community activist Lady Anne Dunbar, who was deeply involved in the fight over Parkchester, has no recollection of this legal action, and a search for court records has not uncovered documents of the case. See "Eae James Mitchell, Togetherness Realty, 1925–1989," in Emita Brady Hill, *Bronx Faces and Voices: Sixteen Stories of Courage and Community* (Lubbock: Texas Tech University Press, 2014), 84.

16 Interview with Lady Anne Dunbar, April 27, 2017; interview with Rosetta Gantt, July 25, 2017. See also Roberts, interview. On the proportion of African Americans in Parkchester as of 1970, see Allan M. Siegal, "In Parkchester, Old Tenants Fear Condominium Plan," *NYT* (June 6, 1974): 39; interview with Sarah Alleyne, June 29, 2017.

17 Interview with Beatrice Franklin, March 30, 2017.

18 Interview with Harold and Dorothy Jackman, June 12, 2017.

CHAPTER 7. "MRS. HELMSLEY SHOULD BE FORCED TO DO HER TIME IN PARKCHESTER"

1 Derivan, interview; Enid Nemy, "Leona Helmsley Dead at 87," *NYT* (August 20, 2007), www.nytimes.com.

2 On Helmsley's aspirations, see "An Appetite for Empire," *Time* (October 4, 1968): 112; Dee Wedemeyer, "Palace Puts Helmsley on Top," *NYT* (February 3, 1980): R1. See also Greenhouse, "Parkchester," 41.

3 On Lowe's memoir, see "Frank Lowe, Just Retired." On Helmsley's initial moves, see "An Appetite for Empire."

4 Greenhouse, "Parkchester," 43; Siegal, "In Parkchester."

5 "State Studies Loss of Tenant Interest," *NYT* (July 19, 1969): 25; "Lefkowitz Alleges Parkchester Defrauds Its Tenants of Interest," *NYT* (November 11, 1969): 78; "Security Money Interest for Tenants Is Optional," *NYT* (February 4, 1970): 45.

6 "The City within the City," *BPR* (November 28, 1968): 1; Siegal, "In Parkchester"; "New Start for Parkchesterites," *BPR* (September 26, 1968): 1, 63. On early perceptions of and apprehensions about Helmsley's plans, see "Parkchester Tenants," *BPR* (March 15, 1973): 1.

7 Interview with Idella Goodman, September 17, 2017; "Now You Can Own a Piece of Parkchester," *BPR* (March 29, 1973): 17.

8 "Parkchester Becoming a Condominium," *NYT* (June 5, 1973): 34; George Dullea, "It's Decision Time at Parkchester," *NYT* (February 4, 1973): 358; "Parkchester Conversion Gains in Court," *NYT* (September 19, 1973): 51; "N. Quadrant Condominium Is Weighed by Tenants," *BPR* (December 21, 1972): 1.

9 Dullea, "Decision Time," 358.

10 Interview with Kathleen Schaefer, February 27, 2017; interview with Bernard Horowitz, April 13, 2017; Napolitano, "Recollections," 27; Hank de Cillia, "Parkchester—The Grand Old Neighborhood," typescript, January 1994 (Bronx Historical Society); interview with Msgr. Donald Dwyer, May 17, 2017. See also a recollection of parents, but not children, being content with one-bathroom life in suburbia of the same time: Perri Klass, "Lessons from Life in a One-Bedroom House," *NYT* (August 6, 2018), www.nytimes.com.

11 Cait Etherington, "New York City before Air Conditioning," *CityRealty* (August 24, 2016), www.cityrealty.com; "Hunter Fans Ad," *Life* (June 27, 1955): 113; James Barron, "No Cooling Hum in This Urban Oasis," *NYT* (August 4, 1988): B1; Daniel Gesslein, "How to Beat the Heat in Parkchester," *BN* (June 10, 1999): 3.

12 Interview with Barbara Francis, September 16, 2017.

13 "Four Generations of One Family in Parkchester," *BPR* (November 11, 1965): 13; Greenhouse, "Parkchester," 43; Dwyer, interview; Sara Wyner, "Parkchester Was Always Too Darn Hot" (unpublished memoir made available courtesy of the author.)

14 Schwartz, "Maintaining the Minyan," 22–24. "Volunteers Needed for Our Morning Minyan," *Young Israelite* (June 1973): 5; interview with Joel Stern, July 25, 2017; Langer, interview.

15 Ralph Blumenthal, "Neighborhoods: First Tenants of Parkchester Have Grown Old," *NYT* (November 11, 1971): 49.

16 Siegal, "In Parkchester." See also Dullea, "Decision Time," 358; Greenhouse, "Parkchester," 43.

17 Krista and Krista, "Reminiscences," 5.

18 Interview with Harry Brown, June 26, 2017.

19 Interview with Fernando Ferrer, July 17, 2017.

20 "North Quadrant Condominium Proposal," *BPR* (December 21, 1972): 20; Siegal, "In Parkchester"; Dullea, "Decision Time," 358; interview with Harry Brown, June 29, 2017.

21 Interview with Philip Schneider, March 19, 2017. See also Winnegrad, interview.

22 "The Cities within the City," *BPR* (November 28, 1968): 1; "Co-op City and Parkchester," *BPR* (November 28, 1968): 16.

23 For discussions of the size of and accommodations available at Co-op City, see James F. Clarity, "Co-op City, Home to 40,000 Is Given Tempered Praise," *NYT* (May 27, 1971): 41; Murray Schumach, "Co-op City: A Symptom of Mitchell-Lama Ills," *NYT* (June 18, 1975): 86; Leslie Maitland, "Co-op City: Paradise or Paradise Lost," *NYT* (January 8, 1979): B1; Samuel G. Freedman, "Co-op City: A Refuge in Transition," *NYT* (June 25, 1986): B1. On Co-op City superseding Parkchester as a destination neighborhood for working- and middle-class people, see Greenhouse, "Parkchester," 38; Blumenthal, "Neighborhoods," 48.

24 Interview with Selma Pickei Glaser, May 31, 2017.

25 Interview with Lenore Greenwald, June 6, 2017; interview with Judy Cohen, June 21, 2017.

26 "Law Suit Attacks State on Condominiums," *BPR* (April 19, 1973): 1, 35. See also "Legal Case Begun vs. Condominiums," *BPR* (March 29, 1973): 1, 22.

27 "Condominium Sales Held Back as Second Suit Is Filed," *BPR* (May 16, 1973): 1.

28 "1200 at Rally vs. Condominiums," *BPR* (June 7, 1973): 1, 22; "Apartment Sales Resume after Ruling," *BPR* (June 7, 1973): 1.

29 "Owners' Group Wins Suit in Parkchester," *NYT* (May 21, 1974): 18. The Defense Fund would continue its struggle until February 1975, when the Court of Appeals, New York State's highest court, upheld the Helmsley position. See "Parkchester Condominiums Upheld," *NYT* (February 18, 1975): 33.

30 "1200 at Rally," 22.

31 Dearie, interview; Dullea, "Decision Time," 14.

32 "Sponsored Advertisement: The Parkchester Tenants Association Cordially Invites Its Neighbors and Bronx Friends to Join Together at 'Unity Day,'" *BPR* (November 16, 1972): 20; "Unity Day's March Set for Sunday," *BPR* (November 16, 1972): 1, 20; "Unity Day Draws 4,000 Asking Aid," *BPR* (November 23, 1972): 1; Joseph P. Fried, "Opinion Is Divided on Base-Rent Bill," *NYT* (May 2, 1973): 49.

33 "Parkchester New Police Patrols Set," *BPR* (June 13, 1967): 1; "Police on Parkchester Tours," *BPR* (June 13, 1967): 16.

34 "Letter to the Editor," *BPR* (October 17, 1968): 17.

35 "But to Most Residents Area Is Liked as Home," *NYDN* (October 5, 1969): 7–8.

36 "Police Figures Show Crime Up," *Journal News* (July 16, 1970): 1, 6.

37 "Parkchester Cops Hearing Date Set," *BPR* (September 28, 1972): 18.

38 "Sponsored Ad," 20.

39 "Tenants Association Files 23,000 Petitions Names," *BPR* (December 14, 1972): 12.

40 "N. Quadrant," 33.

41 "Dearie vs. Lalino for Special 85th A.D. Assembly Election," *BPR* (February 9, 1973): 1; "Dearie Hits Non-Vote on Condominiums," *BPR* (May 24, 1973): 1; Kirk Johnson, "About Real Estate: Parkchester's Labored Conversion a Testing Ground," *NYT* (December 28, 1986), www.nytimes.com.

42 "Parkchester Is at a Crossroads," *NYT* (January 14, 1976): 58.

43 Constance Rosenblum, *Boulevard of Dreams: Heady Times, Heartbreak and Hope along the Grand Concourse in the Bronx* (New York: NYU Press, 2009), 181–83, 189, 203–5; Lee Dembart, "Carter Takes a 'Sobering' Trip to the South Bronx," *NYT* (October 6, 1977): A1, B16. On Cosell's remark, see Rosenblum, *Boulevard of Dreams*, 183.

44 Robert E. Meyer, "How Government Helped Ruin the South Bronx," *Fortune* (November 1975): 143–45; Mathew P. Drennan, "The Decline and Rise of the New York Economy," in *Dual City: Restructuring New York*, ed. John Hull Mollenkopf and Manual Catells (New York: Russell Sage Foundation, 1991), 29–33. See also Thomas Bailey and Roger Waldinger, "The Changing Ethnic/Racial Divisions of Labor," in Mollenkopf and Cattells, *Dual City*, 43; Samuel Kaplan, "The New York Arrangement," *New York* (December 14, 1970): 10; Rosenblum, *Boulevard of Dreams*, 181.

45 Judy Kelmsrud, "Many Elderly in the Bronx Spend Their Lives in Terror of Crime," *NYT* (November 12, 1976): 27, 36. See also "Bronx Strategy Proposal" (November 1986) 13, 17 (Robert Abrams Papers, Box 12, Folder 162, "Demography," Municipal Archives). On the decline of Morrisania, see Naison and Gumbs, *Before the Fires*, xv, 176–77, which emphasizes the "national and global shifts in capital and investment that eventually wrecked similar devastation on many urban areas."

46 "Blackout Light in Parkchester," *BPR* (July 21, 1977): 1, 21.

47 Tom Quinn, "Paradise Lost in the North Bronx," *NYDN* (February 24, 1980): 10.

48 Interview with Camille Redmond, June 26, 2017.

49 Interview with Geri Flowers, August 16, 2017.

50 Rich Mancuso, "New York Times Roughs Up Parkchester and Community," *BN* (May 14, 1982): 1, 9.

51 Quinn, "Paradise Lost," 12.

52 "Aged Pickets Protest Youth Crime," *NYT* (April 5, 1978): 18.

53 Matthew L. Wald, "Parkchester Rally Asks Preservation of Bronx Project," *NYT* (November 21, 1977): 43.

54 "Parkchester Seeks to Slow Crime to a Walk," *New York Post* (July 20, 1979): 14.

55 "Neighborhood Safety Patrol Begins in Parkchester," *City News* (August 2, 1979): 33.

56 "Parkchester Lights Up," *BN* (April 10, 1980): 11; "Back Door Lock Program," *BN* (January 13, 1983): 23.

57 For a sense of the confusion about the future of Parkchester among its residents in the 1970s, see Patrice O' Shaughnessy, "Changed but Still Good," *NYDN* (April 4, 1984). On the legal and legislative struggles over the transformation of the development's southern portion, see Joseph P. Fried, "Condominium Bid in Bronx Set Back," *NYT* (January 20, 1973): 49; Robert E. Tomasson, "Parkchester's Conversion to Condominium Halted," *NYT* (April 1, 1975): 73; Alan S. Oser, "Parkchester Is at a Crossroads," *NYT* (January 14, 1976): 58; Oser, "Rest of Parkchester's Tenants Get Conversion Plan," *NYT* (September 16, 1983): B5; Kirk Johnson, "About Real Estate: Parkchester's Labored Conversion a Testing Ground," *NYT* (December 28, 1984): A19.

58 "Parkchester Cool to Condos," *NYDN* (June 21, 1984).

59 Martin Gottlieb, "Executives Are Offered a City Guide to Housing," *NYT* (March 24, 1983): B3.

60 Victoria White, "If You're Thinking of Living in Parkchester," *NYT* (October 26, 1986): 50.

61 Napolitano, "Recollections," 27.

62 Jackman, interview.

63 Napolitano, "Recollections," 31; "Housing Guards' Firing Affirmed," *NYDN* (April 17, 1986); Philip S. Gutis, "Parkchester Beset by Security Dispute," *NYT* (April 2, 1986): A27; Dan O'Grady, "Dearie Fumes at Firings," *NYDN* (March 24, 1986); "Security Guards Reinstated," *BN* (July 3, 1986): 2.

64 "Guard Dog Seen Helping Crime Fight," *BN* (July 2, 1980): 6; "Suit Seeks to Halt Further Sales," *NYT* (October 26, 1986): 500; Chris Oliver, "Helmsley Slapped with $300M Fed Suit over 'Shoddy' Housing," *New York Post* (January 2, 1987):14; "Parkchester Suit: A New Court," *NYDN* (February 6, 1987).

65 On the need for a mixture of agents and owner representatives, see John Mella, "Condo Election Postponed," *BPR* (September 3, 1986). See also the short biographical sketches in *Parkchester 1940–1990 50th Anniversary* (undated brochure, circa 1990, Parkchester file, Bronx Historical Society).

66 "Going Strong at 50," *NYDN* (August 12, 1990). See also "Teamwork Helps Parkchester Management Get the Job Done," in *Parkchester 1940–1990 50th Anniversary*, 3.

67 Jerry Cheslow, "If You're Thinking of Living in Parkchester," *NYT* (May 10, 1992): R7; Neil A. Lewis, "First Day in First Grade: Tears at P.S. 106," *NYT* (September 15, 1988): B1.

68 Jane H. Li, "Housing Jewel in the Bronx Loses Its Luster," *NYT* (May 29, 1994): CY7. See also Gary Axelbank, "Parkchester Residents Discuss Deterioration of Apartments," *BPR* (March 2, 1995).

69 Xenia Pamulsklakin, "Bitter Rent Battle for Parkchester Tenants," *Bronx Beat* (March 6, 1995): 3.

70 George James, "Lawsuit Filed for 2 Injuries from Toilets," *NYT* (December 29, 1995): B6.

71 "42,000 People on a 129–Acre Site," *NYT* (May 14, 2004): RE6.

72 Interview with Abu Shakoor, July 19, 2017.

73 Pamulsklakin, "Bitter Rent Battle," 3; interview with Edward Watkins, July 26, 2017.

CHAPTER 8. RENEWAL EFFORTS

1 Wedemeyer, "Palace," 4; Sam Roberts, "Helmsley to Quit Rental Market, Tries to Sell Tudor City Buildings," *NYT* (February 7, 1984): B4; Iver Peterson, "Helmsleys' Real Estate: Empire after the Verdict," *NYT* (September 2, 1989): 25.

2 Michael Lappin, "CityViews: The Lessons We Learned from Saving Parkchester," *CityLimits.org* (August 22, 2018), https://citylimits.org. See also interview with Lappin, September 11, 2017; Lappin email to Gurock, September 13, 2017; Lappin, "CPC: A Brief History" (unpublished article, circa 2012): 1–3; Lappin, "A Case Study of Rebuilding Small Multifamily Housing in Low and Moderate-Income Communities: CPC's Efforts in New York City" (unpublished study, circa 2011). Lappin has noted that, notwithstanding his criticism of the Helmsleys, in retrospect, he has described Leona Helmsley as "the Queen of Means." He has suggested that rather than sell the neighborhood as she did to the CPC, she "could have made more money by selling off the retail spaces and/or large numbers of apartments to separate investors, which would have made the restoration of Parkchester infinitely more difficult." On this aspect of the CPC relationship with the Helmsley group, see Lappin, "CityViews."

3 Interview with Andrea Olshan, October 19, 2017. See also company biographies of Morton Olshan, *Olshan Properties* (accessed January 17, 2019), www.olshanproperties.com, and Jeremiah O'Connor, *O'Connor Capital Partners* (accessed January 17, 2019), http://oconnorcp.com.

4 Lappin, interview. See also Melanie Zivancev, "Developers Unveil Plan to Restore Parkchester," *BPR* (July 17, 1997): 9; David M. Halbfinger, "Helmsley's Parkchester Condos Are Sold," *NYT* (July 3, 1998): B6; Jason Sheftell, "Parkchester, BX," *NYDN* (December 4, 2009), www.nydailynews.com; Julia Vitullo-Martin, "A Troubled Landmark Rescued," *New York Sun* (November 19, 2003): 9; Josh Barbanel, "Still a Beacon, Parkchester Climbs Back," *NYT* (March 14, 2004), www.nytimes.com.

5 Ferrer, interview; Bill Stuttig, "Bank Consortium Would Make Parkchester Modern and Sellable," *Bronx Times* (February 26, 1998): 21; Halbfinger, "Parkchester Condos," B6; Lappin, "CityViews."

6 Bill Stuttig, "The Fight for the Future of Parkchester," *Bronx Times* (May 14, 1998); Rafael A. Olmeda, "Vote Moves Condos Closer to Renovation," *NYDN* (November 16, 1998).

7 Halbfinger, "Parkchester Condos," B6. See also Richard Weir, "Parkchester," *NYT* (December 6, 1998): 747.

8 Lappin, interview; Halbfinger, "Parkchester Condos," B6; Weir, "Parkchester," 747; Suttig, "The Fight," 7–8; Barbanel, "Still a Beacon."

9 Interview with Edward Watkins, September 27, 2017; Rafael A. Olmeda, "Vote Moves Condos Closer to Renovation," *NYDN* (November 16, 1978), www.nydailynews.com; Alan S. Oser, "Buyer's Goal at Parkchester: Restoration of a Mini-City," *NYT* (October 27, 1996), www.nytimes.com; Weir, "Parkchester," 747; Lappin, interview.

10 Weir, "Parkchester," 747; "Parkchester Residents Deserve," *BPR* (April 9, 1998); Alan S. Oser, "Starting the Rehabilitation Journey at Parkchester," *NYT* (April 18, 1999): RE 7. On the presence of dissenting voices that raised racial issues, see interview with Kumar Kancherla, November 9, 2017; Lappin, "CityViews," identifying Kancherla as a vocal defender of the CPC.

11 David Critchell, "Tenants' Woes Continue Despite a New Landlord," *NYT* (October 17, 1999): 679. On complaints about the quality of the early rehabilitation work, see also "Architect Blasts P'kchester renovations," *BN* (August 26–September 1, 1999): 10; Oser. "Starting the Rehabilitation," RE7.

12 In both the south and north areas, the CPC and its associates inherited from Helmsley only a minority of positions on the boards. Up north, their minority position was even smaller than it was down south. Lappin wanted to "exercise the right to vote for owner representatives" on the board who would be favorable to the plan. This was opposed by the indigenous board, which led to more than two years of litigation until the courts found in favor of the CPC. See interview with Lappin, October 4, 2017, which also notes Harry Brown's strong support. On Brown's views of the board, see Daniel Gesslen, "P'kchester Prez Blasts Renovation Opposition," *BN* (June 8–14, 2000): 1, 6.

13 Seth Kugel, "Twin Developments Are as Different as Hot and Cold," *NYT* (May 5, 2002): CY9; Lappin, "CityViews."

14 Edwin McDowell, "Parkchester Renovations Is Proving Contagious," *NYT* (December 25, 2002): C4.

15 It also helped that the newly reconstituted board approved an amendment to the rules of Parkchester North requiring that only 50 percent of residents approve the plan, rather than 66 percent as before. See Lappin, October 4 interview.

16 Barbanel, "Still a Beacon"; Elizabeth Lent, "A Successful Experiment in Living: The Evolution of Parkchester," *New York Cooperator* (July 2006), https://cooperator.com. On the problem of squatters during the later years of Helmsley ownership, see Lappin, "Brief History," 4.

17 Jennifer Bleyer, "129 Acres, Renewed Yet Affordable," *NYT* (October 7, 2007): J7. On the earlier newspaper evaluations of Parkchester, see chapter 7.

18 Bleyer, "129 Acres."

19 "Parkchester—The Grand Old Neighborhood." See also interview with Jack Hirschfield, July 23, 2018.

CHAPTER 9. IMMIGRANT ARRIVALS AND OLD-TIMER DEPARTURES

1 *The Newest New Yorkers: Characteristics of the City's Foreign-Born Population* (New York: Department of City Planning, 2013), 159, 163; David M. Reimers, *Still the Golden Door: The Third World Comes to America*, 2nd ed. (New York: Columbia University Press, 1992), 92.

2 Frederick M. Binder and Reimers, *All the Nations under Heaven: An Ethnic and Racial History of New York City* (New York: Columbia University Press, 1995), 227–37; Kirk Semple, "Take the A Train to Little Guyana," *NYT* (June 9, 2013): L11; Joseph Berger, "American Dream Is a Ghana Home," *NYT* (August 21, 2002): B1.

3 *The Newest New Yorkers: An Analysis of Immigration into New York City during the 1980s* (New York: Department of City Planning, 1992), 89–98; *The Newest New Yorkers: An Analysis of Immigration to NYC in the Early 1990s* (New York: Department of City

Planning, 1996), 51–66. It should be noted that in both studies the statistics for Parkchester also include a small section of the Bronx north and northeast of Tremont Avenue called Van Nest. In addition, in listing the many nationalities to be found in the area as of the early 1990s, a full 26 percent were in the "All Others" category that, arguably, includes those from Africa whose presence in this diversified area is noted in other sources. A 1994 study of the "settlement patterns" of the "top ten immigrant cultures" that established large enclaves also points out how Parkchester did not attract any homogeneous cohorts of first-settlement people. These major new arrivals included Dominicans, Jamaicans, Chinese, Guyanese, and Filipinos. See Nikhi Naik, *New York City's Changing Immigrant Population* (New York: Amalgamated Life Insurance Co., Inc., 1994), 20–21, 24–25, 28, 32–33, 44, 50. On recently arriving immigrants being attracted to Parkchester by family members already there, see interview with Parkchester realtor Saleh Uddin, November 9, 2017.

4 Interview with Vera Acquah, October 28, 2017. On the distribution of Mosholu residents by national origin as of 1990, see *Newest New Yorkers* (1992), 60.

5 As far as the area not being a major first-settlement destination, it may be noted that between 1990 and 1994, some 516 newly arrived Dominicans settled in Parkchester, making them the largest Spanish-speaking group coming into the neighborhood. But they were a very small portion of the city's overall Dominican influx: some 30,000 Dominicans settled in the Bronx and close to 27,000 settled in Washington Heights during the same period, for instance. See *The Newest New Yorkers, 1990–1994* (New York: Department of City Planning, 1994), 58, 61, 80. Looking at all foreign-born residents in Parkchester as of 2000, Dominicans were still "the largest group in this section," which included Van Nest. However, it was still home to a very diverse newcomer population. "Indicative of the array of groups on this neighborhood, the top 10" nationalities—including Mexicans, Guyanese, Filipinos, and Bangladeshis—constituted "only 57 percent of the immigrant population, compared to 70 percent in the borough overall." See *The Newest New Yorkers 2000: Immigrant New York in the New Millennium* (New York: Department of City Planning, 2004), 54, 56.

6 Information on these houses of worship is derived from the author's meetings with their imams and lay leaders, facilitated by Tamzidul Islam. The interviewees include Abdul Shahid from Parkchester Jame Masjid, Abul Yahya from Bangla Bazar Jame Majid, Mariamma Cisse from Jamhiyatut Tahaawan Islamic Center (renamed as of 2019 as the African Islamic Center Inc. Masjid Attaiawun), Obaidul Hoque of the Parkchester Islamic Center, and Mohammed Uddin of Baitul Aman Islamic Center. All interviews were conducted on November 13, 2017. See also Daniel J. Wakin, "Safekeeping Faith and Tradition; Bronx Mosque Provides a Place for Prayer and More," *NYT* (November 16, 2001), www.nytimes.com.

7 Interview with Imam Mohammed Uddin, November 13, 2017.

8 Raphael Sugarman, "Hindu Karma an Active Force in Parkchester," *NYDN* (April 16, 1995), www.nydailynews.com. See also interview with Tamesh Motieram, November 12, 2017.

9 Interview with Der Podder, November 12, 2017. See also flyer announcing Sree Sree Shyama Puja and Diwali festival, 2017, provided by Podder.

10 On the background and training of South Asian immigrants in this era, see Reimers, *Still the Golden Door*, 114–15.

11 Kancherla, interview.

12 Michael Horowitz, "Immigrants Living American Dream as Realtors," *Bronx News* (February 26–March 14, 2015): 15; interview with Saleh Uddin, November 9, 2017; interview with Shariful Islam, November 9, 2017.

13 On the problem of maintaining the daily services, see "Young Israel Chatter," *YI* (February 2, 1981): 3; "From the President," *YI* (June–July 1981): 1; "From the Men's Club," *YI* (February–March 1982): 3; "From the President," *YI* (September 1982): 2; "From the President: An Emergency Open Letter," *YI* (April–May 1983): 2; "From the Men's Club: Straight Talk," *YI* (April–May 1983): 4.

14 On efforts to recruit Russian Jews and involvement with the Parkchester-Unionport Jewish Community Council, see "Parkchester-Unionport Jewish Community Council," *YI* (February 1978): 2; "From the President," *YI* (June 1979): 2; "Greeting Our New Neighbors," *YI* (November 1979): 1; "From the President," *YI* (June 1980): 2; "Wanted: Men and Women Translators," *YI* (April 1981): 6. During 1990–1994, some 667 immigrants from Russia settled initially in Parkchester. Though they constituted the largest immigrant cohort in the neighborhood during that period, they were only 16.8% of the total immigrant population in what was described as "an extremely diverse immigrant stream." The religious affiliation of these east European immigrants was not indicated. On these demographics, see *Newest New Yorkers* (1994), 61, 66.

15 "From the President," *YI* (June 1978): 6. For other descriptions of the congregation's financial problems, see "From the President," *YI* (June 1979): 2; "From the President," *YI* (June 1980): 2.

16 B. Horowitz, interview. For reaction of the congregation to the Horowitz family's move out of the neighborhood, see "Young Israel Chatter," *YI* (February 1981): 2. On the congregation attempting to maintain connections with erstwhile members, see "From the Treasurer," *YI* (April 1981): 6; "From the Men's Club," *YI* (June–July 1981): 2; "Notice: Moving?," *YI* (September 1982): 11.

17 "A Message from Rabbi Schwartz," *YI* (April 1984): 2; Schwartz, interview.

18 "Daily Minyan: No Problem," *YI* (September–October 1984): 2. The Jewish Center of Unionport was sold to Mount Zion CME Church in 2001 and as of 2017 was the site of the Glory of Christ Church–Iglesia La Gloria De Christi. See Levitt, *Lost Synagogues*, 83.

19 Interview with Tamzidul Islam, November 13, 2017.

20 On the merger of the congregations, the sale of the property, Rabbi Seymour Schwartz's efforts, and the court case, see Schwartz, "Maintaining the Minyan," 29–33.

21 Ted Regencia and Lindsay Minerva, "A Bronx Tale," *Tablet* (January 23, 2012), www.tabletmag.com; Jonathan Mark, "The Shul in the Mosque," *Jewish Week* (April 30, 2012), https://jewishweek.timesofisrael.com. On additional media attention to the Moslem-Jewish activities in Parkchester, see Daniel Beekman, "Three Rabbis Hike 15 Miles from Brooklyn to Bronx Weekly to Lead Synagogue," *NYDN* (September 25, 2011), www.nydailynews.com; Ted Regencia and Lindsay Minerva, "Mosque, Ultra-Orthodox Synagogue Share One Roof in the Bronx," *Bronx Ink* (December 12, 20012), http://bronxink.org; Ed Hussain, "What the Middle East Can Learn from the Bronx about Religious Tolerance," *Atlantic* (February 15, 2012), www.theatlantic.com. On assistance provided by Jewish communal agencies, see "Students of Multiple Faiths Restore Bronx Synagogue Housed Inside Mosque," *CBS New York* (April 4,

2013), http://newyork.cbslocal.com; "Synagogue in the Mosque Project," *Pluralism Project* (2015), http://pluralism.org. On Bleckman's last activities and his passing, see Amir Levy, "Purim Celebration in a Mosque," *Visura* (March 9, 2017), http://visura.co; interview with R. Paster, July 21, 2017; interview with Rabbi Meir Kabakow; interview with Sharina Drammeh, November 14, 2017; Ed García Conde, "Bronx Building Where Jews and Muslims Worship Peacefully in Danger of Being Sold," *Welcome2TheBronx* (November 14, 2017), www.welcome2thebronx.com; interview with Sheik Moussa Drammeh, December 13, 2017; interview with Sheik Drammeh, September 21, 2018.

22 On the early years of Temple Emanuel, see Beekman, "Temple Emanuel"; Ted Regencia and Lindsay Minerva, "Bronx Synagogue Welcomes Jewish New Year with a Last Goodbye," *Bronx Ink* (October 3, 2011), http://bronxink.org; interview with Jay Korman. September 7, 2017.

23 Interview with Rabbi J. Leonard Romm, September 10, 2017; Romm email to Gurock, September 8, 2017.

24 On the final years of Temple Emanuel, see Beekman, "Temple Emanuel,"; Regencia and Minerva, "Bronx Synagogue" (and reader comment by Ira L. Jacobson [November 9, 2011]); interview with Rabbi Jesse Olitzky, September 7, 2017; interview with Rabbi J. Leonard Romm, September 12, 2017.

25 In addition to the Parkchester churches of long-standing that are studied here from their inception in the neighborhood, there are more than a dozen other Christian houses of worship located in the general vicinity, including the Church of the Revelation on White Plains Road, Fellowship Covenant Church on Castle Hill Avenue and the Westchester United Methodist Church on East Tremont Avenue, not to mention the two churches that took over from the Leland Avenue and Ellis Avenue synagogues. See "The Best 10 Churches near Parkchester, Bronx NY," *Yelp* (accessed January 17, 2019), www.yelp.com.

26 Interview with Rev. Robert Foltz-Morrison, September 25, 2017; Foltz-Morrison email to Gurock, September 25, 2017.

27 Interview with Rev. Clark Bradley, September 13, 2017.

28 Interview with Rev. Hilary Gaston, September 26, 2017; Foltz-Morrison, interview; Charles W. Bell, "Seminary Success Story," *NYDN* (April 13, 2002), www.nydailynews.com.

29 Interview with Barbara Jamison, September 27, 2017; interview with Rev. Dr. Laura B. Sinclair, October 7, 2017.

30 Interview with Evelyn McCatty, October 13, 2017; interview with Rev. Fernando Otero, October 13, 2017. The informal survey of race at the church was done through a head count of the races of the faces of member shown in two anniversary journals, *St Paul's Lutheran Church, Celebrating Our 95th Year* (1974) and *St. Paul's Lutheran Church* (1984). It may be noted for 1974 that a list of members not portrayed is appended, making the head count, albeit useful, not totally conclusive. For the far more definitive 2011 statistics, which were submitted to the Evangelical Lutheran Church in America, see "Congregational Report for the Year Ending December 31, 2011," document provided by St. Paul's Lutheran Church, Parkchester.

31 Interview with Rev. James Thomas, October 18, 2017; McCatty, interview.

32 On the nature of services and the ethnicity of congregants attending services as of October 2017, see Otero, interview; "News and Notes, St. Paul's Evangelical Church,"

October 8, 2017. See also "Getting to Know You: Pastor Fernando Otero," *Metropolitan New York Synod* (accessed January 17, 2019), www.mnys.org.

33 Alan Feuer, "He Knows Every Crack in the Parish Sidewalk," *NYT* (January 9, 2002): B1.

34 Derivan, interview; "Church of St. Helena," *NYDN* (November 13, 2005): 3; *New York State Nonpublic School Comprehensive Information Report* (2016), provided by Richard Meller, principal of St. Helena's School.

35 Graham, interview; *St. Raymond's Parish* (Summer/Fall 2013); "Pastors Appointed in Bronx, Manhattan," *Catholic New York* (September 28, 2016), www.cny.org.

CHAPTER 10. AS A BRONX NEIGHBORHOOD APPROACHES EIGHTY

1 For the latest, prior evaluation conducted by the *New York Times* in 2007, see Bleyer, "129 Acres."

2 Vera Haller, "Living in Parkchester, the Bronx, Working as Planned," *NYT* (October 26, 2016), www.nytimes.com.

3 On the closing of Macy's stores in locations other than Parkchester, see "Here Are 68 of the 100 Stores That Macy's Will Close," *CNBC.com* (January 4, 2017), www.cnbc.com.

4 "Zaro's Announces Return to Parkchester," *News 12 The Bronx* (August 23, 2017), http://bronx.news12.com (see also readers' comments); Stuart Epstein, "Options Dwindle for Bronx Residents Trying to Escape to the Movies," *NYT* (May 25, 2014), www.nytimes.com; Olshan, interview.

5 "Parkchester Neighborhood in Bronx, New York (NY), 10462 Detailed Profile," *City-Data.com* (accessed January 17, 2019), http://city-data.com.

6 On the statistics for 2010, see Table PL-P3A NTA: *Total Population by Mutually Exclusive Race and Hispanic Origin, New York City Neighborhood Tabulation Areas, 2010* (U. S. Census Bureau, 2010 Census Public Law 97–171 file). For comparisons with 2000, see *Total Population by Mutually Exclusive Race and Hispanic Origin by Census Tract, 2000 Bronx Community District 9* (U.S. Census Bureau, 2000 Census PL file). Interestingly, the most recent municipal governmental study of the "Characteristics of the City's Foreign–born Population"—looking at 2007–2011—evidences that for groups like those born in Guyana, Ecuador, India, Russia, and West Africa, among others, none settled in Parkchester in sufficient numbers to make the East Bronx neighborhood stand out among the "top twenty neighborhoods of settlement for foreign-born groups" in New York City. See *Newest New Yorkers* (2013), 34–35, 65–94. The description of the stores on Bangla Bazaar is based on the author's walk through the area on November 6, 2017.

7 "Parkchester: A Great Way to Live," *YouTube* (Parkchester Preservation Management, December 14, 2017), 5 min., www.youtube.com/watch?v=4CkkoMPMX7g.

8 "Parkchester's 75th Anniversary: Thriving @75" (2015).

9 See comments on the "Parkchester: A Great Way to Live" YouTube page.

10 *A View from the Oval: Official Newsletter of the Parkchester South Condominium* (Spring/Summer 2017): 1–8. See also *Annual Report: Parkchester Department of Public Safety* (2016) and *Parkchester South Condominium: Day to Day Operations*, attached to *A View from the Oval*.

11 On these upscale apartments, see "Apartments," *Parkchester* (accessed January 17, 2019), www.parkchesternyc.com.

CONCLUSION

1 For the names of leaders of these war-time organizations from different backgrounds, see, for example, *BHN* (March 5, 1944): 5; *BHN* (March 19, 1944): 5; *BHN* (March 25, 1944): 4.

2 Rodgers, "Life Insurance Investments," 676–79.

3 As a poignant contrast, in the Canarsie section of Brooklyn during this same period, Jews and Italians actively fought the influx of African Americans and Latinos, whom they deemed a great threat to the neighborhood's identity. See Jonathan Rieder, *The Jews and Italians of Brooklyn against Liberalism* (Cambridge, MA: Harvard University Press, 1985).

4 E. R. Shipp, "Integration without Violence," *NYT* (October 21, 1991): E16.

Index

North Quadrant: renovations in, 201; rent
control in, 156; St. Raymond's Church
for, 36; sports in, 171
North Quadrant condominiums, 154–56,
209; board's approval of renovation
for, 205; Dearie on, 175; lack of sales of,
182–83; prices of, 169; tenant for, 172–
73; tenants against, 169–70
NYPD. *See* New York Police Department
NYSCDH. *See* New York State Committee
on Discrimination in Housing

O'Brien-Piper Bill, 18
O'Connor, Jeremiah W., Jr., 198–200
O'Dwyer, William, 120
Office of Price Administration (USA),
69–70
Office of Programs and Planning (NYC), 196
Olitzky, Jesse, 232
Olshan, Andrea, 248
Olshan, Morton L.: CPC and, 198–200; in
video, 248
Operation Open City, 131, 133
Orthodox Jews, 283n3; Chabad as, 227–
30; out-migration among, 161–62
O'Shea, Joseph J., 239
Otero, Fernando, 239
Ovington, Mary White, 103
Owen, Betty, 227

Parkchester: aerial view of, 24, *24*; Board
of Design for, 19; construction concept
for, 19; Co-op City compared to, 166–
68; cost of, 22; crime in, 96, 179–81;
design criticism on, 24–25, 100, 180;
graduate course related to, 23; landscaping of, 22; layout of, 20–21; lease
document rules for, 77, 83, 88, 108–9,
277n10; name of, 20; national news on,
22–23; playgrounds for, 20–21; sale of,
144; site for, 18–19; size of, 18–21; social
class and, 23–24; subway to, 1, 15, 25,
243, 251; tunnels beneath, 67, 276n19;
worthiness of, 208–9. *See also* tenants
"Parkchester: A Great Way to Live," 210–11,
247, 249

Parkchester Alliance, 193
Parkchester Baptist Church, 42, 273n28;
community of, 236–37; membership
decline of, 237; "racial antipathies" at,
236
Parkchester Bronx Reality, Inc., 223
Parkchester Christian Association, 38
Parkchester Committee to End Housing
Discrimination, 111–15, 137
Parkchester Crime and Safety Committee, 186
Parkchester Defense Fund, 168–71, 286n29
Parkchester Department of Public Safety
(DPS), 250
Parkchester immigrants: Afro-Caribbean,
213, 214, 238; Asian American, 214–15;
customs and traditions of, 216; diver-
sity of, 213–14, 293n6; Dominican, 214,
290n5; Ghanaian, 216–17; Guyanese,
215; "open door" for, 214; Puerto Rican,
213–14, 217; "settlement patterns" of,
289n3; South Asian, 193, 217–23, *220*,
246; from Soviet Union, 223–24, 291n14
Parkchester Investigation Department, 32
Parkchester Islamic Center, 226–27
Parkchester Jame Masjid, 218–19
Parkchester Management Corporation,
151, 179
Parkchester Merchants Association, 200
Parkchester NAACP, 136, *136*; community
from, 147–48
*The Parkchester News, Souvenir Opening
Issue 1941*, 272n25
Parkchester North Condominiums, 209;
board approval for, 205, 207, 289n15.
See also North Quadrant condomini-
ums
Parkchester police, *80*, 80–81
Parkchester Preservation Corporation
(PPC), 199–200, 202–3
Parkchester Press Review, 45
Parkchester Real Estate, 209
"Parkchester's 75th Anniversary: Thriving
@75," 248–49
Parkchester South, 183; board for, 202–3;
renovation of, 205–7

About the Author

JEFFREY S. GUROCK is Libby M. Klaperman Professor of Jewish History at Yeshiva University. He is the author or editor of twenty-one books, including the prize-winning *Jews of Gotham: New York Jews in a Changing City, 1920–2010* (NYU Press). He lives in the Riverdale section of the Bronx.

Lightning Source UK Ltd.
Milton Keynes UK
UKHW010246110621
385324UK00006B/240